'In a time when policy-makers throughout the world are questioning the need to prepare teachers to do anything more than mechanically follow teaching scripts, *Critical Practice in Teacher Education* provides us with a clear and compelling case for teacher preparation that educates teachers to skillfully exercise their professional judgment and to be able to respond flexibly to the constant changes that they will face in today's classrooms. Although this case is set in the UK, it should be required reading for teacher educators and policy-makers everywhere.'

Ken Zeichner, Boeing Professor of Teacher Education, University of Washington, USA

'*Critical Practice in Teacher Education* comprises a series of lively essays written by teacher educators in which they take up the challenge of articulating the values and beliefs that shape their work. This is a very timely undertaking, given the way that standards-based reforms have reduced teaching to a set of discrete technical skills that are supposedly transferable from one school setting to the next. The writers draw on a wealth of research and experience as teacher educators to present a range of strategies designed to encourage their students to critically reflect on their professional practice as new teachers. Portfolios, autobiographical writing, reflective discussions about the complexities of their professional practice – through these and other means, new teachers are able to confront their own histories and cultures, reflexively appraising the knowledge and experience they bring to their work. In doing so, they grapple with the situated nature of their professional practice, acknowledging the diverse cultures that young people bring to school as a basis for meaningful communication and social relationships with them. The teacher educators who have contributed to this volume offer a powerful alternative to the sterile educational model of standards-based reforms, which reduces students and their families to consumers, and teachers to the level of delivering goods and services to their clients or customers. *Critical Practice in Teacher Education* speaks back to such reforms, providing grounds for hope that we may one day be able to establish an education system that is genuinely inclusive and truly democratic.'

**Professor Brenton Doecke, Faculty of Arts and Education,
School of Education, Deakin University, Australia**

'For those fighting what may be a rearguard action against the move to a purely apprenticeship model of teacher training, this text provides plenty of ammunition. It presents a case for initial teacher education which values practical experience, intellectual development, reflection, consideration of theory and an enquiry-based approach. The theoretical positioning is very powerful, drawing on 20 years of research and experience. This is very well exemplified through examples of what must be seen to be best practice. The text is an excellent, reflective exploration and justification of a process of learning to become a teacher in the modern world.'

**Professor Kit Field, Dean of the School of Education,
University of Wolverhampton, UK**

'An absolute must have for all teacher educators, mentors and their students at a time when the integration of theory and practice is paramount to not only the introduction of the Masters in Teaching and Learning, but also to the development of outstanding teachers.

The chapters in *Critical Practice in Teacher Education* all view professional learning as a critical practice taken from different perspectives and all succeed in embedding these within the context of schools and universities.'

Tanya Riordan, PGCE MFL Course Leader, University of Portsmouth

'This book gives a considered and realistic account of the debates and tensions around policy, research, theory and practice that currently preoccupy all teacher educators, and it provides some valuable examples of perspectives and approaches to resolving these within the different ITE and CPD programmes of the Institute of Education.'

Cathy Pomphrey, formerly Academic Leader for Initial Teacher Education, London Metropolitan University, UK

Critical Practice in Teacher Education

The Bedford Way Papers Series

20 *Childhood in Generational Perspective*
    Edited by Berry Mayall and Helga Zeiher

21 *Homework: The evidence*
    Susan Hallam

22 *Teaching in Further Education: New perspectives for a changing context*
    Norman Lucas

23 *Legalised Leadership: Law-based educational reform in England and what it does
    to school leadership and headteachers*
    Dan Gibton

24 *Theorising Quality in Higher Education*
    Louise Morley

25 *Music Psychology in Education*
    Susan Hallam

26 *Policy-making and Policy Learning in 14–19 Education*
    Edited by David Raffe and Ken Spours

27 *New Designs for Teachers' Professional Learning*
    Edited by Jon Pickering, Caroline Daly and Norbert Pachler

28 *The Dearing Report: Ten years on*
    Edited by David Watson and Michael Amoah

29 *History, Politics and Policy-making in Education: A festschrift presented to Richard
    Aldrich*
    Edited by David Crook and Gary McCulloch

30 *Public Sector Reform: Principles for improving the education system*
    Frank Coffield, Richard Steer, Rebecca Allen, Anna Vignoles, Gemma Moss and
    Carol Vincent

31 *Educational Resource Management: An international perspective*
    Derek Glover and Ros Levačić

32 *Education in a Global City: Essays from London*
    Edited by Tim Brighouse and Leisha Fullick

33 *Exploring Professionalism*
    Edited by Bryan Cunningham

34 *Music Education in the 21st Century in the United Kingdom: Achievements, analysis
    and aspirations*
    Edited by Susan Hallam and Andrea Creech

A full list of Bedford Way Papers, including earlier books in the series, can be requested
by emailing ioepublications@ioe.ac.uk

Critical Practice in Teacher Education
A study of professional learning

Edited by Ruth Heilbronn and John Yandell

Institute of Education, University of London
Bedford Way Papers

First published in 2010 by the Institute of Education,
University of London, 20 Bedford Way, London WC1H 0AL

www.ioe.ac.uk/publications

© Institute of Education, University of London 2011

British Library Cataloguing in Publication Data:

A catalogue record for this publication is available from the
British Library

ISBN 978 0 85473 859 5

Typeset by Quadrant Infotech (India) Pvt Ltd
Printed by Elanders

Contents

Preface by Ruth Heilbronn and John Yandell

Notes on contributors

Part 1: Professional learning, critical practice

1   The nature of practice-based knowledge and understanding   2
    Ruth Heilbronn

2   Sites of learning   15
    John Yandell

3   The reflective practitioner   29
    Ruth Heilbronn

Part 2: Modes of professional learning

4   From reading into writing: Discovering a personal philosophy   40
    Liz Wright

5   Tasks, audiences and purposes: Writing and the development   58
    of teacher identities within pre-service teacher education
    Anne Turvey and Gill Anderson

6   'A bit of an eye-opener': Critical reflection at Master's level through
    portfolio construction   74
    Karen Turner

Part 3: Case studies of professional learning and assessment

7   Foreign language education: Preparing for diversity   90
    Verna Brandford

8   Playing a part: The case of theatre in education in the professional   102
    education of English with Drama teachers
    Anton Franks

9   Learning to teach Geography   114
    Clare Brooks

10 Music, musicians and learning modes   125
    Pauline Adams and Kate Laurence

11 Performativity versus engagement in a Social Science PGCE   138
    Jane Perryman

12 The principled practitioner: A model of knowledge acquisition   154
    Shirley Lawes

References   167

Index   184

Dedication

We dedicate this book to all the student teachers we have worked with over the years, in schools and university.

Editors' Preface

The focus of this book is on teacher education, which is the most obvious frame of reference for the questions that are addressed here. However, there is a wider relevance to these questions. What does professional learning look like? Where and how does it happen? What processes are involved? What is meant by the notion of 'practice'? For the authors, all of whom now work within higher education, there is particular interest in a further question: What is – or should be – the role of the university in such forms of professional learning?

We recognise, too, that this book constitutes an entry into a debate and that this debate has a history. There are competing models of teacher education, as there are in any form of professional learning. Indeed, it is not possible to begin to write about this field without signalling allegiance to particular theoretical traditions, particular conceptions of practice: we have already done so in adopting the phrase '*teacher education*', rather than the term that has more currency in the world, '*teacher training*'.

If the debate has a history, so do we – and our entry into the debate is shaped by the particularities of our shared history. The contributors to this book, and we as its editors, come from different disciplinary backgrounds, with experience in different phases of education. The history that we share is one of both an individual and an institutional commitment to particular forms and particular sites of teacher education. All of us currently work at the Institute of Education, University of London (IOE). All of us have long experience of working in and with London schools. And everything that is contained in this book is rooted in that history; it is the product of work across time, work involving many people, both at the IOE and in partnership schools across London, and beyond. It is the product, too, of a set of shared commitments and understandings about the nature of teaching and learning, about the relationship of theory and practice, about the complexity of the processes involved in teacher education, and even about knowledge itself.

Our purpose here is not to produce an account of the Postgraduate Certificate of Education (PCGE) course (or courses) on which we all teach, though we hope that a sense of the particular qualities of that course might emerge from the following chapters; rather, we seek to draw on our experience as teachers and teacher educators to make a case for particular ways of understanding, and engaging with, the processes that are involved in teachers' professional development. In our view, it is unhelpful – indeed, positively misleading – to frame these processes as the mere acquisition of a set of easily transferable competences or the demonstration that pre-specified, atomised and separately assessed standards have been met. Our own conception of teacher education, which informs and is informed by our work as teacher educators, needs to be understood in relation to our view of teachers as public intellectuals, and hence our conviction that the formation of teachers must entail the development of qualities of critical engagement with complex questions of policy and practice. The book's title, *Critical Practice in Teacher Education: A study of professional learning,* highlights our view that learning to be a teacher should entail a deep understanding that there are particular values underlying all educational endeavour and that teachers need to develop their own, critical perspective on any theory or research findings. All the contributors believe that learning to teach cannot be reduced to the acquisition of technical skills or a body of theoretical knowledge about teaching.

This book makes its entry into the world at a particular moment, a moment of convergences and contradictions. Its subject is not, in any narrow sense, what it might mean to envisage teaching as a Master's level profession. Nevertheless, one of the triggers – the immediate forces acting on us – has been the transformation of our PGCE course, like others across the country, into one bearing Master's level credits. We do not see this development as marking a rupture with the past; indeed, we are more inclined to the view that the award of Master's level credits on the PGCE is a recognition of the quality of intellectual engagement that has long been characteristic of the course and of students' participation in it. Nonetheless, the formal shift to Master's level has meant that we have all become involved in a series of discussions about the distinctiveness of professional Master's level courses, and these discussions have enabled us to be more explicit than, perhaps, we have tended to be in the past about what we mean by teacher education.

This, too, is a moment when politicians from both main parties have signalled a commitment to teaching quality and to continuing professional development and Master's level study (DCSF, 2008; Gove, 2009). What these commitments mean, and what conceptions of teaching and teacher development inform them, is less straightforward – and less clear. There is, on the one hand, a danger that what is envisaged may be so closely bound up with a narrowly conceived version of school improvement as to leave little space for critical reflection; on the other, the overemphasis on entry requirements as the guarantor of teacher quality may fail to recognise quite how transformative of prior knowledge the processes of teacher education can be. And then there is a further complication: the future of teacher education is unlikely to remain unaffected by the wider economic situation and, more specifically, by the impending cuts in public spending. In these interesting times, it becomes all the more important to make clear what it is that we are about – what is involved in forming teachers who are able to meet the challenge of new times.

The book is divided into three sections. The book's first three chapters in **Part 1** provide *a theoretical perspective on the foundational principles of teacher education* that are further discussed and exemplified in subsequent chapters.

The **first chapter** situates teaching as a practice, in which the knowledge and understanding required of expert practitioners is neither wholly practical nor wholly theoretical. The chapter discusses the nature of teacher knowledge and understanding and the importance of the development of practical judgement, which might be characterised as a capacity to do the right thing at the right time, to respond flexibly and appropriately in the moment.

Chapter 2 explores the nature and function of school experience in the formation of student teachers. It presents a view of this experience as involving both learning by doing and standing back and reflecting critically on practice. What is emphasised here is both the specificity of school experience and the importance of opportunities to gain distance from this experience. The insistence on attentiveness to local circumstance opens up the theme of sites of learning that will recur and be explored further in subsequent chapters.

Chapter 3 establishes how and why engagement in critical reflection is one important way in which practitioners develop a deep understanding of the practice of teaching. All the contributors in the book take as a principle that the ability to successfully reflect on practice is foundational to the integration of theoretical knowledge and practical experience, and hence to professional learning. The notion of reflective practice is slippery – not all reflection is 'good' reflection, such that it brings about new and relevant understandings. The chapter outlines features of 'well-grounded' reflection. The chapter's discussion is set against the background of classical texts on reflective practice.

The second part of the book (Chapters 4–6) directs attention towards *key modes of professional learning*. It focuses on reading, writing and assessment as they are instantiated within a course of initial teacher education. These elements – reading, writing and assessment – are, of course, instantly recognisable as salient features of teaching and learning on almost any accredited course of academic study. Precisely because of this, they may well appear unremarkable, as if these modes of learning might be assumed to operate within a course of professional learning in exactly the same way as they would on a more traditional Master's course. The central argument presented in this section is that this is not the case: that reading and writing are differently framed, serve different purposes, operate in different ways, ways that are attuned to the kind of learning that is accomplished within teacher education.

In **Chapter 4,** Liz Wright examines how student teachers find ways into forms of academic discourse as readers and writers. All texts tend to position their readers; academic texts can sometimes position their readers on the outside, as it were, placing them at the margins of powerful discourses. This chapter explores the ways in which the journal articles that student teachers read on the Professional Learning module of a primary PGCE contribute to their sense of an intellectual identity and their transformation from students to teachers.

In **Chapter 5,** Anne Turvey and Gill Anderson develop the themes of personal learning and critical reflection on practice. Student teachers are always in dialogue with authoritative discourses and writing is one way to articulate this. Student teachers' writing offers a way to represent their experiences during the PGCE year, as well as to stand back and reflect critically on these. It enables the writers to position themselves in relation to these experiences and to address explicitly some of the tensions and contradictions in the advice they are given. Such writing is often uncertain, tentative, a site of departure not arrival, subject to negotiation and shifting contexts. Reflexivity, in relation to both private and professional selves, is also at the heart of this model of writing and development.

In **Chapter 6,** Karen Turner draws on research into a module that requires the creation of a Professional Development Portfolio. Engaging in the assignments in the module involves teachers in a personal construction of the meaning of their practice through critical reflection, in the course of which practitioners articulate how their own experiences are situated within wider socio-historical and politico-cultural contexts. Creating the portfolio facilitates deep learning and the development of practical judgement and provides a focus for professional dialogue on practice with a mentor or tutor.

The first two sections of the book develop key principles that inform our view of professional learning as a critical practice, and these principles are picked up in the individual chapters in the next part of the book. First, we understand that theory and practice are an integrated whole in professional learning. Second, there are different sites for learning, and this raises challenges for professional learning. Third, we hold that professional learning requires the development of professional judgement, which entails the cultivation of a critical disposition.

Part 3 picks up particularly on one of those key elements – that professional learning is developed contingently, in specific situations, and needs to attend to the variety and particularities of context. The third section of the book is principally made up of a series of case studies, each of which tells a particular story from a particular subject perspective. The case studies both represent a need to develop and attend to subject-specific pedagogy, and also invite wider and less specific application. They are presented as neither a blueprint nor a template. What we see in each of the chapters is colleagues wrestling with particular dilemmas and challenges, and working through the implications of our more general commonalities of approach to teacher education, played out in particular and different sites. The particular modules that are discussed in the chapters are diverse in their mode of assessment, ranging from a Geography field trip, a Music ensemble performance, a Theatre in Education project, as well as something closer to a traditional written assignment. The diverse approach to assessment shows that professional learning can be a Master's level engagement that is also an induction into the development of critical practice.

In **Chapter 7,** Verna Brandford introduces a further site for learning in the space of culture and cultures. The chapter opens with a brief exploration of notions of culture, within the context of teaching and learning Modern Foreign Languages, taking as its basis that the student teacher's identity is culturally embedded. In learning to teach, student teachers engage with cultural contexts in schools, classrooms and communities and with the diverse cultures of the pupils, even in schools with apparently homogeneous school populations. The discussion applies across all subjects and phases, as it engages with principles that are crucial to student teachers' development.

In **Chapter 8,** Anton Franks discusses the Theatre in Education module of the English with Drama PGCE, which promotes collaborative work and provides an innovative way of integrating theory and practice. Central to the purpose of Theatre in Education is that it is conceived of as a teaching and learning event firmly situated in the context of schooling. The projects that are the focus of this module contribute to the preparation of teachers as creative professionals, working with limited resources and within particular constraints of time and space. The chapter poses questions about how subject teaching and learning, or the performance of school teaching and its audiences, relate to wider culture and society, and specifically how much learning and teaching are integrated with or abstracted from wider cultural concerns.

In **Chapter 9,** Clare Brooks is concerned with the context in which Geography teachers need to develop a theoretically informed practice and a sense of their role as Geography education professionals, both as subject experts and advocates who can describe and explain their subject's purpose, contribution and scope in a young person's education entitlement. Her portrait of a Geography Master's graduate exemplifies principles for initial teacher education introduced in the first two sections of the book. She shows particularly how the Geography PGCE aims to enable student teachers to synthesise their understanding of theory with their understanding of practice, develop their professional judgement and expertise and use that understanding and professional judgement in new contexts. One of these is the field trip, where learning outside the classroom is captured, using not just written text but video clips, stills and video diaries, leading to a Master's level assignment that takes the form of a poster and presentation assessment.

The focus of Pauline Adams' and Kate Laurence's piece in **Chapter 10** is the challenge of different modes of learning in relation to different student teachers' experiences. In all cases student teachers come to initial teacher education with a variety of subject knowledge and experience. In Music this fact is foregrounded in particular ways, with consequences for course design, as student teachers arrive from markedly different backgrounds and experiences. Some have mainly academic backgrounds in university Music courses, whereas others come from performance-oriented Music college courses. The chapter explores how the Music PGCE course enables student teachers both to exploit the skills and experiences they bring with them and to develop new areas of knowledge and understanding. This process, however, is not so much one of simple accretion – the addition of new knowledge to prior experience; instead, the challenge of arranging, composing and rehearsing for young musicians, often for the first time, enables student teachers to reconceptualise existing skills and knowledge as they engage in authentic, theorised reflection on practice.

In **Chapter 11,** Jane Perryman picks up the theme of student teachers' experiences of two sets of expectations, the first embedded in the performance agenda and the second requiring student teachers to critically engage with all aspects of their Social Science PGCE. She highlights the tensions and dilemmas experienced by student teachers in producing assignments at Master's level, when many are more focused on the rigours of completing their school experience, and also the dangers in setting up a contradictory rather than an integrated view of practice-based knowledge and understanding: performativity versus engagement. The chapter presents two Master's level assignments in detail and explores how these dilemmas are experienced by the student teachers and worked through by the design of the assignments and the teaching on the course.

In **Chapter 12,** Shirley Lawes further reminds us of the wider context of initial teacher education, derived from the research she undertook prior to the introduction of Master's level PGCE courses. She highlights tutors' perceptions of their role, and the experiences and expectations of student teachers in relation to the place of professional and theoretical knowledge in the initial teacher education process. Her study compared a number of PGCE Modern Foreign Languages courses with a dual certification programme, the PGCE and the French *Maîtrise Français Langue Etrangère* (FLE). The research shed light on a number of problems, challenges and dilemmas that teacher educators face in their work, and also on the potential of student teachers to go far beyond the baseline of qualified teacher status competence to become principled practitioners.

Note:

We have changed to culturally and gender appropriate pseudonyms the names of the student teachers whose views have been cited.

Notes on contributors

All the contributors work at the Institute of Education (IOE), University of London.

Pauline Adams is a lecturer in Music Education, teaching on the PGCE and Master's Music Education courses. She started her career teaching in Inner London schools and for some years acted in an advisory role for the Inner London Education Authority. She is the author of *Sounds Musical*, a Key Stage 2 Music scheme (published by Oxford University Press) and is a contributor to *The Curriculum for 7–11 year olds* (1999; in J. Riley and R. Prentice (eds); published by Paul Chapman Publishing) and, more recently, *Learning to Teach Music in the Secondary School* and *Issues in Music Teaching* (both published In 2001 by RoutledgeFalmer).

Gill Anderson taught English in secondary and tertiary schools in London for 13 years before moving into teacher education. She was the English subject leader on a school-based PGCE course for six years and also a subject-specialist consultant in schools across London. In her current role at the IOE she works with PGCE and MTeach students and is interested in creative approaches to English teaching, pupils' development in reading and writing and teachers' professional development.

Verna Brandford is a lecturer in Education, tutor on the Secondary PGCE in Modern Foreign Languages (MFL) and module leader for the BEd Teaching and Learning in Classrooms. She has taught in and trained language teachers for primary and secondary schools as well as adult education. As a consultant MFL adviser and inspector she has worked extensively with several local education authorities giving pre- and post-inspection advice and has worked with staff on curriculum review and development. She was a participant in the Comenius Project Creative Dialogues between 2003 and 2006, which developed Storyline as an alternative MFL teaching approach. Her research interests include MFL and connective pedagogy and overcoming barriers to pupil achievement in the subject.

Clare Brooks is subject leader for the Geography PGCE, and course leader for the Master's in Geography Education. Her research interests include the development and influence of Geography teachers' subject knowledge. She is honorary website editor for the Geographical Association, a member of the IGU-CGE British sub-committee, and a founding member of GEReCo. She is also editor of the online journal *GeogEd*. She has been awarded chartered geographer status from the Royal Geographical Society (with IBG).

Anton Franks was a teacher of Drama and English in London schools and now teaches, researches and writes on Drama and English in Education at the IOE. Publications include *English in Urban Classrooms* (2004) with Kress *et al.*; 'Learning theory and drama education' in *Cultura y Educación*, 2004, 16(1–2) and 'School drama and representations of war and terror...' in *Research in Drama Education*, 2008, 13(1).

Ruth Heilbronn is a specialist in Languages in Education, and Philosophy of Education. She has worked in senior management in schools and held staff development and advisory posts in schools. Her teaching experience at the IOE includes subject leader for the MFL PGCE and module leadership on various Master's programmes. She was a member of the editorial board of ittmfl.org, hosted by CILT, and has published in the fields of teacher education, induction and staff development, MFL and Philosophy of Education, including recently *Teacher Education and the Development of Practical Judgement* (2009, Continuum).

Kate Laurence is subject leader for the Music PGCE and a module leader for the Master's in Music Education at the IOE. She previously taught in Inner London and was director of Music and an advanced skills teacher. She has held professional and advisory roles with the Specialist Schools and Academies Trust, the BBC and for Sibelius Software Ltd. Kate currently leads a number of national CPD courses for Music teachers. She is the author of a number of Music Education resources for Rhinegold Publishing and SFE. Her interests include how Music teachers can develop as researchers, the personalisation of ITE routes for professional musicians and effective CPD in Music Education.

Shirley Lawes is subject leader for the MFL PGCE, a member of the executive committee of the Society for Educational Studies, and a member of National Centre for Languages Advisory Group on Teacher Training. Recent publications include *Modern Foreign Languages: Teaching School Subjects 11–19* (2007; edited with N Pachler and M. Evans) and *Cultural Awareness and Visits Abroad* (2005; in N. Pachler (ed.); *Teaching Modern Foreign Languages in the Secondary School: A practical guide)* and *Practice Makes Imperfect* (2002; in D. Hayes (ed.), *The RoutledgeFalmer Guide to Key Debates in Education*), all with RoutledgeFalmer.

Jane Perryman worked for 10 years as head of Humanities/Social Science in Hackney and Islington. She has been a PGCE tutor since 2002, and is currently the course leader for the PGCE Social Science at the IOE. She also contributes to the EdD and the Master's in School Effectiveness. Her research interests are accountability and performativity in secondary education, inspection regimes, discourses of school effectiveness and school improvement, school leadership and management, and how schools respond to policy. Publications include 'Inspection and the fabrication of professional and performative processes' (2009; in *Journal of Education Policy*, 24(5)); 'Inspection and emotion' (2007; in *Cambridge Journal of Education*, 37(2)) and 'Panoptic performativity and school inspection regimes: Disciplinary mechanisms and life under special measures' (2006; in *Journal of Education Policy*, 21(2)).

Karen Turner has wide experience of teaching at school and at PGCE, INSET and Master's level. Her main responsibilities currently lie with the MTeach where she is module leader for portfolios and tutor. She is also subject leader for the Primary French specialism. She is a member of the editorial committee for the *Language Learning Journal* and the Initial Teacher Training Working Group of the Centre for Information on Language Teaching and Research. Selected publications include 'Portfolios for learning' (2007; with S. Simon in J. Pickering *et al.*, *New Designs for Teachers' Professional Learning*; Institute of Education, University of London); *Learning by Ear and by Eye* (2005; CILT Classic Pathfinder); 'The space between: Shared understanding of the teaching of grammar in English and French to Year 7 learners' (2002; with A. Turvey in *Language Awareness*, II(2)).

Anne Turvey is a lecturer in education whose responsibilities have included subject leader for the PGCE English and Drama; course tutor for the MTeach and the Master's module 'Literature, feminism and the curriculum'; Chair of the London Association for the Teaching of English (LATE) and Committee member of the National Association for the Teaching of English (NATE) ITE. Publications include 'Transformations in learning and teaching through initial teacher education' (2006; with D. Stevens *et al.*, *Literacy*, 40(2)); 'Who'd be an English teacher?' (2005; *Changing English*, 12(1)); 'The space between: Shared understanding of the teaching of grammar in English and French to Year 7 learners' (2002; with K. Turner in *Language Awareness*, II(2)).

Liz Wright has worked in education for 35 years. She currently lectures in primary education at the IOE, works as a SENCO in a primary school and is an associate lecturer with the Open University. Before moving to higher education 16 years ago she worked across primary and secondary education at classroom and advisory level. She is the module leader for the Primary Professional Learning Portfolio at the IOE.

John Yandell taught in Inner London secondary schools for 20 years, including 11 years as head of English at Kingsland School, Hackney, and three years as head of the Ethnic Minority Achievement Team at Haverstock School, Camden. For the past six years, he has led the Secondary PGCE English and English with Drama course at the IOE. He also teaches on the MTeach and Master's English Education programmes. Recent publications have appeared in the *British Educational Research Journal*, the *Cambridge Journal of Education*, *Changing English*, *English in Education* and *English Teaching: Practice and Critique*. He is currently engaged in research on how literature is read in English classrooms.

Part 1

Professional learning, critical practice

Chapter 1

The nature of practice-based knowledge and understanding

Ruth Heilbronn

One preoccupation underpins most of the chapters in this book, one that concerns most people starting to work in professional practice. This concern is epistemological: what does the practice require us to learn; what 'knowledge' underpins it? For teachers working in England, a simple answer might seem to be provided by the TDA (Training and Development Agency) Standards for the award of qualified teacher status (QTS), without which no teacher in England can be registered with the professional, regulatory body, the General Teaching Council.

Standards

The standards for the award of QTS have attempted to address this concern in such a way that makes it possible to understand the practice. Standards were introduced to regulate the awarding of QTS and were intended to ensure consistency over provision and to develop a national assessment mechanism. From September 1997 only those trainee teachers who successfully completed an accredited course and met all the QTS standards were awarded qualified teacher status (DfEE, 1997). Currently, teachers in England and Wales are subject to standards-based assessment at all points in their career (TDA, 2007), moving from QTS through to statutory induction into continuing professional development (CPD) and annual performance management procedures (DfES, 2003; TDA, 2007), and this policy is reflected in similar developments elsewhere.

The introduction of competencies and standards purported to be an attempt to describe good practice, but the attempts that took place between 1997 and 2007 were problematic for a variety of reasons, and there were many critiques of earlier versions of the standards (and their forerunners, competencies) (Carr, 1993: 254; Hyland, 1994; Lum, 1999, 2003; Heilbronn, 2008).

To some extent the 2007 standards are useful in that they enable trainee teachers and their mentors to understand certain areas that need to be covered in order to create competent teachers. However, teaching is an extremely complex endeavour and standards cannot completely provide an account of this complexity, nor encompass comprehensively what 'good teaching' might be. Any definitions of 'good teaching' are contestable and are not as settled a matter as the standards might suggest.

> In common language we created practical discourse that in its concepts, propositions, rules and principles encapsulates our practical experience of our world...practical principles are the outcome of successful practice, generalisations are valid only insofar as they capture what successful practice entails. The more complex the practice and the more it is connected with differences in human attributes and differences in contexts, then the less such generalisations can possibly hope to capture what the practice entails.
>
> (Hirst, 1996: 171)

There appear then to be serious drawbacks as well as advantages in the attempt to describe good teaching through a series of standardised descriptors and to apply these descriptors across a variety of different contexts and circumstances. First, the endeavour is reductive: there is an implicit and underlying belief that 'good' teaching can be reduced to a set of uncontentious descriptors. Secondly, there is no acknowledgement of the variation in the contexts in which the so-called 'standards' are to be attained and verified. In practice, assessors use their own understanding of context-specific factors in interpreting the standards. The standards cannot be applied in a technical-rational way if they are routinely open to interpretation, according to varying contexts. In using the standards, assessors must be applying rationality of another kind. (The term 'technical rationality' was used most famously by Donald Schön, building on the work of John Dewey. A further discussion follows in Chapter 3.)

The current set of standards (TDA, 2007) refers to the knowledge and understanding required to qualify as a teacher. So, for example, for the standard Q10 trainees need to:

> have a knowledge and understanding of a range of teaching, learning and behaviour management strategies and know how to use and adapt them, including how to personalise learning and provide opportunities for all learners to achieve their potential.

To meet standard Q20 they need to:

> *know and understand the roles of colleagues with specific responsibilities, including those with responsibility for learners with special educational needs and disabilities and other individual learning needs.*
>
> (TDA, 2007)

What precisely is the nature of the knowledge and understanding required by teachers, referred to in standards Q10 and Q20? It cannot be covered in a purely technical way by applying technical skills (called 'skills in lesson planning'). Unpicking what is involved in planning lessons, for example, in order to learn how to 'meet' standards Q10 and Q20, demonstrates that no amount of technical information, or knowledge of research and strategies, however useful, can quite account for the complexity of learning to be a teacher. The two standards require a wealth of understanding, experience and judgement in application, which the simplicity of their construction tends to mask.

What might passing the following standards involve? Student teachers must be able to:

> *Standard Q30 – establish a purposeful and safe learning environment conducive to learning and identify opportunities for learners to learn in out-of-school contexts,*
>
> *Standard Q31 – establish a clear framework for classroom discipline to manage learners' behaviour constructively and promote their self-control and independence.*
>
> (TDA, 2007)

Behind the ability to show evidence of these 'skills' lies a great deal of 'knowledge and understanding'. The standards have to be looked at together with a number of other standards, which relate to all the areas covered in other standards, which are categorised under various headings. For example, standard Q10, under the *'Assessment and monitoring'* heading; standards Q11, 12 and 13, under *'Subjects and the curriculum'*; standards Q14 and 15, under *'Literacy, Numeracy and ICT'*; standards Q16 and 17, under *'Achievement and diversity'*, and standards Q18, 19 and 20, under *'Health and well-being'*. Learning to manage a classroom is rooted in a deep understanding of learning, of the particular group of learners and of the individual learners who make up the group, among other things. Learning to manage a classroom depends on how beginning teachers are able to integrate their own experience with the newly evolving learning situation they are confronted with. It is not a simple matter. It is evident that capturing various aspects of teaching and learning is dispersed among many standards. This limits their usefulness as an assessment mechanism, and also as a tool in the 'training curriculum', as conceived by the TDA and ratified in the standards.

Training, education or formation?

It is clear that learning to be a teacher is not just a matter of acquiring a number of technical skills and competencies, but is something that needs to be more broadly conceived. The term 'teacher training' that is used in official education department texts tends to suggest a reductive view of learning to teach. The term 'teacher education' is preferred by many higher education institutions and writers on education (Smith, 1992; Carr, 2003; Moore, 2004). The use of the word 'training' seems to imply that learning to teach is a matter of acquiring a number of skills and competencies, and suggests that reading and critiquing educational theory and research plays little or no role. The term 'teacher education' is broader and encompasses the need for theoretical perspectives. Haynes suggests that using the term 'education' helps:

> *to focus attention on the ends of the teaching act rather than on skill in performing the act. The point of the use of 'education' was to identify the problematic values, standards and purposes to which the teaching act could be put and to argue for a preferred set of those values.*
>
> (Haynes, 2004)

In this book we use the term 'initial teacher education' (ITE) where relevant, but the term 'formation', used in some other countries, overcomes some of the difficulties of terminology and suggests more accurately the nature of theoretical and practical knowledge involved in teaching (Clarke and Winch, 2004; Winch, 2004). Formation relates to the idea of teaching as 'a deliberately conducted practice' (Dewey, 1966: 387). In Chapter 12 Shirley Lawes returns to this theme in more detail.

> *Teaching and learning as a human practice…(involves) not merely a fluency in skills and strategies of communication but also something qualitatively different: a commitment to teaching and learning as a distinctive way of being human in a world that is now one with an unprecedented plurality of lifestyles, value orientations and careers.*
>
> (Hogan, 2003: 209)

Behind the question about whether to talk of 'formation', 'training' or 'education' is the larger one about how we understand the practice of teaching and how we believe people learn to become teachers. Undoubtedly there is an element of theory involved, yet a significant element in making the connections that create an understanding of how to teach well is drawn from practical experience. How does the theory relate to the practice? Many trainees enter initial teacher training and education courses believing that the school is the site of practical experience and learning, and the university is the site of learning about the relevant theory of education and pedagogy. But this perception entails a belief that the knowledge and understanding needed to be a teacher is somehow divided between two different sites of learning. This is not the case, as John Yandell discusses in detail in the following chapter. Learning to teach and continuing to develop practice requires that teachers draw on and apply what they read and discuss, and integrate this with their personal experiences.

Teaching therefore calls upon the personal resources and qualities of the teacher. Chapter 6 on the Professional Development Portfolio is particularly relevant in highlighting the way in which learning to teach means embarking on a particular kind of learning journey, related in some sense to self identity. When embarking on a course of teacher formation, a student teacher learns to relate to others within certain social practices, which gives a structure and a particular form to their self development and hence self identity. Haynes has suggested that 'it is as a participant in the practice of teaching and other practices that I and others can construct the narrative structure of my life, my self identity' (Haynes, 2004). This claim makes sense in the context of the learning journey undertaken by each student teacher, since it is essential to the conception of teaching as a practice to understand that experience forms the foundation of the knowledge and understanding that is required. It is clear then that looking at teaching through the lens of standards and competencies alone cannot identify whether teachers have developed 'rich and connected knowledge and understandings' (Davis, 1998: 19).

A significant factor in the idea of teaching as a practice is the moral significance of both teaching and education (Carr, 2003; MacIntyre and Dunne, 2002; Dunne, 2003). Noddings (2003) talks of teaching as an essentially relational practice, one in which a teacher can only be conceived of in relation to the learner(s). In any case, it makes no logical sense to say that someone has taught something that no one has learnt (Hirst, 1974). The relational nature of the practice of teaching carries responsibilities. As Haynes (2004) reminds us, 'the practices acceptable as part of education, whose ends are significant in shaping and judging the teaching acts, are also a limited set based on moral and other judgements'.

When watching a skilled teacher interacting with pupils, the expert management displayed may seem easy if we lack a deep understanding of the processes and practices of what we are viewing – until we try it ourselves in a similar context. Such teachers work in situations of complexity which demand that they interact with many variables in their daily practice. At any moment they may need to call on a number of elements, including applied theoretical knowledge, and to choose an appropriate mode of action, without having the time to engage in lengthy, or even brief deliberation. Practitioners acting expertly in such situations seem to be exercising some kind of 'practical judgement'.

Practical judgement

Practical judgement might be characterised as a capacity 'to do the right thing at the right time', to respond flexibly and appropriately in particular situations, in which the unique correlation of variables could not be known in advance. In sum, the training curriculum of any individual professional practice is designed to enable such expertise. It is useful to unravel what lies behind this capacity for exercising practical judgement. In so doing we need to think about how the concept relates to the terms 'knowledge and understanding', as used in training curricula, such as the Standards for the Award of QTS (TDA, 2007). Once the nature of such 'knowledge and understanding' is clarified, it becomes possible to address the question of appropriate forms of training, relevant assignments and assessment practices. In this chapter, then, we outline the epistemological basis of the formation we advocate, and in the following two sections of the book we clarify and exemplify in more detail what this formation entails.

The concept of 'practical judgement' goes back to Aristotle's concept of *phronesis*, although this rich and much discussed notion has been translated and interpreted in a variety of ways (Noel, 1999). A relevant interpretation for teachers is found in Dunne's statement that *phronesis* is 'an *eye* for what is salient in concrete situations' (Dunne, 1993: 368). Expert practitioners know what to do in specific situations. They have what seems to be 'an intuitive sense of the nature and texture of practical engagement' (ibid.: 8).

> *Phronesis does not ascend to a level of abstraction or generality that leaves experience behind. It arises from experience and returns into experience. It is, we might say, the insightfulness – or using Aristotle's own metaphor, 'the eye' – of a particular type of experience, and the insights it achieves are turned back into experience, which is in this way constantly reconstructed or enriched. And the more experience is reconstructed in this way, the more sensitive and insightful phronesis becomes.*
>
> (ibid.: 293)

In the above quotation the key term is 'experience'. There can be no split between elements encountered in reading, research, university and schools, because these elements make no sense, have no meaning, bear no significance to the practitioner, until and unless they are integrated and are able to be applied. Understanding develops through the practical situations in which novices are placed, and with which they grapple. This is true for many kinds of workplaces, where novices may be changed by experience into highly proficient practitioners (Hogan, 2003).

It is possible to sort some characteristics of practical judgement into three main dimensions. First, there is an ethical dimension to 'the right' response. Professional practices have their codes of ethics and it is expected that practitioners follow these codes and uphold the values of the profession. If we try to think of an example of practitioner action that seems 'value free' we soon give up the attempt. Teaching, nursing and social work are all thoroughly relational practices. They have 'the other' – the client, the learner, the patient – whose welfare is inextricably linked to their choices and actions. So the right action at any time needs to draw on ethical considerations: a good practitioner will be someone whose actions we can trust as 'wise' or 'judicious'. In acting in a seemingly spontaneous manner, practitioners draw on their own values, qualities and dispositions, as well as on technical know-how and information based on previous, relevant experiences.

Having professional values and living by them are an essential part of being a practitioner involved with others. The capacity for trustworthiness is fundamental to teaching. The practice of teaching involves the ability to see things from the learners' perspective, to show 'pedagogical thoughtfulness' (Van Manen, 1991) and to make adjustments accordingly. Van Manen has described 'tactful' teaching as that which 'locates practical knowledge not primarily in the intellect or the head but rather in the existential situation in which the person finds himself or herself' (Van Manen, 1995: 45–6).

Practical judgement is connected to 'virtue', in the sense that such a practitioner exercises qualities of 'practical wisdom'. A good teacher could be said to be a wise person, someone who exercises an ethical sense of doing what is right, of acting for the good. An example would be a teacher who rejects a strategy for gaining order in the classroom which would involve humiliating pupils, in favour of another which involves more effort and is based on developing trusting relationships. As Smith (2003) has stated, the importance of relationships between pupils, and between them and their teacher, cannot be over-emphasised. Teaching is 'thoroughly relational' (Noddings, 2003: 249) and many of the virtues are exercised in relation to others in a pedagogical space of trust (van Manen, 1991).

A second dimension of practical judgement is its flexibility. Expert practitioners can respond flexibly to changing situations. We cannot know in advance what individual situations will throw up in the way of stimuli that require a response. Experts respond flexibly. Since there cannot be a definitive, right way to respond in every circumstance, it follows that any expert response might not be the best one for the circumstances. Therefore, reflecting on practice, interrogating aims, purposes and outcomes of particular choices in particular situations, can be a fruitful source of knowledge and understanding, and can support the development of practical judgement, as discussed in Chapter 3. It follows too that there can be no universally applicable, infallible theory or pedagogical intervention, given the contingency of individual situations of practice. This is significant in the current climate of government-promoted pedagogical strategies, and educational changes and control over the school curriculum.

A third feature of practical judgement is its rootedness within an individual person, with a particular character, disposition and qualities. When a teacher decides what is to be done in any situation, for example with a recalcitrant pupil, even if her decisions seem intuitive, they are informed by her prior experiences and values. There is always more than one available course of action and individual teachers make choices about what they consider to be the right action in the circumstances. These choices may be based on a number of different factors, involving practical and ethical considerations. A teacher's character, disposition and capacities underlie the exercise of her practical judgement.

Good teachers can be said to exercise sound practical judgement, which involves exercising virtues such as justice, tolerance and courage, and qualities such as patience and optimism. We think of good teachers as acting with integrity and trustworthiness, being open-minded and able to learn from experience. It is an interesting exercise to think of all the qualities required, desired and expected of teachers, an exercise fruitfully revisited at various points in a teaching career (Burbules and Hansen, 1997).

Working at Master's level

When undertaking work at Master's level on an ITE course, it might seem as if there is a kind of 'knowledge' related to theory and another related to practice. Some writers have drawn on a distinction made by Ryle (1963) between 'knowing-how' (procedural knowledge which manifests itself in successful action such as bike riding) and 'knowing-that' (propositional knowledge, such as that found in a textbook about bicycle mechanics). This is where it gets interesting, complex and possibly controversial, because the relationship between 'knowing-how' and 'knowing-that' is complex. Take an example of a traditional skill, such as that of a blacksmith. Apprentices in traditional medieval craft guilds were apprenticed for seven years, during which time they watched and copied the master craftsman and built up their 'know-how' or procedural knowledge. In the case of the blacksmith this might involve learning how to recognise the exact colour of the metal when it needed to be taken from the furnace and worked. The colour indicates the temperature of the metal, and the knowledge of what to do and when to do it is built up by watching the process many times and by trial and error in practising the procedure. Compare this with contemporary apprentices, who may take a course which involves a theoretical element. The propositional knowledge gained on the course may involve some chemistry and physics, to enable the apprentice-students to understand the theory behind the practice. There are also thermometric devices to supply technical information about the temperature attained in the furnace. When these modern apprentices work in their practical placements, which are required sites of learning to become competent in their craft, they are able to use modern technology and applied technical knowledge, that is *'knowing-that'* certain processes depend on certain physical laws. The procedural knowledge (the *'knowing-how'*) is demonstrated in the successful practice.

A blacksmith trained with a theoretical understanding of the processes involved in the craft could articulate the theory behind the practice. However, when engaged in smelting metal the blacksmith works with fluent and tacit understanding of what she is doing – she demonstrates what Gerald Lum has called 'constitutive understandings' (Lum, 2003; Heilbronn, 2008: 70–112). There cannot be a 'split' between the theoretical elements and the practical elements: they need to be integrated into the fluent repertoire of practice. This is certainly the case in teaching. All the writers in this book understand teacher knowledge and understanding in this integrated way.

There may be different ways in which 'knowing-that', or propositional knowledge, is acquired. Some propositional knowledge is gained in evident and overt ways. For example, teachers can find out information about individual pupils' attainment from school records; knowledge of statutory requirements can be gained from reading relevant documents; learning theory research can provide information about how pupils might learn. However, there is always the individual teacher who will make sense – forge meaning – for herself through interpretive processes. How individual teachers interpret what they have read and are told is also influenced by their own personal experience, including their own observations and discussions with other teachers.

This is significant when discussing the issue of theory and practice, and the question of whether or not there are two kinds of 'knowledge', one to be gained from 'theory' and one from 'practice'. If the matter is conceived of in this way, it is inevitable that there will also be a belief that somehow there is a 'split' or a 'gulf' between these two kinds of 'knowledge' that needs to be bridged. But this is to misunderstand the nature of a practice such as teaching, and in this teaching is like blacksmithing, as described above.

Theory is often used as a term for a body of propositional knowledge. We use the word 'theory' with a small 't' in a personal context, for example, to suggest that someone may have well-warranted beliefs underpinning what they do. A teacher might talk about *'her theory about planning or language acquisition'*, for example. When a teacher has read some of the relevant documents and heard about relevant research, she might well then be able to state some general principles that she believes underlie some of her practical teaching. So a teacher of Modern Foreign Languages might say that she had read about language acquisition research and that this has influenced her lesson planning. It would then make sense for her to say, *'Language acquisition research, and particularly the work of x on memory and vocabulary development is the theoretical basis on which I have planned my teaching'* or is *'the theoretical basis of what I do'.*

To talk about 'a theoretical basis of' rather than 'Theory', takes into account the essentially provisional and practice-related nature of the propositional knowledge (the 'knowing-that', the theoretical element) that is *demonstrated in the practice*. This is to be advocated because it is necessary to maintain a critical perspective on any theory or research findings, to subject them to further substantiation in the light of further practice or new evidence. So to think of something called 'Theory' in the abstract, divorced from practice or from practical experience, makes little sense in the context of teacher formation.

Research literacy and criticality

The discussion so far about the 'craft' of practice and the nature of practical knowledge and understanding points to a notion of 'constitutive knowledge', a personal construct of knowledge and understanding which enables the practitioner to act autonomously, in the moment, drawing on a store of known responses in a fluent manner. Practical judgement, as defined in this chapter, is necessary for successful practice and constitutes the capacity and ability to make an informed choice of action or an informed decision in each individual circumstance and, in addition, the ability to do so autonomously. This is how we generally understand a competent or an expert practitioner. A novice would be characterised by the need for help and support in reaching the decision or in engaging with the action.

Experts work within the bounds of their own 'community of practice' (Lave and Wenger, 1991), relating to the norms and regulations of that practice. Experts are able to understand and apply those norms and practices in what seems to be an intuitive way, without submitting their actions to scrutiny in the moment. There is a rationality within the autonomous exercise of judgement. What factors help and support the development of practical judgement? One important factor is the ability to hold a professional dialogue on the developing practice with an expert 'other', in particular circumstances. A further factor central to the notion of a professional practitioner is the ability to understand and articulate a critical stance on the relevant subject knowledge required by the practice. This requires a critical engagement with theory and research, the ability to become and remain – in some sense – 'research literate'.

Teachers routinely use research skills when they engage in curriculum development and in preparing and evaluating lessons and resources. For example, lesson evaluation requires formulating a question, such as whether the pupils learnt what was intended. There then needs to be some kind of data collection, such as evidence of achievement from tasks done in class or observations of pupil responses. The posited question needs to be assessed against the data collected and the findings applied to planning new activities. These steps represent a recognisable research-based methodology. The possession of these research skills is essential for successful teaching.

Teachers also need to be research literate since, without some understanding of the principles and practices of educational research, they will be unable to evaluate theories, policies and strategies, in relation to the aims of their own teaching. In addition, some teachers may benefit from doing their own action research, as a means to understanding and improving their practice.

Educational research in the form of action research is a useful means of developing and improving practice and is undertaken in many ITE courses and Master's courses in education. Indeed, 'the unique feature of the questions that prompt teacher research is that they emanate from neither theory nor practice alone but from critical reflection on the intersection of the two (Cochran-Smith and Lytle, 1993: 15). Currently, there are many varieties of action research, referred to also as 'teacher research' or 'practitioner research' (Dick, 2003; Newman, 2003; Ewbank, 2004; DSEA, 2005). We find:

> *sharp differences between variants of action research in the way they theorise the relationship between research and social (or educational) change: some see it as a technical (or instrumental) connection, some see it as a version of what Aristotle, and Schwab (1969) after him, described as practical reasoning, and others see it in terms of critical social science.*
> (Kemmis, 1993)

Whatever version of action research is followed, there is a key difference between its primary aim, which is to improve practice, and the usual aim of research, which is to produce new propositional knowledge. This does not mean that the findings or conclusion of a piece of action research are only valuable to the researcher who does it, and cannot be useful to others. As Pring points out:

> although such a practical conclusion focuses on the particular, thereby not justifying generalisation, no one situation is unique in every respect and therefore the action research in one classroom or school can illuminate or be suggestive of practice elsewhere.
>
> (Pring, 2000: 131)

Providing that sound research procedures and practices are followed, teachers researching their own practice may come to new understandings about teaching. In Chapter 3, ways of working reflectively in teaching are suggested. A regular habit of reflection, as part of building professional knowledge, lays down ways of working on which practitioner research can be subsequently built. The skills of systematically reflecting on one's own practice can be extended to include reflection on wider educational issues, including developing the skills of evaluating good educational research and distinguishing it from bad research. Embarking on Master's level study on an ITE course helps student teachers to become critical thinkers and to evaluate research rationally for its rigour and validity.

Evidence-informed practice: Teachers as users of research

Both doing research and reading research require an understanding about what research is; how particular theories underpin what is researched; how research is carried out and the relationship of aims and values to the interpretive process of elaborating research findings. It is important for teachers to become research literate, in the sense of being able to question and evaluate educational research. This will enable them to become more informed practitioners, so that they can improve their teaching practice and also develop an informed, independent stance when presented with policies and strategies that are promoted as research evidenced.

Teachers, as *users* of research rather than *doers* of research, need to be trained to differentiate good research from bad, in order to gauge the reliability of findings for their own practice. As Winch has stated, teachers need to develop 'critical rationality as a practical disposition and skill' (Winch, 2006: 45). The nature of critical rationality is a 'settled disposition and set of abilities to subject authorities to evaluation' (ibid.). Teacher education courses at Master's level include work on becoming research literate in this sense.

Finally, undertaking a Master's level course of teacher education and training is to be 'in formation'. While studying and practising in a placement school, student teachers' practical judgement is forming, and their practical experience is informing the development of practical judgement. In learning to teach, student teachers need to develop judgement based on a variety of sources, integrated in their own reflection. The following chapters expand and illustrate this conception of teacher education and training.

Chapter 2

Sites of learning

John Yandell

Learning activity appears to have a characteristic pattern. There are strong goals for learning because learners, as peripheral participants, can develop a view of what the whole enterprise is about, and what there is to be learned. Learning itself is an improvised practice: a learning curriculum unfolds in opportunities for engagement in practice. It is not specified as a set of dictates for proper practice.

(Lave and Wenger, 1991: 93)

What I want to do in this chapter is to explore the place of school experience within initial teacher education (ITE). In so doing, I want to challenge two widely held views about the development of teacher identities, both of which were mentioned in the previous chapter. One is that there is a clear divide between theory and practice; the other is that becoming a teacher is a process that can best be conceptualised as the acquisition of a set of context-independent skills and attributes.

Simple binaries: The New Right and the move to school-based training

In the 1980s, a number of influential voices, from what has been characterised as the New Right (Furlong *et al.*, 2000), argued that there really wasn't much need for university-based courses for ITE – indeed, that the very existence of such courses was a barrier to the recruitment into teaching of able people, people with 'knowledge and talent' but with neither the time nor the inclination to waste on irrelevant theory (Hillgate Group, 1989: 1; Lawlor, 1990: 42). According to this view, the defining characteristic of effective teachers is subject knowledge, allied to a particular orientation towards the subject:

the true teacher or educator is one endowed with knowledge of his subject, but over and above that, with a love and respect for it.

(O'Hear, 1988: 15)

Such disciplinary knowledge is acquired, and such love is instilled, so the argument goes, within the potential teacher's undergraduate studies. Thus the assumption is that subject knowledge is a necessary precondition of entry into teaching: it is something that the neophyte already possesses. What remains to be imparted is the craft of the classroom – and this is best acquired on the job, as it were, by serving an apprenticeship working alongside more experienced colleagues:

> It is small wonder that many newly-qualified teachers say that the most valuable part of their course in education was their teaching practice, because...teaching being preeminently a practical skill is something one learns how to do by doing it.
>
> (O'Hear, 1988: 18).

This viewpoint is that learning to teach is accomplished by teaching. The model is culturally conservative, in two significant ways: first, the best that can be hoped for from such a system of training is that the neophytes will gradually come to emulate their colleagues more and more successfully – so that becoming more skilful is the same as becoming more like one's mentors; second, the subject is treated as a stable, pre-existent entity – both the body of knowledge and the disposition towards that body of knowledge have already been learnt before entry into teaching. The craft of the classroom thus becomes conceptualised as the efficient transmission of an established body of knowledge and of the appropriate attitude of reverence towards it (see also Lawlor, 1990).

O'Hear, like Lawlor and the members of the Hillgate Group,[1] was engaged in an argument for a more decentralised, school-based route into teaching.[2] The Hillgate Group explicitly acknowledged that this model was intended to be a counterposition to university-based ITE:

> a new kind of route into a career in teaching, based primarily on an apprenticeship served in school, which would exist alongside, and in competition with, the teacher training courses run by institutions of higher education.
>
> (Hillgate Group, 1989: 2)

The New Right's support for school-based training was part and parcel of their distrust of 'theory'. Theory, associated with higher education, was represented as simultaneously irrelevant and, largely because of its association with equalities projects (feminism, antiracism and gay and lesbian rights, in particular), dangerously political (Hillgate Group, 1989; Lawlor, 1990). What happened in the 1990s was that the emphasis on the school-based component of ITE received the endorsement of policy: circulars 9/92 (DfE and the Welsh Office, 1992) and 14/93 (DfE, 1993), covering the secondary and primary phases of school, respectively, enforced an enlarged role for schools in the training process.[3] And the paradigm of 'training' that was promoted in the circulars was, likewise, derived from the New Right, foregrounding as they did two core elements: subject knowledge and practical teaching skills (Furlong *et al.*, 2000).

It would be a mistake, however, to imagine that it was only the theory-averse pamphleteers of the New Right who were arguing for a reconceptualisation of the role of school experience within ITE. Practitioners, too, were involved in the local development of collaborative partnerships between universities and schools: in Sussex (Furlong *et al.*, 1988), Oxford (Benton, 1990) and at the IOE. I have first-hand experience of the last of these, as a student on the 'alternative' Secondary PGCE (1984–85): my course was constructed around cross-curricular investigations conducted by teams of student teachers working in partnership with school-based mentors. In all of these partnerships, there was an explicit understanding of teaching as theoretically informed; hence all were quite distinct from the New Right's preference for an anti-theoretical model of practice.

What such approaches had in common, too, was a readiness to pose problems, to maintain a position of critical engagement with the processes of schooling that is diametrically opposed to the notion of merely learning by doing. These approaches have proved durable, even in unfavourable climates. The Oxford internship scheme is alive and well (Ellis *et al.*, 2007), while at the IOE there remains a commitment to a partnership with schools that includes an explicit orientation towards collaboration in research (Heilbronn and Jones, 1997). What such approaches have achieved, at least some of the time, has been a repositioning of the student teacher:

> As the beginning teachers moved through their course in the school[,] the research element in the work led them to continually question us, the so-called experts, i.e. the teachers from the school and the Institute of Education.
>
> (Jones in Heilbronn and Jones, 1997: 77)

Standards and central control: The teacher as context-free individual

As has been explored in the previous chapter, the maintenance of central government control over all routes into teaching has been accomplished largely through the Training and Development Agency (TDA, formerly the Teacher Training Agency or TTA), whose *Professional Standards for Teachers* map out the characteristics to be demonstrated by teachers at every stage of their careers. These standards are presented as 'statements of a teacher's professional attributes, professional knowledge and understanding, and professional skills' (TDA, 2007: 2).

The categories, which group together the 33 standards that must be met before qualified teacher status (QTS) can be awarded, map neatly onto O'Hear's adumbration of the three essential qualifications required by a 'good teacher':

> He needs, first, a qualification in his subject [knowledge and understanding] and, secondly, practice in teaching leading to a satisfactory ability to teach [skills], and thirdly, the emotional maturity to work as a teacher [attributes].
>
> (O'Hear, 1988: 19)

Many of the problems that are associated with the attempt to describe the development of professional identity in terms of a set of separately identifiable competences or standards have already been addressed in the previous chapter. The universalising tendency of the standards approach is what concerns me most here, since it carries the implication that the particular site in which attributes are honed and demonstrated, in which skills are developed and refined, in which knowledge is acquired, is unimportant. From the New Right 20 years ago, through the government circulars of 1992–93, to the current TDA regulations which continue to specify the number of days that PGCE students are expected to spend in school, there is, simultaneously, an emphasis on the centrality of school experience in the formation of teachers and a lack of specificity about how school experience functions in the process. There is a shared assumption that 'practice' will lead, in due course, to the acquisition of the requisite skills – the 'ability to teach'. Since what is learnt is universally applicable, the local is reduced to the status of the merely accidental, the circumstantial.

The standards/competences approach to teacher education should be seen in the context of policy-makers' more general insistence on 'standards not structures' (the slogan of New Labour; see Fitz et al., 2005); likewise, the universalising effect of the standards/competences lists of teacher attributes is part of a wider shift in policy away from local democratic accountability towards a model of centralised control. The comment made by Furlong et al. on the orientation of government policy in the 1980s has remained pertinent throughout the past two decades:

> As in many other areas of recent government policy, 'consumer demand' has been presented as the guarantor of quality, relevance and democracy. Yet as elsewhere the Government has at the same time taken upon itself to determine what that demand actually is; once again the democracy of the market place has been accompanied by the reality of greater central control.
>
> (Furlong et al., 1988: 12; see also Jones, 1989, 2003; Jones et al., 2008).

The TDA's *Professional Standards for Teachers* map out a linear progression from QTS through to Excellent Teacher and Advanced Skills Teacher: each rung on the ladder of professional advancement is defined as a set of properties of the individual, properties that exist within the teacher, not as a function of more complicated interactions or circumstances. The skills and attributes ascribed to the individual teacher are assumed to be as portable as the portfolios in which these are to be demonstrated (Yandell and Turvey, 2007).

As Michael Apple has observed, such an approach leads to 'the dismissal of any types of situation-specific and qualitative understanding that is grounded in the lived experience of teachers in real schools' (Apple, 2001: 188). Teachers' expertise is always situated: it is developed over time and in relation to specific contexts and conditions. As has been shown in Chapter 1, this is, in effect, an epistemological argument – an argument for certain kinds of knowledge, acquired in certain kinds of ways. Closely allied to this is the argument for methodologies that are properly attentive to the local, the contingent. Thus Peter Freebody, in making claims for the usefulness of a case study approach, insists that:

> *teachers are always teaching some subject matter, with some particular learners, in particular places and under conditions that significantly shape and temper teaching and learning practices. These conditions are not taken to be 'background' variables, but rather lived dimensions that are indigenous to each teaching–learning event. In that important respect, case studies show a strong sense of time and place; they represent a commitment to the overwhelming significance of localized experience.*

> (Freebody, 2003: 81)

For teachers (and those involved in the formation of teachers) not to pay sufficient heed to the 'lived dimensions…indigenous to each teaching–learning event' is to indulge in reductively simple paradigms of teacher effectiveness, to foster explanations that focus exclusively on the attributes of the individual teacher. Such explanations place an insupportable weight on innate talent (the paradigm of the charismatic teacher, born, not made, who succeeds and inspires through sheer force of personality [see Moore, 2004: 51–74]) or on the acquisition of straightforwardly transferable skills (the paradigm of the competent craftsperson, who becomes effective through training, by attaining competence in a set of pre-specified and isolable skills [ibid.: 75–99]).

Ethnographic perspectives: Attentiveness to local knowledge

Changing Teachers − Finland Comes to England − Secondary, a programme that appears on Teachers TV (TTV), shows what happens when a highly experienced Science teacher from Finland, Maija Flinkman, comes to spend a week in a girls' secondary school in South London. The classroom footage in the programme is atypical of the output of TTV, which tends to present 'good news stories', whereas this is not a shiny example of best practice. Instead, what we are treated to is both deeply uncomfortable and − for anyone who has spent time in secondary schools in England − instantly recognisable. The teacher, for all her previous experience and all her professional attributes, knowledge and skills, is treated as a supply teacher by pupils who pay her scant respect, who are by turns bewildered and alienated by the differences between her approach and their expectations. What the film demonstrates is thus not the superiority of one education system over another but the crucial importance of precisely those features of schooling that are peripheral to the standards discourse: local knowledge and the development of pedagogical relationships over time.

Student teachers on the PGCE course on which I teach are encouraged to watch this programme as a pre-course task. We hope that it might help them begin to understand something of fundamental importance in the construction of teacher identities, namely that such identities (like any identity) are relational, situated products of history. Context − the school, the department, the classroom − exerts a shaping influence on the very identity of the teacher. To suggest this is not to deny the teacher's agency or responsibility, but instead to insist that an adequate account of a teacher's work must remain attentive to particular contexts, must acknowledge the contingency of all teaching and learning. At the opposite pole to Maija Flinkman's week spent in a South London school is the account of an experienced teacher's practice presented in Turvey *et al.* (2006), where what is most salient is the denseness of the teacher's knowledge of her learners, her deep attentiveness to their histories, their relationships, their development.

Generally speaking, student teachers begin our course with well-established disciplinary commitments. Most have degrees within the field that is their chosen subject and for the vast majority there is a strong sense of what the subject has to offer, a sense of its value and importance: they might represent the aims of education as 'the preservation of knowledge, skills, culture and moral values and their transmission to the young' (Hillgate Group, 1989: 1). What they might reasonably expect from their PGCE course, therefore, is an induction into the skills that will enable them to effect this transmission process. Part of what happens on the course might be construed as the transformation of subject knowledge into pedagogic content knowledge (Shulman, 1999). Part of what happens on the course − and particularly in the classroom – is that questions are posed about what O'Hear (1988) described as the teacher's 'emotional maturity': children and young people can be searingly direct in probing the pressure points in new teachers' sense of self – and the vulnerability of new teachers is directly proportional to the urgency with which they confront what seems to them to be the most important question: 'Can I do it?'

Much of our – the university tutors' – interventions, particularly in the first half of the course, might be construed as attempts to divert our student teachers' attention away from that question and towards more interesting ones (summed up, in the first lecture of the course, in a formulation that we derived from the title of a former student teacher's final assignment: 'Who are the learners, and what do they know?'). Much of what we ask them to do is designed less to enable them to demonstrate their attainment of particular pedagogic skills and more to encourage them to become attentive to the particular classrooms in which they find themselves, to the particular learners whom they encounter. Their first task, emanating from the week that they spend in a primary school at the start of the course, is to write a 'profile of a reader', based on one of the primary children whom they have been observing. A couple of weeks later, they are expected to write a 'language autobiography', in which they focus on their own history as a language user. When they begin their first period of practice in a secondary school, they are asked to construct a 'focused lesson observation' – an account of a single lesson. The reading that they engage with in connection with these tasks (Minns, 1997; Barrs and Cork, 2001; Gregory, 1996; Gregory and Williams, 2000; Kress *et al.*, 2005) might all be characterised as displaying ethnographic tendencies.

Ethnographic insights exert a shaping influence on the course. There is, inevitably, an historic dimension to this approach, arising out of a long-standing interest in London classrooms and the diversity – of language and culture, history and class – in which they are constituted. As I have presented it above, this might appear to be merely a local idiosyncrasy, a product of the course tutors' research interests, having only peripheral relevance to the formation of teachers. What I want to suggest, on the contrary, is that the ethnographic turn, made at the outset of the course and revisited thereafter, enables our student teachers to approach that part of the course that is labelled 'school experience' from a fundamentally different perspective, and that this perspective allows them to engage intellectually with the particular schools in which they find themselves. (The use of the term 'school experience' is an attempt to indicate something of this emphasis: this is a deliberately broader formulation than 'teaching practice', since practice is only a part of what is to be accomplished.)

The move to Master's-level PGCE courses might encourage an O'Hear-like reaction, a renewed questioning of the role of theory in the formation of teachers and a widening of the imagined gulf between university- and school-based elements of the course. The written assignments which we ask our student teachers to produce are designed to cut across such simple oppositions. The act of writing is intended to enable them to bring theory to bear on practice and to mobilise their school experience in the reading and critique of theory. Part of what is involved in school experience is, necessarily, learning by doing; an equally important part of the learning entails standing back and reflecting critically, asking not only 'How is this done?' but also 'How might it be otherwise?' In this sense, student teachers are confronted with two kinds of text: one is the body of research and scholarship that might, for the sake of convenience, be labelled theory; the other is the particular site of schooling – the institutional setting, the department, the classroom – in which the student teachers are placed. They should be encouraged to reflect critically on both kinds of text and to move from such reflection to the production of new knowledge, new theory and new practice.

Reading the school through the lenses of policy and theory[4]

Halfway through our PGCE course, at the point when the student teachers begin their second block of school experience, they are asked to write an essay on the place of English. In preparation for this assignment, they are presented with extracts from a variety of policy documents, ranging in time from the 1862 Revised Code (Maclure, 1969: 80) to English 21, part of the Qualifications and Curriculum Authority's (QCA) recent consultation on the future of the subject (Hackman, 2006). They explore these texts collaboratively, then are invited to consider points of continuity and discontinuity with the present and to think about the practice that they have met as observers and participants in schools. This is the brief for their written task:

- Drawing on your knowledge of policy and practice, now and in the past, write about the place of English in the curriculum.
- What place does English occupy?
- Why is this, and how might it be differently imagined in the future?

This assignment encourages student teachers to engage with the discourses of policy; it presents the curriculum subject as a changing and contested space, as the product of historical processes. At the same time, this assignment asks them to consider how the subject is instantiated in the singular, specific sites of their teaching practice schools. What, in effect, does it mean to study English here, now, in this school? What histories lie behind these practices? How can such practices be theorised? How else might the subject be imagined, here, for these learners?

This assignment seeks to enact precisely the integration of practice and theory that we see as constitutive of the PCGE course. It demands, simultaneously, engagement in the local, the particular, of practice, and in critical reflection, stepping back from practice to gain a wider perspective. And the student teacher is reflecting in writing on a problem that exists in the world.

I want to look in some detail at the response that this task elicited from one of our student teachers. Roy takes as his starting point Zancanella (1998), a course reading that opens up issues of canonicity and curriculum design:

> *Don Zancanella in 'Inside the Literature Curriculum' examines two opposing philosophies of English pedagogy: one that encourages students to assimilate into the dominant culture of literature, providing a point of access into high socio-economic statuses; the other encourages students to make an evaluation of several different kinds of literature, especially ones more locally relevant to the area and ethnicity of the school.*

Zancanella's essay is an account of a literature and language arts curriculum developed by a single teacher in a school in New Mexico. It presents the possibility of a local curriculum – one that was constructed by a teacher sensitive to the lives, experiences, histories and cultures of his pupils – while acknowledging that the majority of the department remained committed to a more traditional curriculum, on the grounds that they believed that such a curriculum would better prepare their pupils for the demands of the next stage of their education. Roy's summary indicates his understanding of the terms of this debate: it shows, in effect, that he can 'do' scholarly reading. The question that confronts him, though, is a much more demanding one: what light can Zancanella's account shed on the different context of his own school? Can a curricular initiative in New Mexico simply be transposed onto a school in East London?

What gives urgency to this enquiry is Roy's sense of the specific characteristics and needs of the school where he has been placed. It is an Inner London school, situated in an area of acute poverty and deprivation, a school where almost all the pupils are from minority ethnic communities, the large majority of them of Bangladeshi heritage. In this site, questions of the relationship between school and community, questions of curricular design and access, questions of culture and identity, are sharply posed.

> *After reading this essay I was struck by how unworkable both these teaching approaches would be if transferred into my new school. I am very much of John Hardcastle's opinion in 'Carlos' Task' [Hardcastle, 2002] that by ignoring a student's origins you are reducing the boundaries of that child's self-expression. English, the subject, suddenly becomes a means of devaluing certain voices; self-knowledge is discarded in favour of social assimilation.*

*However, with the range of ability in English in the school so great,
and the overall prospects of advancement in the area surrounding the
school being so small, a less 'traditional' method of English teaching
might be unpopular with students, and their parents, who would
perhaps be appreciative of any chance to study the dominant culture
as a crucial point of social and economic access. One could argue
that diverting from the current curriculum to suit the students would
be more patronising to the community, as if they required exclusive
assistance, than if their culture had been ignored at all.*

Roy's reading of Zancanella and Hardcastle provides him with
perspectives from which he can (re-)examine the issues that confront him
in his placement school, partly because these readings, too, challenge any
easy notion of generalisability: to say that both papers are engagements in
specific, situated debates is not to deny their wider resonance, but to insist
on an attentiveness to local circumstances. Roy's reading of his school, of its
pupils, their parents and the local community that the school serves, is equally
crucial to his developing argument. And Roy's attentiveness to the context of
his school leads him to recognise that the question of the place of the subject
cannot be dissociated from the bigger question of the function of education.
What, in this place, is schooling for? Whose interests must it serve?

Roy's understanding of what is at stake here is a product of the space
he has been given – and the opportunities he has taken – to explore the
problem of the subject and the problem of the site of schooling. At work is the
kind of reflexivity described by Moore (2004) and which is further discussed in
Chapter 3. Such reflexivity moves beyond the kinds of questions 'embedded
in the competences and standards discourse' (ibid.: 149) – questions such
as 'How did my classroom management strategies work?' – and towards a
consideration of how the immediate activity of self-evaluation might be
located in a much bigger picture: a picture that may include the practitioner's
own history, dispositions, prejudices and fears, as well as the wider social,
historical and cultural contexts in which schooling itself is situated.

Roy recognises that schooling cannot be separated from issues of
power. He acknowledges that some configurations of the subject can exclude
and demean pupils' subjectivities and affiliations just as surely as other versions
of English might create curricular spaces in which important identity work
can be accomplished. And yet this does not lead him to a position of simple,
programmatic support for localised curricula because he recognises the
legitimacy of the demands from pupils, their parents and communities, that the
school should provide them with access to cultural capital, to 'the dominant culture'.

Roy starts with a binary opposition – the binary of Zancanella's essay
– a curriculum constructed from local and locally valued texts, reflecting the
particularity of pupils' cultures and histories, or a curriculum whose content is

derived from the high-status texts of the dominant culture? He uses writing his assignment to reflect on what these poles of attraction have to offer – to him and to the school pupils whom he has just started to teach. What enables him to resolve, or at least to move beyond, this opposition is that he shifts the focus from curricular content to pedagogy:

> *attention should be diverted away from which texts are taught and towards the status a text should assume in teaching. From my small experience in my new school, deciding how ethical one text is above another can be mind-bendingly complicated.* **What is important is how texts are taught.** *Students should be allowed to build up a range of perspectives to inform their reading, rather than possessing a set of useless nuggets of information gleaned from the usual series of texts, knowledge that might come in handy in a pub quiz, but with little application elsewhere* [emphasis added].

What is entailed in this moment of professional learning? Subject knowledge, to be sure, and pedagogical content knowledge, too – but much more than this. Big questions of policy are inextricably linked here to immediate (practical) questions of how best to organise teaching and learning, how to meet the needs of particular pupils and groups of pupils. Roy's professional learning has much in common with that of the Australian student teachers described by Doecke and McKnight:

> *Essential though it may be for these student teachers to gain the kind of experience embodied in the notion of pedagogical content knowledge, their professional learning is ultimately dependent on the way they handle the ideological issues with which they are faced. Their learning is driven by their beliefs and values.*
> (Doecke and McKnight, 2003: 305)

Writing the assignment enables Roy to work towards a properly theorised practice – and one which restores, both to him as beginning teacher and to his pupils, a sense of their shared agency.

And then there's the question of what kind of teacher we want to produce. If it's O'Hear's model, then Roy's lines of inquiry don't help. But if we see teachers as public, organic intellectuals (Gramsci, 1971), then they need the opportunity to interrogate processes of schooling as part of finding their own way into productive pedagogic relationships.

Student teachers as legitimate peripheral participants?

I want to return now to O'Hear's view of teaching as 'pre-eminently a practical skill' (1988: 18) and to the model of teaching practice which is, in effect, an apprenticeship in the craft of the classroom. The intention and the effect of this way of representing school experience is to construct a counterposition between practice and theory, between workplace and seminar room, between doing and thinking.

Lave and Wenger's (1991; Wenger, 1998) development of a theory of situated learning is helpful in deconstructing these binaries. Starting from an ethnographic interest in particular instances of craft apprenticeship, Lave and Wenger move towards a general theoretical perspective on situated activity – a perspective that calls into question the possibility of conceiving of learning as anything other than situated. For them, the situatedness of activity constitutes:

> *the basis of claims about the relational character of knowledge and*
> *learning, about the negotiated character of meaning, and about the*
> *concerned (engaged, dilemma-driven) nature of learning activity for*
> *the people involved.*
>
> (Lave and Wenger, 1991: 33)

The case studies of apprenticeship on which Lave and Wenger draw indicate very clearly that, no matter how 'practical' the work may be, learning is never simply about doing. Always and everywhere, it would seem, learning is sociocultural, involves observation and talk, involves narrative; it is through such means that the neophyte gradually moves from legitimate peripheral participation to full participation in a community of practice. What Lave and Wenger's empirical data show, too, is that even in cases where apprenticeship involves a specified dyadic relationship of master and apprentice, 'it is not this relationship but rather the apprentice's relations to other apprentices and even to other masters that organize opportunities to learn' (Lave and Wenger, 1991: 93; see also Clark, 2001).

This account of learning from peers and 'other masters' speaks directly to our PGCE course and how professional learning is conceptualised and operationalised within it. Becoming a teacher is not accomplished merely by practising to be one, but by participating in a community of practice, and participating entails questioning and reflecting as central activities. For Roy, relations to 'other masters', including those – such as Zancanella or Hardcastle – at some distance from the specific site that is his placement school, significantly shape his learning in the school.

The community of practice of the PGCE student teacher, therefore, is not coterminous with the school, let alone the single department: it encompasses peers, placed in different schools, as well as tutors – and it also includes those voices they encounter in their reading. It might, indeed, be more helpful to conceptualise the position of the PGCE student as one who participates simultaneously in different, though overlapping, communities of practice – including those of the course, of the discipline or subject, as well as the more localised community of the individual school. Participation, in relation to each of these communities, is, as Lave and Wenger recognise, 'always based on situated negotiation and renegotiation of meaning in the world' (1991: 51).

As a legitimate peripheral participant in these different arenas, the student teacher is necessarily implicated in power structures and relations. These are not necessarily comfortable relations, and there are frequently tensions and contradictions both within and between intersecting communities of practice. Studies of workplace learning that draw on the central concepts developed by Lave and Wenger have sometimes tended to underplay these tensions and contradictions, to treat communities of practice as more stable, more harmonious and more homogeneous than they really are. Lave and Wenger themselves emphasise that all communities of practice are subject to change – and, indeed, that is one of the effects of the legitimate peripheral participation of the newbies. They also recognise that all communities of practice need to be seen as part of larger activity systems, systems which are themselves fractured, unstable and subject to change, both gradual and sudden.

For much of the time, the student teacher's position may be one of relative powerlessness, where their peripheral status is synonymous with marginalisation. The experience, reported by Doecke and McKnight (2003: 298), of Australian student teachers who are silenced and physically marginalised within the school staffroom, is an equally familiar one in the context of London schools. But peripheral participation can also be a privileged vantage point, a position from which to make sense of the hurly-burly as well as 'a position at the articulation of related communities' (Lave and Wenger, 1991: 36). Again, this seems to me to capture well what is happening with Roy, as he brings different communities into productive relationships and thereby renegotiates meaning in relation to his own practice in the specific site of his placement school. Roy, of course, is both unique and also stands for other student teachers as they negotiate their way into and among different communities of practice. The next section takes a closer look at some of the resources that our courses provide to enable teachers to accomplish this.

Notes

1   The Hillgate Group was a right-wing pressure group that produced a series of pamphlets on British education in the late 1980s. Its leading members were Caroline Cox, Jessica Douglas-Home, John Marks, Lawrence Norcross and Roger Scruton.

2   This argument has resurfaced recently in another pamphlet from the Centre for Policy Studies: Burkard and Talbot Rice call for the abolition of the TDA on the grounds that 'teacher training can be provided more effectively within schools, as an employment-based system, or via short courses like Teach First' (2009: 19).

3   These interventions by central government marked a development from circular 3/84 (DES, 1984), which prescribed, for the first time in the UK, the number of weeks that trainees should spend in school (Furlong *et al.*, 1988: 12).

4   An earlier version of this section appeared in Heilbronn *et al.*, (2009).

Chapter 3

The reflective practitioner

Ruth Heilbronn

The previous two chapters have shown that becoming an expert teacher is not a simple matter of acquiring theoretical knowledge and applying it to practice: such learning cannot be reduced to the acquisition of technical skills. Each individual situation of practice is unique and complex, and knowing what to do in any moment requires more than the ability to apply formulaic, technical knowledge. Teachers, and others in high-skilled vocational practices, need to engage successfully in the practice and also reflect critically about the practice, stepping back from it to gain a wider perspective.

Promoting and developing critical reflection in teacher education has proved problematic in the climate of performativity that has prevailed over the past 30 years in England, since teacher education came under centralised government control and became subject to performance criteria in the form of standards and the establishment of centralised regulatory bodies. In Chapter 2 Yandell developed some of the implications of this, and the story of this increasing control from the mid-1970s onwards has been well documented (Benn and Simon, 1972; Chitty, 1990; Hirst, 1996). The era following the 1944 Education Act was characterised by a general consensus about many aspects of education and educational practices. Education then was generally seen to provide 'the foundations of a good life for everyone, through the promotion of their development as rationally autonomous individuals' (Hirst, 1996: 167; see also Corbett, 1968; Peters, 1965; Peters and White, 1969). It was generally accepted that 'education has a value for the person as the fulfilment of the mind, a value which has nothing to do with utilitarian or vocational considerations' (Hirst, 1974: 31). The introduction of the first national curriculum (NC) by the 1988 Education Reform Act, and the subsequent emphasis on the performance indicators of test results, was significant in changing this general consensus about the aims of education.

Changes in teacher education ran parallel to those in the school curriculum. As Chapter 2 explored, the role of practical experience in school as the major part of the trainees' curriculum was decisively extended (DFE and Welsh Office, 1992, 1993). Once it was decided that a substantial amount of trainee teachers' time was to be spent in school, initial teacher education (ITE) programmes were significantly altered. It then became debatable what the particular role of the higher education institutions (HEIs) might be in developing a scholarly approach to teaching, and providing access to and sites for research and scholarship in education. Despite widespread reference to Schön's notion of the fundamental importance of 'reflective practitioner' knowledge (1983, 1987), most ITE courses in England are under pressure to 'deliver' a national accreditation through the award of qualified teacher status (QTS), and the notion of practice and theory in the QTS standards (TDA, 2007) threatens to overwhelm the process of developing a critically reflective stance. A limited conception of reflection is articulated in the QTS standards, which are constructed with a view of professional development that is reduced to achieving a series of standards. So, in Standard Q7 teachers need to be able to 'reflect on and improve their practice, and take responsibility for identifying and meeting their developing professional needs'. In Standard Q9 they need to 'act upon advice and feedback and be open to coaching and mentoring', and while Standard Q8 does identify having 'a creative and constructively critical approach towards innovation', this approach is characterised by 'being prepared to adapt their practice where benefits and improvements are identified'. Defining 'a critical approach' in terms of what seems to be a performance management process casts the notion of reflection more in the discourse of technical rationality than within the rich concept of well-grounded reflection.

The spirit of reflective inquiry discussed in this chapter involves some of the behaviour identified by Roth (1989), including:

- questioning the basis of what is done;
- reflecting on how others do things;
- seeking alternatives;
- keeping an open mind;
- seeking the theoretical basis and/or underlying rationale;
- viewing various perspectives;
- asking hypothetical questions about alternatives;
- challenging prescriptive models that are not adapted to the situation;
- considering consequences;
- hypothesising;
- synthesising and testing;
- seeking, identifying and resolving problems.

Schön's concept of the 'reflective practitioner', which he based on Dewey's idea of reflective inquiry (Schön, 1992: 121–3), is widely applicable to other practices, as can be seen from the literature in diverse fields such as nursing (Johns, 2004), management and training (Swenson, 1999), conservation and ecology (Davis-Case, 2001), government (Schall, 1997), computer science (Hazzan, 2002) and sports coaching (McShane, 1999). Currently the term 'reflection' is variously used in literature on practice-based learning and suffers from an instability of definition. A continuum of meanings can be found, from pondering on trivial details on the one hand to systematic data analysis on the other (McLaughlin, 1999). So what precisely are we advocating when we design and develop opportunities for critical reflection in our courses?

Some of the important questions that Schön's account of the reflective practitioner attempts to answer relate to *how* experts know what to do in the heat of the moment without rationally thinking through each individual action they take. How does a procedure, followed at first with rational guidelines, become instinctive? What is involved in highly skilful and responsive action that seems intuitive? We know that this faculty can be developed, as most skilled workers in complex practices start out as novices and only develop expertise after several years in the job.

Reflection builds on the fundamental human process that Giddens has called 'reflexivity'. Giddens points out that:

> *all human beings continuously monitor the circumstances of their activities as a feature of what they do, and such monitoring always has discursive features…agents are normally able, if asked, to provide discursive interpretations of the nature of, and the reasons for, the behaviour in which they engage.*

(1991: 35)

The teaching and learning affordances outlined in this book are based on the notion that reflected-upon personal experience is a basis for developing knowledge and understanding. Our view of teacher education is one that facilitates and enables 'discursive interpretations' of the experience of practice, in which applied theory is implicit. Acting reflexively means acting in response to experience. In teaching, 'the moment' may be one in which many variables are apparent, and the teacher's response requires skill and judgement. The various learning experiences are designed to support the development of practical judgement, as defined in Chapter 1, to gain the necessary 'strategic knowledge' (Schulman, 1986), in order to exercise the 'professional artistry' that Schön has defined as 'the kind of professional competence practitioners display in unique, uncertain and conflicted situations of practice' (Schön, 1987: 22).

Several writers in this book refer to a performativity agenda that limits teacher development. To rely on 'technical rationality' is to misunderstand the nature of practice and to fail to recognise that 'we need to think...about knowledge...in a different way' (Schön, 1971: 49). Schön rightly points out that practitioners making decisions in the heat of the moment about what to do are expert performers, capable of highly skilful action, which 'reveals a knowing more than we can say' (ibid.: 51), not abstracted technical knowledge but 'knowing-in-action' (Schön, 1987). Highly skilled practitioners come to depend on this 'knowing-in-action' to perform their work apparently effortlessly and without going through a rational thought- and decision-making process (Gilroy, 1993; Eraut, 1995: 12).

Teachers may read statements about what constitutes teacher knowledge and understanding, such as those that are found in competency and standards-based approaches, but without some kind of mediated experience of how their technical knowledge relates to their own practice, 'intuitive' and fluent practice does not follow.

Schön argues that 'knowing-in-action' is not limited to expert practice but is also shown in everyday situations and everyday routines. There are many occasions when we are able to act spontaneously, without apparently thinking, and when this happens, 'knowing-in-action' is revealed by action and is tacit, in that it cannot be fully described (Schön, 1983: 49–50; 53–4). It is 'the knowing we manifest in the doing' (Schön, 1987: 230). He states that 'knowing-in-action' might commonly be called 'intuition' or 'instinct' and is evidenced, for example, in the successful performance of physical skills such as crawling, walking and juggling or when engaging in ordinary social interactions and conversations (Schön, 1992: 124). 'Knowing-in-action' for Schön is the first and simplest component of reflective practice and it is this kind of expert action that practitioners aim to develop.

Contexts for reflection

Practitioners may engage in reflective practice in various contexts. Teachers are situated individuals within the contexts of one classroom or various classrooms; of a group of pupils or various different groups; within a team or teams of teachers; within the large context of a particular school, with all the various aspects of management, leadership, policies and practices. These nested contexts are situated in the wider framework of government policies, and have political and evaluative dimensions. As practitioners develop, the scope and content of what they reflect upon also tends to develop from an initial emphasis on self and survival to understanding the wider contexts, as Reynolds (1965) and Dreyfus and Dreyfus (1986) have found.

Because reflection entails engaging with personal experience, different modes of reflection may appeal to different teachers, at different times, for varying purposes, and can take different forms, including the production of a personal narrative, a case study or a reflective journal. Reflection can take place within various 'sites' (Moore and Ash, 2002), such as one's own teaching and learning or through engaging with research literature or personal practitioner research. The examples and case studies given in the following chapters of this book further illuminate the nature and scope of successful reflective practices in practitioner learning.

In the learning journey the first preoccupation is often with surviving the practice, and 'the reflexive turn' (Moore, 2004: 141–67) tends to take on the primary sense of developing expertise in the classroom. Understanding the wider contexts, and how they influence and position the individual, generally takes longer to develop. Developing a critically reflective disposition and capacity is crucial to enable student teachers to 'go beyond accepted ways of thinking and behaving and to invite and welcome various alternative ways of understanding' (Scott, 2000: 126). In this second sense of the concept of reflective practice, personal experiences need to be considered within wider socio-historical and politico-cultural contexts (Hatton and Smith, 1995: 35), and to draw upon academic literature and research. Reflexivity is crucial to understanding the wider contexts that create and construct immediate experience. Our stance as course designers assumes that being a 'good' teacher means acting with wide and deep understanding. This leads to rejecting the notion of the teacher as 'technician…whose primary function is to develop the skills to put into practice a set of behaviours determined by policy-makers' in favour of 'the educationally literate teacher' (Scott, 2000: 4). To achieve educational literacy in this sense means understanding the origin and functions of 'policy documents, press and research reports as constructed and ideologically embedded artifacts' (ibid.). Barnett has suggested that critical reflection might therefore be transformational, so that a person changes from 'being critical' to developing 'critical being' (Barnett, 1997: 7). Our assignments and interventions with our student teachers are designed to enable them to develop their own critical stance, in order to inform their teaching, which ultimately needs to be fluent.

Well-grounded reflection

Successful reflection might be termed 'well-grounded reflection', by which I mean reflection that develops new understandings, leading to more competent practice and to a growth in expertise and confidence in the practice (Heilbronn, 2008: 48–69). Well-grounded reflection enables 'tacit understandings' to surface, so that they can be examined, critiqued, developed and re-framed (Elliot, 1991). It enables practitioners:

> *to problematise situations and to challenge existing views, perspectives and beliefs, promoting or leading to development or change in terms of work-related understandings and/or outlooks.*
> (Moore and Ash, 2002)

Not all reflection achieves these ends. Britzmann (1986) has identified ways in which reflection might be badly grounded (see also Moore, 2004). It may be, for example:

> *'ritualistic' reflection that actually reinforces current thinking and perceptions and becomes a shelter within which to hide from more challenging explanations of circumstances and events.*
> (Moore and Ash, 2002)

Mentoring is a fundamental practice-based process for teacher development. Yet all parties in this mentoring process may fall prey to 'bad' reflection. We have seen several cases in which mentors appear to follow reflective processes with their trainees in weekly meetings; seem to work collaboratively to identify 'targets' for their student teachers' development; hold weekly discussion meetings when they seem to be engaged in a reflective, developmental process. But the meetings have been merely occasions to tick off various QTS standards, without deep engagement with the actual practice of the student teacher.

Sometimes the mentor may be genuinely engaged in a deeply reflective process, but the student teacher may not. In another example of a mentor–trainee partnership, the mentor had been through a process of explanation, modelling, narrating a way for the student teacher to engage pupils, by giving her signposts, bridges and 'scaffolds'. Weekly mentoring meetings were held, lessons were analysed and suggestions for future lessons were made. The student teacher participated in this reflective process and said that she would implement the suggestions made. However, the suggestions were poorly understood and the student teacher failed to engage the pupils. Although the mentor took the student teacher through a reflective process, based on their joint experiences, knowledge and understanding, he could not 'get through'. The student teacher did not understand how to create lessons in which the children were able to engage with the learning tasks. The pupils become restless through lack of engagement with the lesson and presented the teacher with challenging behaviour. The student teacher acknowledged that the lessons were not successful but blamed the pupils, making comments such as 'What can you expect with children like these?' or 'They're thick aren't they?' Despite repeated attempts on the mentor's part, the student teacher persisted in her belief that the pupils' lack of intelligence determined their failure to follow her lessons.

Well-grounded reflection can be distinguished from ritualistic reflection 'in moving the practitioner to a position which is simultaneously more critical (both of "self" and "system") and more confident' (Moore, 2004: 152). It can also be distinguished from 'pseudo reflection' (Britzmann, 1986), which can happen when a trainee prejudges a situation and is not open to reassessing situations from new perspectives. A case in point concerns a teacher who decided that a particular pupil was playing up in class because he had Asperger's Syndrome. The teacher had read about this condition and thought it fitted the profile of his misbehaving pupil, although no diagnosis had been made by anyone else. The teacher 'reflected' on classroom incidents and constructed an explanation in psychological terms to explain the pupil's non-compliant behaviour. This 'diagnosis' was in fact wide of the mark and did not help matters. It led the teacher to respond inappropriately to the pupil's behaviour, which exacerbated the situation. Some headway was made in changing the pupil's behaviour to a learning stance, when the teacher in question stopped using the Asperger's label to describe what was going wrong, and understood some factors in play, such as that pupil's high reading age for the class was implicated in boredom with the material set by the teacher, together with general dissatisfaction with the teacher's expectations.

'Teaching' is contingent, conjured up in a particular classroom, at a particular time, with particular people, so being able to evaluate the particularity of the pedagogical experience in order to improve upon it is essential for any future learning to happen with the particular group of people involved. Also, experiencing more and more examples of such practice builds up a store of instances, and reflected-upon experience builds up a store of digested experiences. This is how a teacher constructs a repertoire of actions on which she can draw in the heat of the moment. It is therefore important to provide opportunities and guidance for the achievement of well-grounded reflection from the beginning of teacher education courses, without them becoming ritualised affordances. Simply providing opportunities, such as procedures for evaluating lessons or for peer discussions may not establish personal, critical questioning. Well-grounded reflection does not even need to follow systematic procedures: it may arise through 'day-dreaming' or some kind of metaphorical thinking, which might happen to produce a good solution to a dilemma or question.

Reflexivity, self and others

However well-grounded reflection may be, it is not in itself sufficient to good practice.

> *Teaching involves more than reflection. We would think little of a teacher who was rich in the capacity to reflect (in whatever sense) but who was unable to establish appropriate relationships with pupils, or was disinclined to invite them to engage in any work.*
>
> (McLaughlin, 1999: 17)

There is a normative dimension to teaching, and we generally expect teachers to be exemplary figures (McLaughlin, 2004). We want teachers to hold to certain values, but we also want them to exercise judgement in how their values apply to particular cases. So flexibility is required and we cannot allow:

> *a certain tendency to construe teaching in the...sense of social or professional role (to) obscure our vision of the wider non-institutional human and moral significance of both teaching and education.*
>
> (Carr, 2003: 255)

The way in which the individual practitioner responds to the situations of the moment can be developed through a critically reflective process, but fundamental to any response is that person's values, personal qualities and dispositions, as well as technical and theoretical knowledge and understanding. For example, 'motivation' is a topic that teachers routinely read about and think of as a highly significant factor in pupil learning. Reading and discussing empirical studies on how to motivate pupils or how learning comes about does not in itself inform teachers about how learning comes about *in their own classrooms*. In order to enable pupils to learn, teachers need to engage deeply with their pupils. A primary capacity for well-grounded reflection is the ability to see things from the learners' perspective, to show 'pedagogical thoughtfulness' and engage in 'tactful teaching' (Van Manen, 1991, 1995), which means being sensitive to pupils' reactions and having the ability to respond appropriately. The dialectic of teacher–learner requires constant adjustment to what is going on in the moment, as well as the ability to work to a plan. Certain teacher qualities and dispositions are implied, such as the ability to 'think on one's feet', open-mindedness, resilience to having one's fundamental assumptions challenged, and a willingness to welcome advice and support. Others are the ability to make connections between one's own experiences so as to be able to generate new learning and changed behaviour. Another could be the capacity to trust in one's own judgement while keeping an open mind. A capacity for optimism is certainly called for, as – I believe – is courage.

The development of reflexivity is drawn back to the development of the self in social situations, with others and to the underlying emotional commitment to such development. Trust, hope and courage are relevant to such commitment.

(Giddens, 1991: 38)

Dialogue, community and others

All the writers in this book engage in some kind of professional association. When engaged in a professional practice we are, by definition, embedded in a community of other practitioners and are subject to the distributed process of that learning discourse community (Hoffman-Kipp *et al.*, 2003; see also Lave and Wenger, 1991). Schön's reflective practitioner is therefore necessarily embedded in a community of practice, and in a social process. The 'experts' defined by these communities have a responsibility towards conveying:

a sense of relative values or perspective: a sort of scale by which we can appreciate the relative worth and significance of things…for when we come to practical life it is not merely knowing that two and two make four which counts, it is putting together this two with that other two; in other words, the ability to size things up at their right value.

(Dewey, 1990: 337)

Articulation develops out of experience, through reflection, which can be aided to a large extent by good mentoring processes and practices. A successful mentoring experience can help to develop shared understandings about the meanings of that practice, through a collaborative exchange. It follows that the mentee's experiences need to form the basis of the process of interpreting meanings. Freire has expressed this requirement as 'the context of authentic dialogue between learners and educators as equally knowing subjects' (1972a: 32). Mentors should have a broader perspective than the mentee and have a role to play in mediating external conceptualisations, but the two parties are 'equally knowing', in the sense that they both bring to the dialogue their own experience of what they discuss, through and on which they build a mutual comprehension, which is itself a conceptualisation.

Finally, teachers need to have the ability to reflect critically so as to develop practical judgement, in order to exercise fluent expertise in any situation. This expertise relies on integrating theoretical understanding with personal capacity. There are various sites for reflection and it is possible to see if reflection is well-grounded: not all reflection is necessarily good. Reflection on practice can be thought of as well-grounded, if it enables the practitioner to reach new and productive understandings. It should lead to a critical review of what has gone before, to open up some 'new' possibility of action or conceptualisation. The chapters in Part 2 deal with how this capacity is enabled and developed in specific ways.

Part 2

Modes of professional learning

From reading into writing: Discovering a personal philosophy

Liz Wright

Often I did not leave my classroom except to go to the toilet or to go to the staffroom. I had my lunch there. I did my work there and occasionally I would cry there. It was a refuge from prying eyes but also it was my ball and chain…my weaknesses were played on and my strength of character was really tested.

(Cai, student teacher, 2009)

This quote from one of the papers written by a primary student teacher doing the Professional Learning Portfolio (PLP) module illustrates some of the tensions experienced by student teachers. It also illustrates the power of student teachers' voices – and all this emerged from a module whose aim was to provide primary student teachers with a space for critical reflection. The module was included alongside more tutor directed skills and knowledge based modules. Both types of modules are important and contribute to a primary teacher's knowledge base. The PLP module is premised on a socio-cultural view of learning where pedagogy is learner-centred. It provides a space where student teachers are supported in co-constructing the professional knowledge that will support them as they move into teaching their own classes. The PLP was introduced onto the primary PGCE route at the IOE in 2007; in 2009 the module was taken by 120 student teachers.

The module does not provide 'a package of knowledge'; instead, it offers space for critical reflection (Daly *et al.*, 2004), a space in which students are encouraged to create their own knowledge. Some students found this a risky and daunting project, but as the module progressed they began to recognise how productive such spaces can be (Galton, 2007). A minor challenge was presented by the significant number of the students who were taking the module but were unclear about why they were embarking on it at all. For some students this module was their third choice from a selection of modules where the teaching content was much clearer and the focus was on knowledge as product rather than process. However, as the PLP module progressed there was a change in the students' motivation. At the beginning, students could be heard muttering, 'Why do we need a module that focuses on professional learning?' As the module drew to a close, they were all able to explain very convincingly the rationale behind the module.

The students' voices in this chapter are a testimony to the learning that emerged as they began to feel that the focus of their writing could be on their ideas. This chapter explores the relationship between the journal articles that framed the students' learning and the writing that they produced for their portfolios. The journal articles supported the students in developing their own philosophy of teaching and, consequently, a sense of agency in the face of the targets and standards that at times threatened to obliterate their own learning. In their writing the students discovered that they have their own ideas. The traditional student–lecturer relationship was disrupted and recast within a more transparent pedagogy of mutual reflection (Noel, 2000). In this chapter the students' voices stand alongside mine as we reflect critically on our developing understandings of primary education. The chapter begins by raising questions about the role of the academy in student teacher learning.

Joining the academic community

Students choose the route that they want to take to gain qualified teacher status (QTS), with some opting for work-based routes that do not require input from a higher education authority. They are content to gain accreditation as teachers without studying at a university. Chapter 2 has raised issues around understanding the role of theory and the school as a site for learning. As teacher educators we need to be very clear about what the academy contributes to primary student teacher learning on the PGCE route. Student teachers who take the university route are taking the opportunity to continue their involvement with the academic community. As undergraduates their experiences are generally as recipients of knowledge; as postgraduates taking a Master's level course they have more complex expectations. The academic route in initial teacher education (ITE) moves between two cultures – the school and the university. It is increasingly important that the university is able to account for the contribution that it makes to the professional learning of primary teachers as it is now – both here and abroad – just one of several paths into teaching; it is no longer the default route (Grossman and McDonald, 2008).

Increasingly, student teachers are selecting other ways into teaching – drawn by the practical routes that focus on the rich learning that takes place in the primary school. Views have been expressed that university courses are sometimes too idealistic and impractical (Wray, 2006). Many teacher educators have not taught in a primary classroom for years; given the pace of change, this can be a source of some concern to those who are about to enter these classrooms. This is in contrast to other professional routes such as medicine where lecturers are still practising consultants, and probably has more to do with the high status of medicine and the low status of primary teaching. In the academy, to be a teacher educator is often seen to be on the margins of academic life (Maguire, 2000).

The nature of higher education is changing, but joining an academic community still requires students to be readers of journal articles and competent writers within high-status academic genres. Unlike the oral culture of school, the more prestigious academic culture is built upon public conversations in the form of journal articles. The tensions between these two cultures have been well documented (Gitlin, 2004). School-based teachers are often less convinced by the debates in journal articles; the students' writing in their PLPs often hinted at the disdain and barely concealed contempt for academia shown by some of the school-based teachers they had encountered. One student teacher was assured by a teacher in her placement school that when she was a real teacher she would not have time to think about 'ivory tower ideas'. As ITE has been upgraded to Master's level, there is an increased expectation that the process of becoming a teacher will be explored within the context of these high-status texts. Is this a wise move?

Journal articles as a pedagogic tool

There are four components in the PLP module. The first two are compulsory. In the first component students explore their developing identities as teachers. In the second they explore the differing knowledge bases that they draw upon as they carry out their school-based tasks. The third component focuses on policy perspectives, and the fourth on the role of journal articles in stimulating debate. For the latter, students must choose a journal article that they would recommend for inclusion in the module and they must explain how the article supports critical reflection and professional learning. Students must choose between the third and fourth component.

Ritter (2007) writes of developing pedagogy in teacher education and how he eventually constructed teacher education as a 'learning problem'. I find this a helpful approach and, like Ritter, constantly look inward at my role in this enterprise. Ritter's view of being a teacher was originally that of someone who knows their content area and deposits appropriate information in students' minds; a 'banking' model of education (Freire, 1972a: 45–60). He describes how working with student teachers changed his ideas; he began to notice their fear when faced with assessment and their view that the teaching course was just something to 'get through' rather than an experience during which learning might take place. I have had similar conversations with student teachers on the PLP module as they have reflected on their experiences on the PGCE course.

The journal articles that were used as readings for the PLP module were carefully selected. I attempted to read them through the eyes of student teachers. I wanted articles that would speak to the student teachers, not in a patronising way but in a way that validated their experiences and contributed to their thinking. I sought 'writerly' texts that invited the active participation of the reader (Barthes, 1974). The lack of synthesis between theory and practice in some students' writing may be because the gap between the theory in the readings and their own practice is too wide for them to cross. Rather than construct deficit models of student teachers who cannot write in the required academic genre, it can be useful to consider whether the journal articles themselves are a barrier to the students' learning.

On the PLP module, journal articles are used as pedagogic framing (Siraj-Blatchford and Sylva, 2004) for student learning; they represent the 'behind-the-scenes' aspect of pedagogy. The journal articles are introduced to students via a study guide which provides a context for the articles and links them to the course themes. There are always five or six journal articles per session to encourage the students to make a choice about which articles to read in depth. Having to make a choice involves a more active approach to the reading than just being given one or two articles that have been selected by the lecturer. Pedagogically, choice is an important element of active learning; it is evident in early years practice where very young children are supported in making choices about which areas of the nursery they will work in. Craft et al. (2007) discuss the ways in which pupils' agency in learning diminishes from the Foundation Stage to KS3 as children's choices become increasingly restricted. The element of choice meant that the sessions could not be dominated so easily by the lecturers as can be the case when just one or two articles are selected.

As a primary phase teacher educator I regard early years pedagogy as one of the most powerful approaches to learning; the concept of 'sustained shared thinking' within a pedagogy of cognitive co-construction between teacher and learner (Siraj-Blatchford and Sylva, 2004) is central to our approach on the PLP module. The most effective early years pedagogy is sensitive to children's cultural values and takes account of their agency as learners. Accordingly, the student teachers sit in groups to discuss the articles that they had chosen to read and the lecturer's role is to listen and observe and to try not to leap into the discussion too soon. As they watch children make choices about where they will direct their energies, early years practitioners become very good at observing learning. Early years pedagogy distinguishes between pedagogical interaction and pedagogical framing (Siraj-Blatchford and Sylva, 2004). As we listened to the student teachers talking, we became more confident that the debates in the journal articles made sense to them; they recognised their experiences and thoughts, and their ideas were mirrored in the words of the journal authors. Texts position us as particular kinds of readers and sometimes the texts that are given to student teachers are written solely for an academic audience, thus positioning student teachers as outsiders. Burke (2008) has written powerfully about the ways in which particular authorial voices in higher education are privileged.

An important aspect of learning therefore takes place as the students engage with texts in their discussion of both the article and their school-based experiences. In the fourth component of the PLP module the student teachers are required to select an article that they believe should be included in the reading list for PLP. Jane, one of the student teachers, wrote about an article by Pearce (2004) that dealt with issues of race in the primary classroom. Jane had chosen and researched this article herself. She felt that the article 'spoke to the profession in a way that many academic articles do not'.

Jane felt that Pearce's article legitimised her own thinking and provided a frame for her own professional learning. Sarah Pearce, the author of the article, is a teacher-researcher who is exploring her changing perceptions of race as a result of work with her class of 8 and 9 year olds. There has been a lack of transparency regarding the reader–writer relationship in journal articles where theoretical knowledge is historically privileged over practitioner knowledge. Jane was searching for journal articles that respected practitioners' knowledge; such articles position student teachers as insiders rather than outsiders.

The student teachers explore new territory through their reading. Some of them are empowered to research their own texts and to argue for their inclusion in the course reading list. Through such activities they begin to understand that the construction of reading lists is not a neutral process. The silences that exist in course literature can tell stories too. Carnell *et al.* (2008: 21), through their conversations with published writers at this university, have further contributed to our understanding that reading can be a resource and inspiration for writing. It matters what we give our student teachers to read.

Writing within the academy: My experience

When I studied for a Master's at this university my supervision tutor allowed my concerns to move from the sidelines to become a central part of my dissertation through the 'collaborative and talkback dialogue' that he adopted during the tutorial sessions (Lillis, 2001). Lillis points out that the dialogues of participation employed by tutors when discussing written work with students are not neutral and reflect their underlying beliefs about professional learning. In 'talkback' the tutor acknowledges the partial nature of text and opens up a space, just as my supervisor did. For me, the use of 'talkback' enabled me to begin my dissertation by reflecting upon my concerns. These centred around what I perceived to be the obliteration of my cultural identity as a practising teacher as I became caught up in the hegemonic practices of a powerful research university – the university where I now teach. I suspect that some of my reflections made uncomfortable reading for my supervisor:

> *I want to speak of the struggle to describe the reality of education. It can be described as a struggle between a benevolent academic elite who have access to the written public arena and oppressed teachers who mainly carry out the debate in the private arena. There will be those who protest at such a description of the debate. Nevertheless, it is my description, and it is rooted in my experience of that debate…I think it is important to validate teachers' experiences of education as well as academics' experiences. The suppression of teachers' voices is part of a wider arena…It is important to be clear about why teachers' voices are not heard.*
>
> (Wright, 1992: 12–13)

Over the years I have become more familiar with academic discourse; I acknowledge its power to analyse the familiar world of the classroom where I also still teach. My schizophrenic existence reflects that of the student teachers as they, like me, move between university and their school placements, crossing the cultural boundaries that sometimes seem to separate academic and practitioner knowledge. I have become more fluent in academic language – both spoken and written – but not yet bilingual. My practitioner voice always feels more comfortable but I am increasingly aware of the cultural capital attached to my fledgling academic voice. Student teachers need the insight that this flexibility of approach offers.

Writing within the academy: Today

On many modules writing is seen by the academy as simply part of the summative assessment of the course; students write so that their knowledge can be assessed against course criteria. Again Burke addresses these issues, suggesting that writing needs to be understood as being 'enmeshed in wider power relations that construct the "author" in classed, gendered and racialised ways' (2008: 200). If the production of writing is constrained by such powerful forces then the assessment of writing will also be caught up in the same 'hegemonic discourses of assessment; which speak of objective, rational and transparent procedures and processes' (ibid.).

On the PLP module the student teachers' writing is integral; they discuss and, twice during the module, submit their writing in the form of papers. Before their papers are submitted they are peer reviewed when they read a draft of their writing to each other. For some student teachers this is the first time that they have ever shared their writing with a peer group. It may be the first time that they have been aware of their own writing voice. At first, many find the process quite daunting. In her paper Tifani quoted from Nias (1992) who researched the culture of primary teaching. The course literature, where possible, privileges journal articles that focus on primary education. Tifani understood the growth in her own professional learning through her reading of Nias' observation that 'teachers grow and develop only when they "face themselves"' (1992: 5). Tifani describes how vulnerable she felt when she shared her paper:

> *Initially I was apprehensive; apart from feeling fear of sharing my paper with my peers I felt vulnerable exposing my inner thoughts and running the risk of being judged. However the process was not as horrific as I imagined; in listening to the different papers I realised writing is 'a tool for understanding' (Attard and Armour 2005: 198)… it was refreshing to hear each individual's unique journey.*
>
> (Tifani, student teacher, 2009)

I also write in response to the students' papers, read my writing out to them, and invite their responses. The use of the term 'paper' rather than 'assignment' is intended to create a more authentic writing experience where writing is seen as a way of sharing ideas rather than just providing knowledge to be graded by the tutor.

Like Lillis, I believe that dialogue must infuse all aspects of pedagogy from teaching the module to preparing the writing for assessment. There must be space for 'talkback' where students are able to engage in critical reflection and challenge pedagogic practices so that we 'explore ways in which alternative meaning-making practices in writing can be institutionally validated' (Lillis, 2001: 44). This, however, was not something that we were able to achieve on the module as many of the student teachers were so fearful of the assessment process and so unconfident as writers that challenging pedagogic practices was not something that was high on their list of priorities. Sam captures the views of some student teachers:

> *I find myself caught between the desire to question what I am learning and the necessity to just learn what I am told in order to pass.*
>
> (Sam, student teacher, 2009)

Despite their hesitant start, most of the student teachers, including Sam, gained confidence as writers. They began to take ownership of their writing and to see it as something more than a dumping ground for their knowledge, more than just part of a summative assessment process. The journal articles that formed part of the course literature modelled ways of writing and themes which resonated with their experiences.

Student teachers' views of writing on PLP

Tifani wrote about the changes that took place as she became more confident working within the parameters of the module.

> *Through writing papers and engaging in discussions personally I found I was more reflective…I felt less isolated, frustrated and felt safe to question and critique my own paper…*

> *…my initial response towards this module was contrary to my current views, the thought of having to recall, reflect and question my motives for my conduct appeared frightening; I was content in acting and responding without thinking why…Through studying two terms of this module my initial ideas, thoughts and fears about reflection have drastically changed. I now integrate reflection within my daily routine, to help me absorb the process to grow, change, question. Rather than dreading the process of reflection I now feel more resilient towards reflection and have recognized the implications of reflection within the process of learning.*
> (Tifani, student teacher, 2009)

In her paper 'Mirror mirror on the wall, does a reflective practitioner gain much at all?', Sameera also wrote of her struggle to engage with a module in which she was not a willing participant. She had wanted to enrol on a more conventional module which offered an attractive-sounding package of knowledge, as opposed to PLP which seemed to her just to offer space for reflection and debates. Sameera described how at the start of the course she was:

> *against the idea of undertaking a module which 'forced' me to write about my thoughts and reflect when I could be enrolled on the 'Inclusion' module which at the time I thought would benefit me more. I thought I would learn about something that I would find valuable and could apply to my practice as a teacher.*

> *However as my time on the PLP module progressed, and I think back on my thoughts towards this module at the very beginning, I see how flawed they were and how completely wrong I was. By being given the opportunity to engage in reflective writing, I feel that it has been the only real chance that I have had during the whole course to reflect upon different aspects of my practice…I got the opportunity to reflect upon my experience as a whole.*

I feel strongly that had I not been enrolled on the PLP module I would not have been able to reflect upon my practice…there is not much room on the course to step back and think about our practice and theoretical knowledge, which is surprising given the fact that a lot of research has argued that it is an integral aspect of learning to become a teacher.

(Sameera, student teacher, 2009)

In the fourth component, Sameera chose Calderhead's (1987) 'The quality of reflection in student teachers' professional learning' as an article that all PGCE student teachers should read. Sameera's understanding of reflection had developed and her link to Calderhead enabled her to critique not just reflection, but different kinds of reflection. Sameera had become interested in the concept of 'in-depth' reflection and quoted from Heilbronn (2008) to highlight concerns about 'ritualised reflection'. Her journey, like Tifani's, had been transformative. They had both used their papers to articulate the changes that had taken place in their thinking.

Writing as a tool for reflection: Identity

There can be a gulf between the input of seminars, where content knowledge is delivered to students, and the act of writing an essay. Questions and queries raised in discussion in seminars do not always find their way into writing. Also, spoken situations can be teacher-dominated rather than participatory. For some student teachers the gap between the conversations that they have had and the act of translating those conversations onto paper can be daunting. Writing is often under-utilised in learning as speech is considered to be the most effective mode for exploring ideas. But writing can also be a place to explore thinking, to develop questions and to generate ideas. Although writing can add another layer to understanding, it may (less productively) just be used to record the knowledge of others rather than to explore critical positions and raise questions.

So often debates about teaching are dominated by academics, while teachers' voices are confined to the oral culture of the staffroom. The issue of voice is an important consideration in writing. Reflection is easiest in a voice with which the writer feels comfortable. Writing in *Liberating Scholarly Writing,* Robert Nash, an academic at Columbia University, suggests that: 'To write is to demonstrate with a degree of certainty that we truly matter' (2004: 22). Nash challenges academic genres that demand the suppression of the personal voice, believing that 'personal stories contain within them the germs of many intellectual and experiential truths' (ibid.: 42). He views narrative scholarly writing as a balance between establishing an intellectual context and an honest personal voice. Primary teachers know that children write best when they write from first-hand experiences; that 'human engagement is high at the point when we exchange stories of experience' (Watkins, 2006: 124).

The first component of the PLP module starts with narratives of the students' experiences – their developing identities as beginning teachers. The voices of the student teachers emerge as they reflect upon the journey on which they are embarking. Here they are provided with a model for the kind of academic writing that is legitimised on this module.

Cai, whose voice introduces this chapter, describes how her relationship with her school mentor was fragile. This was partly because of the tensions between university-based systematic knowledge and school-based craft knowledge. When Cai tried to explain her reasoning behind one of the numeracy activities that she had taught, which drew upon theoretical knowledge gained from her university lectures, she felt that this knowledge was perceived as irrelevant by her class teacher. Cai drew strength from Maynard's (2001) article, which she had selected in the fourth component as the article that she believed all PGCE students should read. Cai describes how:

> *Constructing a teacher identity as a newcomer in a community was extremely difficult and this 'uneasy' relationship was heightened by the tension between my 'internal pressures' for personal survival and the 'external pressures' to impress my class teacher, pupils, management and supervision tutor.*
>
> *We construct identity in relation to others and on the PGCE course, one is given a unique opportunity to engage in learning about oneself. In the community of learning, I am aware that schools often do not foster this sense of shared learning. However, Maynard's (2001) article highlights the critical relationships and the fact that one's social context is important as a student teacher. I gained comfort from reading her article, which confronts my fears of teaching being a lonely profession.*

(Cai, student teacher, 2009)

The themes of identity and the experiences of teaching in the first term of the course position the student teachers as experts. They are writing about their experiences, their struggles, their achievements and their disappointments. For many – at the start of a demanding PGCE course – this feels like a productive space to explore.

Writing as a tool for reflection: Policy

As the module progresses its content moves further away from student teachers' experiences, and the third component of the module explores policy issues. This is the most challenging of the components, as an understanding of policy is often outside the students' experience. One of the articles offered is Alexander's (2004) 'Still no pedagogy? Principle, pragmatism and compliance in primary education'. It is an article that is written out of sheer desperation with a state-dictated primary curriculum. In this article Alexander locates the primary strategy within a debate that problematises pedagogy. He sees *Excellence and Enjoyment: A strategy for primary schools* (DfES, 2003) as an ambiguous policy document which, while claiming to hand over control to primary teachers, in fact keeps tight control over the literacy and numeracy targets, and therefore over primary pedagogy. For some student teachers Alexander's article offers a different lens through which to view policy; others are critical of what they see as his 'rant'. There are times when I glimpse Day and Alexander, eminent primary phase academics, through the eyes of some of the student teachers: my heroes are reduced to old-timers with a 'chip on their shoulder' by the next generation of teachers who embrace the planning frameworks that have become part of the state's machinery for curriculum delivery.

While some student teachers take issue with Alexander, others, like Nancy, found the article transformative. Nancy began to see policy through Alexander's eyes. Reading Alexander as one of her chosen articles helped Nancy to develop:

> an appreciation of the extent to which educational policies and initiative are set within a political context...The article highlighted for me the danger of reading any policy document in isolation and without setting it within an overall political and social context...The article also provided me with a better understanding of the pressure on teachers to comply with government policies and initiatives in the current climate of testing, targets and performance tables, and it helped me to appreciate some of the factors contributing to the apparent gap between the pedagogical theory promoted at university and what I have observed on school experience...Alexander's critique of Excellence and Enjoyment *serves as something of a template on how to read other policy documents.*

> His article has supported me in realising the importance of analysing policy and adopting an enquiring stance about why it has arisen and what the underpinning arguments and evidence are. It has made me realise that I need to take responsibility for my own professional learning and for developing my professional knowledge if I want to respond in an intellectual way to policies. This will enable me to take

a wider perspective within teaching, to move from being a technicist to a professional who recognises the social and political issues that surround teaching and which affect children in school…Through the PLP module I have come to understand the importance of developing a robust professional identity based upon my educational values and beliefs.

(Nancy, student teacher, 2009)

Quoting Crick and Wilson (2005: 372), Nancy argues for the importance of a vision 'of what things might be'. Crick and Wilson's article is one of the articles included in the readings for the fourth component. In it, they explore both children's and adults' learning from a relational aspect. Like some of the other articles selected for the PLP module, this article moves seamlessly between academic debates and the primary classroom. The article ends with a warning that Nancy quotes: 'Without a vision, regularly revisited, of what things might be, we shall as a society ossify' (Crick and Wilson, 2005: 372).

Nancy believes that Alexander's (2004) article highlights the complexity of pedagogy and the need to look beyond prescriptive approaches towards a broader understanding of what education might be. She does not underestimate the challenges of critical reflection but believes that without it there is a danger that the restrictive curriculum where 'the space for reflection is lacking in over-regulated classrooms' (Crick and Wilson, 2005: 372) may erode any possibilities for authentic learning. She reflects that:

No doubt it is challenging to sustain intellectual enquiry and critical reflection as one's role and circumstances change. However the alternative could be to run the risk of losing sight of the values and beliefs that motivated the decision to teach in the first place.

(Nancy, student teacher, 2009)

Professional learning

Another article that is used in the fourth component of the module is by Attard and Armour (2005): this is one of those rare articles where a practising teacher's voice can be heard without it being mediated by a 'higher status' authorial voice. Karl Attard is a PE teacher who is engaged in doctoral study. He describes the 'reflective odyssey' that he has embarked upon, and believes that writing is a tool for reflection to support conversations with himself. For Attard such lone conversations are a poor substitute for a community of writers who would provide 'professional intimacy', which he believes would be a very effective environment to support professional learning. Attard applauds university routes that create spaces for student teachers' voices; he sees auto-ethnographic writing as a supportive genre.

Mike (student teacher, 2009) recommends Attard and Armour's (2005) article for student teachers who are interested in professional learning. For him, professional learning is 'an ongoing process of enquiry where understanding is deepened; it can be a transformative experience'.

> *[In the seminar many students] viewed Attard as a sad individual, picturing him alone at his computer with only a desk lamp on, writing about his emotions and how isolated he felt. They criticised him and I didn't understand why.*

Mike felt that the student teacher reactions may have reflected a cultural taboo in reaction to Attard's overt expression of feelings in an academic article. Mike developed his defence in his paper:

> *Attard is on a mission here to get his readers to see that this type of writing is a way to achieve professional development…I believe that writing is a beneficial and effective way of developing personally and professionally…I commend Attard for his bravery in expressing his emotions in such a public manner…The article presents reflection as a possible solution to reducing the theory-to-practice dilemma, to better understand oneself and gradually develop professionally.*
> (Mike, student teacher, 2009)

The student teachers' evaluations of the module often referred to the impact that the module had had on their thinking. They used phrases such as 'opened up thinking', 'clarified thinking', 'think about deeper issues', 'opportunity to consolidate my thinking', 'given me a very healthy and enduring educational philosophy'.

The sense of stepping back in order to create space for thinking is captured in this quote, taken from the end-of-module evaluation. The student teacher appreciated how the module had 'helped me to take a step back from the fast paced PGCE and begin to understand the bigger picture of teaching and learning'.

For some students this 'stepping back' had created with it a sense of 'agency'. One wrote that it was 'very nice to be given a "voice" and made to feel that my views were worthwhile'.

The module was described as 'a sanctuary within the PGCE course'. A sanctuary where one student felt able to:

> *reflect, think and progress professionally and personally in ways I will never forget and I am extremely grateful. It has felt like a safety net.*

Other student teachers wrote about the focus on learning:

> *The module helped me to focus on learning that I might have otherwise missed/been unaware of. It is necessary to be forced to articulate your learning to enable you to evaluate what you have learned.*

I strongly feel that all PGCE students would hugely benefit from this module, in particular the emphasis on critical reflection and professional learning.

Developing personal philosophies

Teacher education is a complex terrain in which to work. It exists at the nexus of multiple institutional and policy contexts (Grossman and McDonald, 2008: 185). The PLP module is part of a PGCE route where almost every minute of every day is filled with a lecture or a workshop. The PGCE course is fast paced, and there is a sense of urgency about the amount of knowledge that has to be assimilated. It feels like the 'hurry along curriculum' (Dadds, 2001).

Some student teachers did not take up the PLP module willingly – either because they did not think that reflection had any part to play in becoming a teacher or because they felt daunted by the prospect of reflection. It is not always easy to persuade student teachers that the PLP module has anything productive to offer. Many come to it believing that all they need is to be given a set of skills to equip them for life in the classroom. And they do need skills and knowledge – but that is not all they need. In a performance-driven culture, Rob described how he had imagined his journey to becoming a teacher:

> *Initial memories of my first week at the institute are of the size of the section of the library dedicated to reflections on teaching. I had never before considered that teaching would be such an introspective past-time, with so many questions that people would need to address. My thoughts prior to starting had been mostly about the period from 9.am to 3.30 pm when I would be teaching my class. I had envisaged encountering a library full of books, but expecting them to be teaching aids, learning materials, children's books and subject knowledge development tomes…before starting the course, I had always considered myself as a plumber might before taking his apprenticeship. I was waiting to be tooled out in everything I would need to enter my first classroom…I imagined seminars where teachers would play the part of unruly children and we would be given a series of routine techniques for dealing with them; in short my questions satisfied with answers. The reality is that we have been asked to 'zoom out' from what we know about education and view the entire landscape of teaching and learning from a much more academic standpoint…*
>
> *I begin to realise that I am constructing a personal philosophy; just as questions in the classroom can help children to develop their meta-*

cognitive abilities and therefore learn new skills…not just knowledge, questions can lead me to a reflective attitude…This doesn't mean that I now have the answers. But it does mean that I shouldn't be worried about not having them, and that the answers will come as my personal (and therefore individual) philosophy as a teacher develops.

(Rob, student teacher, 2009)

The concept of a personal philosophy of teaching was a theme taken up by several student teachers as they began to realise how the space created by the PLP module could be filled with their own thoughts.

Pring's (2007) reflections upon the Nuffield Review of 14–19 Education and Training for England and Wales cause him to muse upon the declining role of philosophy in educational debates. The issues that Pring raises are as pertinent to primary education and the education of student teachers as they are to the 14–19 sector of education. Pring suggests that the fact that the introduction of externally imposed standards and the concept of what 'works' in education are no longer considered as non-controversial notions is significant. His is a reminder of how this impoverished view of education moved learning away from 'the struggle to understand' towards 'the capacity to behave according to the targets set' (Pring, 2007: 325).

Taking up this theme, another course article 'The hope and practice of teaching' by Ayers (2006) asks some challenging questions of teacher educators. Just as Alexander's (2004) is an article of despair, so Ayers' is an article of hope that taps into the idealism of those new to teaching. In this article teacher educators are in the firing line as Ayers suggests that they need to move beyond the 'cramped thinking' that currently surrounds education with its talk of grades, targets and testing. Ayers suggest mutiny rather than obedience, while acknowledging the harsh reality of some classrooms where student teachers are learning to teach. Ayers, in a rallying call, which acknowledges the pitfalls of rhetoric, says:

I want beginning teachers to resist, to rebel against all of it, to reject these clichés, to stand on their own feet, and to make their way toward the moral heart of teaching at its best…we have to refocus on teaching as intellectual and ethical work, something beyond the instrumental and the linear…It demands that we embrace the humanity of every student – that we take their side. Easy enough to say, excruciatingly difficult to enact in the daily lives of schools.

(Ayers, 2006: 271)

Articles such as these give student teachers permission to take risks and critique both the modules that they are taking and the framework within which they are learning to be teachers. Ayers' article was one of the most cited in the students' papers. It led one student teacher to reflect upon our attempts to 'churn out a tribe of semi-efficient practitioners to fill the gaps in the inner London state school system'. Critical reflection can make challenging reading.

In my almost 20 years of experience as a primary teacher educator it seems to me that we have stopped asking questions about primary education because we have somehow been persuaded that others will do that for us. When I moved from being a secondary Drama and English teacher into primary education, I was struck by the passivity and obedience of many of the school-based primary teachers with whom I worked. There were, of course, notable exceptions, but they were the minority. One of the successes of the PLP module has been to encourage primary student teachers to ask deep and, at times, challenging questions. Teacher education has to equip our students with the courage to think deeply and ask challenging questions: that must be part of professional learning. The university should be a good place to do this.

Today's primary teachers have to be braver than primary teacher educators have been in their acquiescence to the strategies and policies that have engulfed and strangled the primary curriculum. Many primary teacher educators have just watched events unfold in stunned silence. Watkins writes of the need to 'reclaim learning' within the context of educational policy that has required us to focus on the 'space invaders of teaching, performance and work' (2006: 121). Watkins' distinction between a performance orientation and a learner orientation is helpful. It is the learner orientation that provides the agency and the impetus for critical reflection; Watkins suggests that 'successful schools are not compliant organisations' (2006: 125).

Learning to become a teacher

The students' papers provide insights into the world of the student teacher where dreams are shattered, relationships are tested and confidence is gained. One student teacher said that the PLP module had given her – for the first time in her life – an 'intellectual identity'. Some student teachers took up the theme of learning and recognised that focusing on their own learning was crucial to their success as educators. However, some seemed less than convinced that this was the route that they were being offered. Rosalie was not the only student teacher who wondered whether she had come on the PGCE route to learn or to become a teacher. That she felt able to make such a distinction illustrates her awareness of the different pathways, and (I suspect) her partial disappointment with what she was being offered. The technicist, skills-based route of training that teacher educators are increasingly being required to offer student teachers still remains a safe and seductive route, particularly within a climate of Ofsted inspections. However, such an approach can be counterproductive and misguided.

Reflecting upon her interrupted journey to becoming a teacher – she had abandoned the PGCE course and then returned the following year – Rosalie said of her first attempt:

> I had begun to convince myself that I had to know everything immediately…learning became an arduous task and I started to even resent its existence, similar to the feelings of a child who loathes school.
>
> (Rosalie, student teacher, 2009)

Rosalie struggled with her identity and, in particular, the importance of retaining a learner identity when she felt that there was such a focus on performativity. She describes how the university tasks threatened her learner status, which she felt became submerged as she focused on targets and the QTS standards (TDA, 2007) that she was required to meet. In her paper she argues that some of the school-based tasks that student teachers are required to carry out – the 'gifts that they bring' (Edwards, 1997) – can sometimes put their learning needs in direct conflict with children's learning needs. She describes how the second time around she had the confidence to adapt the university tasks and take ownership of the learning:

> I am learning to be a learner without fear of failure. I am finding the PLP module a source of strength and validity – it is giving me confidence to be a learner and the confidence to value my own views. My personal thoughts are being validated by academic writings. I think that PLP will be the making of me and of my future pupils… True learning takes the external on board but is rooted within the personal…A big barrier to my learning is my confidence and fear of failing…when I relax about my learning it becomes easier.
>
> (Rosalie, student teacher, 2009)

The way forward

The route to becoming a primary teacher is complex because teaching is complex. Teaching across nine or more subjects requires intellectual rigour; analysing the learning of young children requires the highest level of observational skills. Taking part in policy conversations and action research from the perspective of a practitioner with a wealth of experiential knowledge, which those outside the classroom can only dream about, is a challenge. Yet that is what this century will demand of its primary teachers. Knowledge can no longer be parcelled up and recycled second-hand to teachers by outsider researchers. We need a more effective pedagogy as transmission models of learning are increasingly discredited. The PLP module draws on a pedagogy of mutual reflection by empowering student teachers and developing the listening skills of their teacher educators.

Becoming a teacher must mean becoming part of a professional and intellectual community; in this the academy has a key role to play. Initial teacher education needs to move to the heart of the academy; it needs to be the powerhouse, with academics at all levels eager to talk to the next generation of teachers. As teacher educators we need to understand the ways in which we can support postgraduate student teachers, to read carefully what they have to say and then – if we must – continue to use extrinsic rewards and grade their writing. We need to think carefully about the nature of postgraduate study at Master's level because that is what we are now required to 'deliver'. Ten years ago Hagger and McIntyre (2000) alluded to the increasingly impoverished view of teacher education that was resulting from an increase in directives from government bodies. Since then that influence has increased dramatically. It is therefore timely to reassess where we have got to in our work with student teachers.

Hagger and McIntyre suggested that teacher education might be understood as involving interactions and negotiations 'among intelligent people in very different positions, each with their own agendas and their own rational ways of pursuing them' rather than the more seductive and simplistic view of 'rationally planned courses with clear objectives' (2000: 487). An emphasis on 'negotiation' rather than 'delivery' can potentially provide a space for lively debates and transformative learning within a pedagogy of mutual understanding. In the hands of skilled and confident teacher educators this is not a recipe for anarchy but rather a framework for teacher education that is learner-centred rather than teacher-centred.

The PLP module focuses on negotiation and student learning rather than a delivery model of teacher training. It is for this reason that it is initially resisted by many of the student teachers. However, as those who took the module became more confident as learners they began to understand how to use such a learning environment productively. To quote one student teacher:

> I am eternally grateful that this module focuses on the journey rather than just the end point. The journey to becoming a teacher is a special one – not to be missed.
>
> (Helen, student teacher, 2009)

Chapter 5

Tasks, audiences and purposes: Writing and the development of teacher identities within pre-service teacher education

Anne Turvey and Gill Anderson

In common with other courses in initial (pre-service) teacher education (ITE), during the course of the year we set our student teachers a series of written tasks as part of their development. What we want to consider here are three questions that arise out of the tasks we set:

- What model of writing underpins the tasks?
- What does the sequence of tasks on our particular list suggest about conceptualisations of progression and the development of teacher identities?
- What principles inform the university tutor's feedback and what does this contribute to student teachers' development?

A model of writing and development

Student teachers on a PGCE course encounter a variety of ideas about what it is to be a teacher. Some of these ideas predate their entry onto the course and arise from different sources – from media and film representations of teaching, from their own experiences as pupils in school, from the expectations of friends and family, from their earlier explorations developed in their academic field of study. Once on the course, student teachers need to negotiate their way through two different sites – the university and the school. And in each of these sites they meet different demands and expectations, many of which challenge their previous ideas of being a teacher. Each site also comprises a different community of practice, with its own professional identities, habits and ways of talking (Lave and Wenger, 1991; Wenger, 1998). Student teachers encounter these communities of practice as authoritative voices: they listen to university tutors and schoolteachers, always knowing that both of these groups of people will be influential judges of their own professional development; they begin to adopt and use the words, attitudes and perspectives of these communities. In other words, they struggle to inhabit these competing discourses as they begin to deal with overlapping – and sometimes contradictory – models of professional identity and practice; simultaneously, they work to maintain a sense of their own identities and of the possibility of their own agency, as people who will be able to make a difference in the classroom.

So what function does writing fulfil for these student teachers? First, it enables them to look forward, to explore private and professional selves, to begin to construct, in a medium over which they have control, the professional identity that they wish to inhabit. Second, the act of writing puts the writer at a distance from experience. Writing creates the space, therefore, for reflexivity, for an exploration of an experience that is necessarily remote from, not the same as, the experience itself. But this distance is also a distance from the authoritative voices that, within the school or the university, can be so powerful as to leave little space for the student teacher's voice.

For writing to fulfil this function, it has to be of a particular kind, and has to be set up in particular ways. Some forms of traditional academic discourse, where what is privileged is performativity, conformity to generic norms and the demonstration of officially sanctioned knowledge, constrain thought and development. The forms of writing that our PGCE course promotes, on the other hand, are those that encourage student teachers to believe in a voice that is uncertain, creative, tentative, a site of departure. Student teachers are encouraged to write in the first person – something that many of them find difficult, precisely because they have become habituated to meeting the demands of the kinds of academic discourse described above: to be asked to put yourself back into the picture creates a vulnerability and an uncertainty about expectations. The impersonal academic voice, like the impersonality of some conceptions of a teacher's role, can appear to offer a safe space, a means of preserving a separation of private and public, personal and professional identities and enactments (see Yandell and Turvey, 2007).

Implicit in our conception of writing and its role in the development of professional teacher identity is understanding the teacher's identity as necessarily drawing on and inflected by that teacher's history, dispositions and values. Asking student teachers to use the first person entails the expectation that they will consider, and be explicit about, their positionality. Writing, like teaching, is enacted from a particular position. It is an activity-in-context:

> *[Writing] is about a means of saying who you are, and locating yourself in the world, and representing yourself in the world.*
>
> (Kress, 2008: 131)

The kinds of writing fostered on our course are underpinned by the principle of reflexivity (Moore, 2004), an idea that draws attention to the multiple contexts in which an individual acts and her identities are formed. Student teachers are encouraged to explore the past in order to analyse the taken-for-granted beliefs and assumptions that they have of the defining features of the profession's practices and values. This reading of reflexivity is linked to:

> *an understanding that discourses such as that of the competent craftsperson with its universalising turn, or the charismatic subject discourse with its essentialist turn, or variants of the reflective practice discourse that over-emphasise individual over collective responsibility, operate against such a perception and understanding.*
>
> (Moore, 2004: 142)

Reflexivity moves the student teacher beyond such forms of self-evaluation, which are increasingly embedded in the language of competences and standards, and places it in 'a much bigger picture':

> *a picture that will include the practitioner's own history, dispositions, prejudices and fears as well as the wider social, historical and cultural contexts in which schooling itself is situated.*
>
> (Moore, 2004: 149)

At this stage, we should be clear about two possible (mis)readings of our claims on behalf of particular forms of writing within the PGCE course. First, the fact that on our course writing has such a prominent role does not mean that we assume that writing, always and everywhere, is the semiotic mode that should or does perform this representational function. The crucial point in our argument is not, therefore, about writing as such but rather about writing as one possible form of representational work. Second, we are alert to the dangers of autobiographical and narrative approaches that simplify identity and development, approaches that present the self as singular or lacking in complexity and contradiction, approaches that abstract identity from specific histories and from wider social movements and tensions.

What we are putting forward is a specific approach to specific pieces of writing. But we should make clear that this approach arises out of a more general conceptual framework, a social semiotic theory and a sociocultural theory of learning. Writing tasks are set up in ways that reflect our understanding that all language, written and spoken, is always and everywhere multivoiced. Language is always produced with a consciousness of others, of others' prior utterances and of others' potential responses. Meaning, in this model of language, is not passively received but always actively made and remade, from the resources that are available, in particular sites.

> *The word in language is half someone else's. It becomes 'one's own' only when the speaker populates it with his own intention, his own accent, when he appropriates the word, adapting it to his own semantic and expressive intention. Prior to this moment of appropriation, the word does not exist in a neutral and impersonal language (it is not, after all, out of a dictionary that the speaker gets his words), but rather it exists in other people's mouths, in other people's contexts, serving other people's intentions: it is from there that one must take the word, and make it one's own.*
>
> (Bakhtin, 1981: 293–4)

This has implications for our view of teacher agency, the development of teacher identities and of the role of discourse in these processes. Student teachers adopt, interrogate and navigate their way through the powerful, public discourses of school and university: they are not just, as Foucault might have it, the subjects of these discourses.

Education teems with other people's words – 'literacy', 'ability', 'gifted', 'level'. The common-sense view is that these words have meanings that are stable, shared and unproblematic. But for student teachers, entering as outsiders into sites where these words seem to constitute a common currency, there is work to be done to make these words their own. What complicates matters further, though, is that the student teachers negotiate between different sites – different schools as well as between school and university – and in each site they will find that the same words are populated with different meanings. Writing puts these different meanings out in the open, available for scrutiny and critique. It allows the writer to consider these competing meanings, but – more especially – to consider these meanings in relation to practice, to test out what such words might mean in the context of their developing understanding of real learners in real classrooms.

Bakhtin, Britzman argues, draws attention to the 'power struggle' involved in any person's 'becoming', between authoritative discourse and internally persuasive discourse. Authoritative discourse demands allegiance:

> *It is 'received' and static knowledge, dispensed in a style that eludes the knower, but dictates, in some ways, the knower's frames of reference and the discursive frameworks that sustain them.*
>
> (Britzman, 2003: 42)

In contrast, it is 'internally persuasive discourse' that

> *pulls one way from norms and admits of a variety of contradictory social discourse. Discourse that is internally persuasive provisions*

creativity, the play of meanings…[It] is the site of departure rather than a place of arrival. A tentative discourse, subject to negotiation and shifting contexts, and able to voice possibilities unforeseen, internally persuasive discourse is a discourse of becoming.

(Britzman, ibid.)

These ideas are helpful in exploring the tensions experienced by student teachers, for example, in the ways they encounter the principles and practices of assessment. In education there is an authoritative discourse that absolutely dictates 'the knower's frames of reference' in relation to what can be said about children's learning and progress. These frames are constructed from such terms as 'current and target levels', 'grades', 'attainment targets', 'objectives and success criteria' that are not only 'dispensed in a style that eludes the knower' but are emptied of any sense of their historical and theoretical origins or of their contested nature.

When we ask our student teachers to write a case study of a pupil's development, we are inviting them to consider learners in all their particularity, and this means, necessarily, to consider their individual learning as always socially and culturally embedded. This leads student teachers to look critically at those norms Britzman refers to, which is the main language sanctioned by powerful institutions for representing learning and progress to the individual child as well as to the world. A contradictory discourse seeks to understand learning in relation to a child's potential and to the ways in which progress might be seen as social, collective and occurring over time. This view of assessment is always in dialogue – difficult, unequal and often bad-tempered dialogue – with the dominant discourse.

The idea that words are slippery, elusive and not necessarily faithful to the speaker's intentions is of particular interest to us in what we are saying about writing as a search for a voice and teacher identity. For example, when our student teachers write their case study they grapple with ways of making sense of data, of evidence of their chosen learner's progress (or lack thereof), and of how to bring these ways of defining learning and the learner into contact with their own experience of the learner. The act of writing foregrounds – brings into consciousness – tensions between competing approaches to defining and measuring progress and between all these approaches and the student teacher's first-hand history of an unfolding relationship with a particular learner. Writing can, therefore, enable the writer to render explicit the provisionality of any and all of these accounts – and their limitations. It is not that the writing privileges the writer's grounded perception, but rather that it enables the writer to appropriate for their own purposes the more authoritative voices of others, to populate these words with their own understandings of a particular learner, and hence to consider the value and implications of future interventions.

The sequence of writing tasks

The writing that we ask student teachers to produce is sequenced and set up in particular ways. Writing is preceded by discussion, the purpose of which is to locate the emerging professional self in relation to immediate others (peers and tutors) as well as the more distant, more powerful voices of researchers, academics and policy-makers. Writing, in other words, is initiated in and through dialogue and is construed as contributing to ongoing debates. Student teachers are expected to draw on autobiographical experiences and to examine them in the light of their reading, their discussion with peers and tutors and their exploration of and participation in school classrooms.

Figure 5.1

Compulsory Core Tasks for English and English with Drama STs

- **Subject knowledge development**: pre-course writing assignment for the tutor *'who will discuss with you the contents of what you have written. It is also an opportunity for you to introduce yourself to your tutor as a writer… The organisation and presentation of the writing is important'* (1,500–2,000 words).

- **What constitutes a good teacher?** PGCE generic pre-course task (1,000–1,500 words).

- **Profile of a reader in the primary school**: a case study based on observation of an individual learner. Ideas presented and discussed in seminar groups before writing (1,500 words).

- **A lesson plan for teaching a KS3 novel and a commentary on the collaborative planning process that led to this plan.**

- **A language autobiography:** *'focus on an aspect of your own language history that interests you'*; *'How you write this, how it is organised and what you choose to include is up to you'* (1,500 words).

- **Focused observation task**: *'what can you say about the way language is used, and the purposes for which it is used in the lesson? How does this provide you with evidence of learning'?* (1,500 words).

- **Language teaching and the place of grammar in English and MFL:** writing up a collaborative research project with an MFL ST in school (1,500 words).

- **Students write a scheme of work on myth and complete the 'cover sheet' themselves, answering the question: what have you learned about planning from planning a complete SoW?**

All the above submitted during the first term.

- **Reflection on School Experience 1**

- **Case study of an individual pupil's learning development** (submitted early February, at least 2,000 words)

- **The place of English in the curriculum** – *'drawing on your knowledge of policy and practice, now and in the past'* (submitted end of February; 1,500 words)

- **Reflection on School Experience 2**

- **English, Media and Drama module assignment**: *'three essential aspects...*
  1) sustained critical reflection on some aspect of your teaching
  2) substantial reading to underpin the assignment
  3) pupils and some moments of their learning'
  (submitted end of course; 5,000 words).

Looking at the list of core tasks in Figure 5.1, one thing is immediately striking. We ask our student teachers to do a lot of writing. This begins before they start the course and continues throughout the autumn term as we expect them to write short pieces every week or two. As tutors, we respond to each piece, giving feedback on a cover sheet. This considerable investment of time from student teachers and tutors is repaid by the way in which student teachers are encouraged to see writing as *a resource*, a way to access their own experiences of English and education, and a space where they can begin to develop a distinctive professional voice. Although some of the writing might be included later in the year as assessed work for portfolios, it seems important to us that in framing the tasks, the way they are mediated by the tutors and in the kind of feedback we give, that we hold off from the language of criteria for assessment. In a way, we want to provide a protected space for the development of a voice which can begin to embody a strong sense of teacher identity. We want to release them into writing. Discussion of assessment criteria can be inimical to this because it shifts the terms of the tutor/student relationship – and we want to avoid closing down the opportunity for them to see writing itself as central to the development of professional skills and *thinking* about practice.

Throughout the first term of the course, the priority is to establish a personal relationship and *professional dialogue* between the tutor and the student teacher, to move the tutor's role as an assessor within an assessment framework into the background. In the comments that frame the subject knowledge development task we emphasise this personal relationship and professional dialogue by drawing attention to the audience and purpose of the task, and defining these specifically in relation to the development of teacher identities rather than assessment of the writing in relation to academic criteria. We say that the writing is 'for your tutor who will discuss with you the contents of what you have written. It is also an opportunity for you to introduce yourself to your tutor as a writer.' So, from the beginning, the writing itself is constructed as being at the centre of the professional relationship and the process of becoming a teacher. 'Getting to know you' is inseparable from 'getting to know you as a writer'. The task itself is a familiar one on many pre-service courses, but it is often framed as an 'audit' of prior knowledge with the notion of measuring up the student teacher's competence and subject knowledge in relation to a range of authorised frameworks, the national curriculum in particular. Not uncommonly, the tutor's role here is constructed as that of assessor, gatekeeper, or perhaps at best critical friend, in the process of prescribing or negotiating an 'action plan' to address areas of perceived deficit. Such framing shapes the writer's response. Because it is highly contingent on approval within a framework for assessment, the writing is likely to be more cautious, less exploratory and more defensive than in a context where the purpose of the task is 'to get to know you as a writer'. We want student teachers to feel instead that the writing will constitute a professional dialogue about two things – the nature of the subject itself and their positioning of themselves in relation to the subject.

It would be possible to see progression within higher education as a process of acquiring the skills and conventions of academic writing. This approach tends to prioritise extensive reading and referencing to policy, theory and research, and an ability to critically evaluate these in relation to teaching practice and pedagogy. Such a model of progression might generate a much shorter list of written tasks designed to practise the form of the long academic essay. A different notion of progression underpins our list of assignments. As a way of thinking about progression in writing and its relation to developing teacher identities we might identify three polarities within this:

- *autobiographical narrative* and *conventional academic forms*
- *personal experience* and *knowledge of literature and policy*
- *specific (individual learners)* and *general (whole classes, subjects and curriculum)*.

This has implications for the form and content of the tasks set.

Autobiographical narrative and conventional academic forms

From the first task in the list, we emphasise that the organisation and presentation of the writing are important and that we expect the students to attend to the aesthetics of the writing process as well as the content – to craft and shape their ideas. In terms of the form of the writing, considering the *sequence* of the tasks, we could say that they tend to move broadly from being fairly open in form towards more prescribed and conventional forms. This openness is made explicit and central in the way many of the early tasks are framed. For instance, when we ask our student teachers to write their own language autobiographies, we say: 'How you write this, how it is organised and what you choose to include is up to you.' It is clear that there is a choice about what they focus on and that this should be based on professional and personal interest: 'Focus on an aspect of your language history that interests you.' Autonomy and judgement are important qualities here because we want student teachers to develop a strong, independent voice as professionals. If writing is to be a site where this happens, then, *as writers*, they need to do much more than jump through the hoops required to show competence in rehearsing conventional academic forms of writing. They need to practise exercising critical and aesthetic judgement about their own writing before operating within the genre of the academic assignment.

Writing never happens in a vacuum and the notions of openness and autonomy here are relative ones. In producing these written tasks, student teachers will inevitably be drawing on their experience *as readers* of a wide range of writing as well as operating a set of assumptions about 'the writing that we want' in this context. That said, it is important that the writing tasks are set within the context of a programme of readings and to acknowledge that we see student teachers' reading as an important resource for their writing in perhaps a rather different way from that inscribed in academic criteria. These tend to construct reading on ITE courses as the mining of an established body of respected literature for ideas that student teachers might 'apply,' more or less 'critically,' to their own practice. Our view of criticality is that it is to be located relationally, not in certain texts but between texts and in the connections that readers make between texts and classroom experiences. If the aim of developing teacher identities is prioritised, it is possible to see how reading might be conceived of as a more planned and targeted resource for student teachers' writing.

Personal experience and knowledge of literature and policy

In terms of the content of the students' writing, the tasks set in the early part of the course require student teachers to dig deep into their own histories and to use their writing to unearth for themselves and others their formative experiences of English and education. This writing allows them a space to gain some perspective on where their values, ideas and assumptions come from, and to begin to make sense of this in relation to their earliest experiences of teaching in school. Tasks such as 'subject knowledge development', 'what constitutes a good teacher?' and 'a language autobiography' are designed to help student teachers write in an autobiographical way in order to explore who they are as learners and what knowledge they bring with them.

As student teachers begin to draw on their own experiences of learning and using language throughout their lives, they begin to probe the relationships between language, culture and identity from the inside. Again, this kind of task offers them the opportunity to reflect on their own complex relationship with language. They *all* discover that they have a particular history of standing in a variety of positions in relation to powerful forms of discourse. They also reflect, often with great pleasure, on the power, creativity and playfulness of non-standard or unofficial forms of language – the process of learning to talk and write, 'mistakes' they made, family words and jokes, slang and dialect, code switching, and combining the language of the home and the school. Many student teachers comment on the fact that they thought they would have nothing to say about their own language, but by distancing themselves from it through writing they were able to write themselves through to a new perspective, often exposing powerful emotions and memories along the way.

All of this, then, makes it more likely that when they first meet pupils in school, they will do so with an awareness of the power of language to shape identity and of the complexity of the way in which we all continue to construct and reconstruct multiple selves through our interactions with language. This in turn means that they will be able to pose questions or at least problematise common-sense terms which have strong currency in school – for example, EAL (English as an Additional Language), Standard English, literacy – and see through them to the individual learners. By engaging in writing of this kind first, they can begin to hear their own voices, before dealing more thoughtfully, confidently and personally with tasks such as 'the place of English' which require engagement with more established and authoritative forms of discourse in academic literature and policy documents.

Specific (individual learners) and general (whole classes, subjects and curriculum)

A number of the early writing tasks ask student teachers to look very closely at individual pupils or particular classrooms. Writing enables the students to describe and explore what they see about learning in a specific context and, at the same time, to begin to develop their understanding of learning itself as always context-specific. We want them to experience the possibilities of the case study as a genre of writing which can support their professional development throughout the course and beyond. Here, we have to go back to the point about the link between student teachers' experience as readers and writers on the course and the way in which the writing tasks we set are placed very carefully within a programme of reading. We ask our student teachers to read two books before the course begins – *The Reader in the*

Writer (Barrs and Cork, 2001) and *Read it to Me Now!* (Minns, 1997) – both powerful texts that use case study methodology to throw a spotlight on individual learners. The particular power of case studies lies in the apparent paradox whereby the sharp focus on particular examples of learning leads to an enlarged picture of learning as a whole. There is an ideological dimension to the choice of this genre of writing, as it is one that embodies a view of learning as something that is always socially constructed and context-dependent and, crucially, one in which the writer is involved and committed, positioned by the writing as an actor inside the scene as well as observing and reflecting on it.

It is these qualities we want to encourage in our students as writers and as teachers. When we set the case study tasks, we mediate them with discussion in seminars about reading the texts above, with the aim of encouraging student teachers to take on the spirit of this genre. In particular, we want them to see that their own experience of classrooms and their emotional as well as intellectual reactions are valid within their professional writing. In supporting the development of their identities as teachers, we want them to begin to weave together their own story of being in the classroom and thinking about it in the context of the stories of individual pupils and their learning. We want them to see learning as an ongoing story made up by the interactions of pupils and teachers in particular classrooms around texts of various kinds.

It is important to qualify and clarify the notion of progression itself that is being discussed. We do not conceptualise these three polarities as representing a spectrum of difficulty. We do not think, for instance, that writing from personal experience or very closely describing the observation of a particular pupil is easy and that evaluating policy documents or writing a 5,000-word academic essay is hard. Rather, to be meaningful and useful *in terms of developing teacher identities,* the writing tasks that come towards the end of the course need to be infused with the reflective qualities, perspectives and confident voices of the earlier pieces. The way in which student teachers are able to operate within more established genres of professional and academic writing will be changed by their early experiences of writing in more open, personal and specific ways. In formulating the notion of progression on a PGCE course, we need to be clear about where we have come from and where we are going. We think that the goal ought to be newly qualified teachers who have a strong sense of their own professional responsibility and autonomy based on their reading, their own experiences as learners and their interactions with particular pupils and classes. It follows from this that the progression we plan through the sequence of written tasks is not one that prioritises the mastery of highly prescribed academic genres; instead it encourages student teachers to use writing to work things out for themselves and to pose questions, to circle around issues of learning and view them from different angles, and to resist easy or reductive solutions and explanations they may meet in their professional lives. The teacher identities our student teachers take with them into their first year of teaching will continue to evolve. It is our hope that writing will continue to play a part for many of them in interrogating their own classrooms, developing ideas about their own practice and contributing to the wider debates around the subject as a whole.

Dialogic practice and the tutors' feedback

In thinking about how the student teachers' writing is framed, we need to consider not only how the tasks are set up and their sequence but also the ways in which we as tutors respond to them. Here, too, dialogic principles inform our practice. To explore this, we will focus on the function of the cover sheets, the medium whereby tutors respond to student teachers' writing.

Figure 5.2

English Subject Task

Profile of a reader
For a description of the task, see pages 59–60 (63–64 E/D) of the Course Handbook.

Name of ST:

Name of Institute Subject Tutor:

The contribution of this task towards meeting the Standards for Qualified Teacher Status:
This task helps BTs to reflect on their observations of KS 1/2 curricula and teaching arrangements (Q 11) and on the range of developmental factors that affect learning (Q 18).

The PSE week marks the start of the process of learning from the effective practice of others (Q3, Q 10) and of becoming aware of the statutory and non-statutory frameworks within which teachers work (Q 15). The task's focus on individual learners introduces BTs to aspects of differentiation (Q 19, Q23, Q25).

This task contributes to the **Professional Practice** and **Subjects** in a **Wider Context** modules. The Profile of a Reader may be included for assessment in the **Language, Culture and Learning** portfolio.

Feedback: I wonder if after the presentation on 'the multilingual classroom' and after some time in school, you have had further thoughts about Abdul and his progress in reading. 'Home' stands in your account as a 'problem' in terms of Abdul's development, at least his development in English. The picture you present is what is sometimes called a 'deficit model' of bilingualism: it's a 'lack', almost a disadvantage. BUT you are clearly interested in learning about Abdul as well as in helping him, not just to 'read better' (although of course that is crucial to his progress in school), but to 'get on' generally and feel that there is a place for him in school. You hit the nail on the head when you say: 'Trying to identify what would best aid Abdul's learning is complex'. I do think that his enthusiasm and his desire to join the school community that you are very sensitive to, as well as his desire to 'succeed' academically, are real strengths in his profile. What happens in Year 7 will be crucial and I understand your apprehensiveness. I do recommend the work of Josie Levine when you have some time: *Bilingual Learners* and the *Mainstream Curriculum*, not new but still wise. If you choose to include the Profile of a Reader in the portfolio later in the year, let's talk about some other critical reading you might include.

The cover sheets are located in a complicated web of related texts and, as such, refer to and consequently act as a reminder of the fact that they cannot be separated from the business of assessment. So, to give just one example, a box that takes up a significant amount of space in the upper half of the cover sheet (see Figure 5.2) contains a formal reminder that the task under review contributes in ways that are explicitly linked to detailed specifications in *Professional Standards for Teachers* (TDA, 2007) towards meeting the Standards for the award of qualified teacher status (QTS). It states in spare, impersonal terms the function and purpose of the task: 'This task helps STs [student teachers] to reflect on their observation…' and so on. Thus it addresses different audiences, including inspecting bodies and examiners as well as the student teachers themselves. Inscribed in the very design of the cover sheet, then, is a set of social and professional relationships and orientations. Unavoidably, the relationship between tutor and student teacher is shaped by these complexities. Part of this relationship is the unequal one of assessor and assessed. In this context the tutor's feedback seeks to manage a particular social nexus.

The tutor's words are framed by a box that occupies the bottom half of the cover sheet. Looking at Figure 5.2, the contrast between the tutor's personal voice and the impersonal discourse of standards in the upper half is striking. The tutor writes as though picking up the threads of an ongoing conversation. She swiftly establishes a sense of a shared world with her student teacher by referring to a relevant moment from the course, and she takes care to suggest that the student teacher may have moved on since she wrote the piece in question. There is an implicit assumption here that the writer will continue to develop her ideas, not in isolation, but rather in close contact with a tutor who shares an interest in the same issues. The feedback begins:

> *I wonder if after the presentation on 'the multilingual classroom' and after some time in school, you have had further thoughts about Abdul and his progress in reading. 'Home' stands in your account as a 'problem' in terms of Abdul's development, at least his development in English.*

The way is cleared for the tutor to introduce a substantial consideration that stands opposed to what the student teacher suggested in her piece. The way the tutor does this is more than just diplomatic: it promises further discussion. She writes, 'The picture you present is what is sometimes called a "deficit model" of bilingualism: it's a "lack", almost a disadvantage.' She evokes a history of debate, a contested discourse about bilingual learners within which the student teacher's piece is positioned. This involves a major repositioning that foregrounds negative implications, tensions and contradictions that the student writer may not have noticed at the time of writing. And, though the evocation of such a history may seem to diminish the value of the student teacher's contribution in relation to the larger debate, it is plainly intended to prompt further thought.

The tutor's next move is pivotal. She restores a sense of the worth that attaches to the processes (writing and reflecting) in which the student teacher is engaged by acknowledging the fact that she is committed to helping a child, a real person from a minority ethnic background, with a particular heritage and personal history. 'BUT,' she writes, 'you are interested in learning *about* Abdul.' She further implies that the source of the student teacher's miscalculation or flawed evaluation (offering a deficit view of Abdul's language and background) lies in her apprehension that Abdul will not do well in secondary school. The overall implication in the tutor's feedback is that the student teacher's writing is a milestone in a learning trajectory that will occur over time. Her feedback closes with a recommendation for further reading and a strong hint that the conversation could be continued at a definite point later in the course.

Before moving on to the second cover sheet, we want to mention another shift that happens in the tutor's feedback. When the tutor evokes a history of debate about the place of bilingual learners' first language, she also makes a judgement about the student teacher's writing and gives appropriate feedback against a backdrop of subject knowledge and values that are both larger and more enduring than the detailed specifications set down in *Professional Standards for Teachers* (TDA, 2007).

In the second instance of feedback (see Figure 5.3), the tutor writes as though she is intervening in a widening conversation. As in Figure 5.2, she conveys a sense of a shared world, but this time the sense is established through a suggestion that the content of the student teacher's piece might be shared with another, named, member of the tutor group. This suggestion implies participation in a collective, professional enterprise in which experiences and insights are circulated for everyone's benefit.

Figure 5.3

Feedback: Share your 'three major elements of my identity' with Katie: something happened in a classroom at her school that would interest you and, conversely, you have light to shed on her questions about 'the names we give ourselves as well as those others give to us' (I like her phrase!). Your language autobiography is fascinating and so encouraging in terms of your own 'writing style': you seem to me to have found a powerful voice here, one that 'speaks' of your particular, individual experiences of language and identity but one that also communicates to a wider audience. Take one example – what you say about your name: this illuminates beautifully the complex ways in which language is bound up with issues of family, history, migration, power and culture, and takes the reader back to what you say at the beginning about those three major elements of the phrase: 'British Bengali Muslim'. What you say about 'hybridity' is interesting too and you might like to have a look at Ben Rampton's work with London adolescents and their 'new languages'. I want to talk more to you about your experiences as a school student: I think you are saying that you now think it was a 'mistake' to retreat into Bengali ('retreat' is my choice of verb here, not yours). Is that right? And of course, I know you are interested in issues around 'gender and cultural expectations'. I recommend Jane Miller's book *Many Voices*: she interviewed a number of bilingual learners and some speak about their status as girls within both family and community, something that you refer to in relation to your own history.

Crucially, the tutor's response is attuned to the nuances of identity formation that lie at the core of the student teacher's piece. Further, there is an implicit acknowledgement that the student teacher's voice is authoritative when she speaks about what the tutor calls 'the three major elements' of the student's phrase: 'British Bengali Muslim'. While recognising the significance of what the student teacher has written about her personal history, she recommends recent research that could afford a theoretical framework for analysing not just what the student teacher has to say about her own formation of identity, but additionally about the situation of many bilingual children in London schools. In future, it is suggested, the student teacher's writing could be strengthened by referring to relevant scholarship. There is a suggestion, too, that the insights that inform the individual story will have special relevance for generating professional understandings of the learning needs of bilingual pupils within a wide constituency, including teachers and policy-makers.

The tutor's personal, engaged tone is, again, striking: 'I like her phrase!...I want to talk more...I think you are saying...Is that right?' This seems most appropriate, given the nature of the student teacher's writing and the tutor's interest in the issues it raises. Finally, the overall orientation of the feedback is directed towards generating a professional conversation that will continue beyond the PGCE course.

The argument that we have been constructing here is about the role of writing in ITE and about the role of the university in relation to producing this writing, but it is also – crucially – about the development of teacher identities. Education remains subject to the changing fashions of policy, felt nowhere more keenly than in teacher education. Yet, despite all the currents and eddies generated by policy-driven interventions, writing has allowed our student teachers to continue to pose questions – sometimes quite critical ones – about what they see in schools and how they might conceptualise their own roles within them. Writing, surrounded by and arising out of talk and reading, creates a space for student teachers to reflect on those tensions and equips them to go into schools, maintain a critical perspective and always be ready to ask *'How might things be otherwise?'*

Chapter 6

'A bit of an eye-opener': Critical reflection at Master's level through portfolio construction

Karen Turner

In this chapter I discuss the role of portfolios in the professional learning of teachers engaged in the Master of Teaching course at the IOE. I begin by providing details of the course, its philosophy and the principles which underpin the design of the portfolios. I then report on the outcomes of two interview studies in which we investigated students' notions of critical reflection as evidenced in one-to-one interviews and in their portfolios. Notions of critical reflection are explored by referring to the academic literature. The chapter ends with a discussion of the role of critical reflection in the construction of the portfolio and the contribution of the portfolio to professional learning.

The Master of Teaching

The Master of Teaching (MTeach) is an award-bearing Master's level course at the Institute of Education designed for practising teachers in all phases of education. It differs from traditional higher degree courses where academic study is separated from professional practice. For MTeach participants, the scholarly activities and investigative work they engage in are situated in their own classrooms and are shaped by their own professional development interests and needs. MTeach students are part of a 'community of practice', a group of people who 'share a concern, a set of problems, or a passion about a topic, and who deepen their knowledge and expertise…by interacting on an ongoing basis' (Wenger *et al.*, 2002: 4). The interaction in this case takes place through computer-mediated communication in cross-phase, cross-subject online discussion groups and is stimulated by briefing papers referenced to relevant academic, research-based and professional readings. The co-constructivist approach to professional learning is characterised by many of the elements that national and international research have shown to be fundamental to effective teacher learning, in that it supports opportunities for reflection and personal development beyond government priorities and extends professional identify through boundary crossing into other phases (Hodkinson and Hodkinson, 2005: 124). It is connected to and derived from participants' work with learners (Yates, 2007: 214), and it provides intellectual stimulation and sets up learning networks beyond the school (Lovatt and Gilmore, 2003: 208).

The Master of Teaching is part of the IOE's 180-credit Master's programme. Two portfolios of 30 credits each comprise part of the assessment framework. They were designed to serve the dual purpose of assessment and scaffold for professional learning, and to reflect the key elements of collaboration and reflection on theory and practice which define the course. For the purposes of consistency in summative assessment, the contents of the portfolios are prescribed, but within the prescription there is choice and flexibility which gives teachers the scope and discretion to demonstrate individual capability and achievement (Dinham and Scott, 2003). The components of the two portfolios are shown in Figure 6.1.

Figure 6.1

Contents of the two MTeach portfolios

Professional Development Portfolio 1 (PDP1)	Professional Development Portfolio 2 (PDP2)
A Philosophical Statement	A Philosophical Statement
A critical appraisal of an article from a professional or academic journal	A review of online learning as part of an electronic tutor group
A piece of reflective writing related to an oral presentation by applicants to peers at the course interview	An evidence study carried out in school and critically reviewed. The study might relate to development of the teacher as a subject or phase specialist, or as a researcher; to the study of pupil progression; to the use of teacher narrative in understanding professional development

Three pieces of evidence (for example, schemes of work, lesson observations, projects) showing professional development which are prefaced by reflections on the way the evidence contributes to development.	A critical review of an academic article or chapter or of a writer and the influence of the work on the teacher's practice.

The first portfolio (PDP1) is submitted in the early part of the first term of the course and is the first piece of assessed work. It is concerned with accrediting prior learning. The second portfolio (PDP2) is submitted at the end of the first or second year of the course (depending on the sequence of modules taken). It focuses on learning during MTeach studies and requires students to review their practical and theoretical learning.

The portfolios require students to reflect critically on teaching and learning. The components are designed to support reflection that is *critical* by inviting students to look back over time and to look beyond their own practice to the wider field. Moreover, they must look outside their specialist phase or subject to consider educational values more broadly as well as the wider role of the teacher as educator. This is the purpose of the philosophical statement. When teachers write their first philosophical statement, they may go back to a statement they produced during the initial training year; when they write the second philosophical statement, they go back to their first statement to review whether their fundamental beliefs about the purposes of education remain the same, a process which might be transforming or reconfirming. We consider looking 'long' and looking 'wide' to be key elements in critical reflection.

Portfolios and professional learning

Since the inception of the MTeach, we have carried out two interview studies into the effectiveness of the portfolios as a tool for professional learning, initially in 2004 when our first cohort of MTeach students graduated and again in 2006 as a follow-up to the first investigation. On the second occasion, we also carried out an analysis of aspects of the interviewees' second portfolio. In the first study, we interviewed students at the end of their first year of study who had completed the first portfolio and graduates who had completed both portfolios. We were particularly interested in students' understanding of the dual role of the portfolio as a summative assessment requirement and a support for professional learning, as we were concerned that students might experience some conflict in addressing both purposes. In the second study, we interviewed course graduates about the second portfolio and we focused on their understandings of critical reflection. We asked interviewees to define what they understood by critical reflection and to share with us passages of critical reflection from their second portfolios.

The outcomes of the first interview study (Turner and Simon, 2007) showed us that students were able to appreciate and manage the dual purpose of the portfolios. This was, we concluded, because of the high degree of synergy between a learning portfolio (as defined in the academic literature), the philosophy underpinning the design of the course and the assessment criteria at higher degree level. A learning portfolio requires thinking, talking and knowing about teaching, and involves a process of discovery (Grant and Huebner, 1998). In order to understand 'the complex, messy, multiple dimensions of teaching and of teacher learning' (Lyons, 1998: 15), teachers need to 'engage in professional dialogue with colleagues' (Klenowski, 2002: 25). Such collaborative talk about teaching is fundamental to the MTeach online discussions. To understand better the complexities of teaching and learning, portfolio writers need to reflect critically, a process which involves analysis and questioning: querying why things are the way they are, challenging assumptions and exploring alternatives. Taking up a position of 'reflective scepticism', as Scott (2000: 126) calls it, cannot result from a review of practical experiences alone but requires the consideration of other forms of professional knowledge such as the findings of research and theoretical insights derived from the foundation disciplines (Furlong *et al.*, 2000: 138). Such intellectual activities are essential to Master's level study where students are assessed, among other things, on their capacity to 'refine professional knowledge through scholarship', 'to analyse pedagogy within immediate and wider professional contexts' and on their 'ability to draw from appropriate intellectual perspectives through their knowledge of the related academic literature' (IOE, 2009).

In the first interview study, when interviewees were asked to talk about their understandings of critical reflection, they recounted personal experiences that did not go beyond their own classrooms and which focused on the effectiveness of skills without any broader critique, or which provided some reasons for action but which were limited to personal judgement. However, in talking about the construction of the philosophical statement, interviewees expressed wider conceptions of critical reflection, linking classroom experiences to scholarly reading and research, and referred to the purposes of education and the articulation of educational values. Interviewees who had completed both portfolios explained that the first philosophical statement served as a sort of landmark by which they located change and professional development over time. Constructing the second portfolio enabled them to draw together theory and practice.

As a result of our findings in the first interview study, we wanted to nurture more complex understandings of critical reflection, so we introduced some changes to the ways in which we supported students with the construction of their second portfolio. We began with the clarification and elaboration of our own understandings of critical reflection through a literature review and we shared this with the students. We then created opportunities for reflective conversation (Bold, 2008; Ghaye and Ghaye, 1998) through workshop sessions. As a result of these changes, we felt that the second portfolios showed a stronger critical edge. In 2006 we carried out a second interview study in order to look for more elaborate and purposeful notions of critical reflection and its application through the components of the second portfolio.

Understanding and nurturing critical reflection

The ability to reflect critically on practice is fundamental to learning through portfolio construction (Klenowski, 2002; Lyons, 2002; Hatton and Smith, 1995; Dinham and Scott, 2003; Orland-Barak, 2005; Pedro, 2005) to teacher learning more broadly (Schön, 1983; Ghaye and Ghaye, 1998; Dinkelman, 2000) and to professional learning more generally (Boud *et al.*, 2006). Reflection is both retrospective and anticipatory because it is concerned with learning from experience through systematic and purposeful enquiry into practice (Schön, 1983) for the purposes of improvement. It involves deconstruction and reconstruction of practice and the creation or deepening of professional knowledge. There is, however, no consensus in the literature on what makes reflection critical (Dinkelman, 2000: 198). There are certainly connections between the different conceptions of 'critical', but there is also confusion, which is highlighted in the longer discussion on critical reflection in Chapter 3 of this book. Furlong *et al.* (2000: 138), for example, suggest that reflection is *critical* when practical experience is reviewed in the light of theory and research, but for Hatton and Smith (1995: 40, 45) engagement with the literature is part of *descriptive* reflection, and for Ghaye and Ghaye (1998: 30) part of *receptive* reflection. For Hoyrup and Elkjaer (2006: 32), the 'hallmark' of critical reflection is confronting the taken-for-granted and the unnoticed, but 'clarifying assumptions underlying the educational process' and 'explicating rationales for educational goals' is termed *practical* reflection by Dinkelman (2000: 198).

We found three relevant and useful conceptions of critical reflection in the literature: critical reflection that brings together theory and practice (Furlong *et al.*, 2000); critical reflection that interrogates accepted routines and confronts the taken-for-granted (Ghaye and Ghaye, 1998; Hoyrup and Elkjaer, 2006; Lyle and Handley, 2007; Bold 2008); and critical reflection that considers practice within the wider socio-historical political context (Hatton and Smith, 1995; Ghaye and Ghaye, 1998; Dinkelman, 2000) and encompasses a consideration of educational values (Ghaye and Ghaye, 1998), including 'deliberation about the moral and ethical dimensions of education' and the contribution of education to 'the construction of a more equitable, just, and democratic society' (Dinkelman, 2000: 198, 199).

The interrelationship between these three conceptions of critical reflection lies in the need to situate individual practice and personal beliefs within the dominant cultural belief system underpinning government policy for education. 'Teachers are not free agents' (Ghaye and Ghaye, 1998: 34) and they must learn 'to decode the symbolic landscape' (Ghaye and Ghaye, 1998: 18). So critical reflection begins by analysing the individual's classroom practice and moves increasingly outwards to draw on the knowledge and practice of others, to seek out theoretical perspectives and to consider the wider socio-political context in order to understand how teachers are positioned by policy and how pedagogy is shaped and directed by changing views of 'good practice' over time.

These three conceptions of critical reflection are all relevant for Master's level portfolio work and connected well with our own conceptions of critical reflection as being 'long' – requiring time and distance in order to look back less subjectively – and 'wide' – needing to go beyond a consideration of an individual's classroom practice to the wider field of educational research and theory because new visions of education are more likely to be stimulated by engagement with the ideas of others. The literature review enabled us to elaborate on our own conceptions and to see ways in which different forms of reflection might scaffold the writing of the four components of the portfolio and lead to deeper learning. Our understanding of some of the fundamental tenets of critical reflection in all its forms helped us to see ways in which we could nurture its development in our Master's students.

We made the following changes to support the preparation of the second portfolio:

- Through face-to-face presentations, we shared different aspects of critical reflection from the literature and related these to different components of the portfolio. For example, in the philosophical statement, in order to articulate their own educational values, we encouraged students to situate their beliefs about schooling within the wider socio-political context and to consider the ways in which they are shaped by a particular cultural system. In preparing the evidence study, students were encouraged to reflect on classroom practice by referring to the ideas encountered in their scholarly reading.
- We created opportunities for 'reflective conversation' (Ghaye and Ghaye, 1998; Bold 2008) in workshop sessions where students shared draft components with a critical friend or 'dialogical other' (Ghaye and Ghaye, 1998: 21). This involved students in core reflective activities such as explaining, justifying, listening to different perspectives, questioning and confronting.

- We encouraged students to look back over time and with fresh eyes by returning to their first philosophical statement as part of their preparation for the second statement. At the end of each online module, we required them to include reflective annotations on significant learning elements from their electronic discussions so that the review of the online learning component for the portfolio became a sort of 'reflection on reflection' which illuminated professional learning over time.

The second interview study and its findings

In 2006 we conducted a second interview study which focused on students' understanding of critical reflection and its expression in the different components of the second portfolio. We interviewed nine students, two male and seven female, selected as representative of the whole cohort. Six students were campus-based and three students were based in a secondary outreach institution. The nine students had a range of teaching experience: two had begun the MTeach post-PGCE; two had begun the course in their second year of teaching, post-Induction; and five were experienced teachers who held posts of responsibility. Finally, two of the teachers were primary specialists, one teacher was a further education foreign language specialist and six were secondary teachers, each with a different specialism (Geography, Science, English, Business Studies, Physical Education and Media Studies). We were interested in how they constructed the second portfolio, the order of preparation, what they enjoyed about writing it and which component(s) they learned most from. We asked them to define critical reflection and to share examples of critically reflective writing in the portfolio (which they had identified in advance of the interview).

In reporting the outcomes of the second interview study, the focus is on student definitions of critical reflection and its manifestation in their selected portfolio extracts and the interview transcripts. In places, we draw on other parts of the portfolios where we believe critical reflection is evident to provide a fuller picture of professional learning as evidenced in the construction of the second portfolio. In analysing the data, we were looking for conceptions of reflection which go beyond personal recounts of experience to encompass theoretical perspectives and educational values through engagement with others and with the literature, leading to analysis of practice and changed pedagogy.

Beyond personal recounts: Engagement with others

In their definitions of critical reflection six out of nine of the interviewees referred to the importance of looking beyond their own classrooms to the work of others. They talked about 'looking outside yourself' (Linda), 'looking at other people's work' (Michelle), 'being open to the opinions of others' (Rowena) and 'taking on board the advice of others' (Paula). Natasha talked about engaging with 'those rich discussions that you have with other colleagues and other individuals in schools'. By 'other individuals', she means the children in her primary school and also the Teaching Assistants and Learning Mentors who have the time and opportunity to talk with individual children and who 'notice a lot about children's learning that a teacher can't access' (Natasha, interview). Having worked very closely with support staff as part of a classroom research project, Natasha had realised how much 'rich information' about individual learners teachers have access to, and yet they rarely have time to engage in professional dialogue with teachers and their feedback on learning is often 'maligned' (Natasha, interview). For Valerie, critical reflection was not simply about 'one set of thinking' (her own), but about 'involving others which could be distant friends like authors of research or literature or real physically present friends, like colleagues or even students' (interview).

Michelle and Valerie chose extracts which illustrated critical reflection from the review of the online learning component of the portfolio. These elaborated on their understandings of the need to work with others in order to interrogate one's own practice. Michelle wrote about the role of her online tutor group as a 'supportive forum' where members were not afraid 'to challenge and prompt divergence in thinking' and were encouraged to experiment with the ideas of others (Michelle, extract and interview). In her interview, Valerie talked about her selected extract from the review of online learning in a way that clearly illustrated 'epistemological development' (Moon, 2008: 101). Through engagement with the ideas of others, she was able to take a more relativist position, to understand that multiple interpretations of ideas are possible and that knowledge is constructed according to sets of beliefs and/or according to context (Moon, 2008: 103):

> We had all read the same article and that's when I think it becomes interesting because we've all read the same thing but because we are all so different and we are working and professionally speaking, acting in so many different contexts, the way I will understand it is maybe completely different from the way somebody else will understand it. And that's precisely why it becomes more interesting and enriching because I've got my vision or my view point on the reading and then somebody else comes along and says 'no but maybe it actually means something else', or' have you thought about this other interpretation' let's say. And then you think well that's true. It is also that, so it enriches you because it's like as if you are having a dialogue with the writer although he's not present, with the author, so you're talking to him or about him with others and we all input based on our context.
>
> (Valerie, interview)

Gareth, one of the interviewees whose definition of critical reflection did not include engagement with others, nevertheless selected an extract from the portfolio in which he reflected critically on the importance of others in the development of professional knowledge. In this extract from his review of online learning, he wrote about turning to online peers for ideas to engage his own classes:

> *I increasingly find myself looking to appropriate the method and ideology of different group members into my own industry.*
>
> (Gareth, extract from review of online learning)

He reflects, however, that this is not a straightforward transfer because he needs to understand the ideas underpinning activities to make them work in his own context:

> *In the past, when I have tried to incorporate a 'jigsaw'-style task in my lessons, I have often failed to direct this activity within a suitable learning framework – i.e. what am I doing and why am I doing this?*
>
> (ibid.)

Engagement with the literature

Five out of the nine interviewees included the role of academic literature in their definitions of critical reflection or in their selected extracts. For these students, reflecting critically involved bringing together practical experience and theoretical insights from module and personal readings. Engagement with theoretical ideas widened perspectives on pedagogy, deepened understanding of learning, encouraged a questioning stance and offered alternative visions of teaching.

> *Being critically reflective is also acquiring, I suppose, the confidence to question, so I question everything. I question who I am, I question what I do, I question why I do it…And all because of the literature I've read. It's given me the confidence to question and reflect on things that have gone before.*
>
> (Rowena)

This perspective on critical reflection is reinforced by Rowena's chosen portfolio extract which illuminates the way in which encounters with the ideas of a particular writer have not only changed her pedagogy but also caused her to reflect on what it means to be a 'good' teacher, as these extracts from her philosophical statement show:

> *This year, as I have developed, so has my focus and understanding of pedagogy. My main focus point this year has not been what I can bring to my lessons but what knowledge and perceptions my students*

bring and what strategies I can employ to encourage them to learn how to learn.

Instrumental and a springboard in the development of my thinking has been the literature of Chris Watkins and his views regarding promotion of the meta-cognitive processes of students.

In analysing last year's (philosophical) statement, it was evident that at that time my impression of what a good teacher was amounted to no more than a dossier of what skills I had to bring to lessons.
(Rowena, philosophical statement)

Freya does not refer to engagement with literature in her definition, but her two portfolio extracts, chosen because they show how she developed as a teacher over time (interview), provide evidence of the importance for her practice of engaging with research literature. From initial feelings of being 'overwhelmed with the research and reading' involved in her very first online discussion work, Freya reflects that 'reading research material and doing my own research are now part of my classroom practice' (Freya, selected extract from the philosophical statement). This includes keeping a reflective journal because she has come to value teacher narrative alongside academic research and to realise its importance in relation to enhancing her own learning (Freya, selected extract from the review of online learning).

Literature as a vehicle for thinking and seeing differently, and for supporting critical reflection that challenges the taken-for-granted in individual practice or more widely, is confirmed by Valerie and Linda:

Critical reflection is when there is that element of the literature that helps you see also in a different way.
(Valerie, definition of critical reflection)

As I understand it, it's looking back at what you've done with a different hat on…thinking with wider perspectives, with ideas, with theoretical perspectives…looking outside yourself back on what you've done…I think the theoretical perspectives help because apart from anything else, you get another opinion on what you're doing and it's an opinion that appears in print, and so it holds some weight, and in a library.
(Linda, definition of critical reflection)

The power of literature to bring about 'perspective transformation' (Askew et al., 2005: 5) is evident in the writing of Valerie, Michelle and Paula. These transformations are concerned with changing power relationships in the classroom and a shift from teacher-at-the-centre-of-control to shared teacher-learner responsibility. Valerie developed a 'more democratic relationship' with her learners, 'encouraging them to lead their own and others' learning' (Valerie, selected extract from philosophical statement).

Michelle and Paula did not refer to the role of literature in critical reflection in either their definitions or their selected extracts, but pertinent examples of the role of literature as an aid to thinking differently could be found in their philosophical statements. Engaging with socio-constructivist theories of learning as part of Master's level studies led Michelle to relinquish her 'long held almost stereotypical view of a teacher, based on (my) schooling, upbringing and what I thought was expected and valued whilst I was training' and to become 'more vulnerable in the classroom' by which she meant 'taking more risks, letting the students dictate the direction of the lesson' and being more spontaneous.

Paula turned to the literature for different perspectives on managing a very challenging Advanced Level group. She reflected critically on this and made resulting changes in her practice:

> After reading in Van Merriënboer and Kirschner (2001) about inquisitorial and expository approaches to educating and that collaborative learning takes place when 'students can negotiate the material they are to deliver and interact with others to achieve their desired aim' I adapted my teaching material in order to accommodate this. They responded better than I could have imagined and were more motivated by the task. Reflecting on this activity gave me the courage to adopt similar practices with my lower school groups.
>
> (Paula, philosophical statement)

For Natasha, critical reflection involves engaging with 'reading literature, scholarly or not scholarly' (definition) and her two selected portfolio extracts both illustrate ways in which the literature has challenged her thinking. The transformations as a result of critical engagement with the literature are more philosophical than pedagogic. In the second extract from the evidence study, she reflects on the way in which the work of a particular writer resulted in an understanding of how teachers can be agents for educational and social change in urban areas:

> Keyes was a powerful piece of writing because of the social context of what he's saying because he's talking about basically educational agency and teachers being [a] kind of powerful element of being able to change educational advantage for children…And that's what makes the kind of engagement with literature, I think, quite powerful when it actually challenges me or I get a sense of their passion for a particular area and it's similar to mine.
>
> (Natasha, interview)

These reflections, which brought together her own inner city classroom experiences and challenging reading, resulted in new thinking about the purposes of education and a realisation of 'the power' she had as an educational professional to shape children's lives for the better (Natasha, selected extract from the evidence study).

The socio-political context of learning and educational values

For Michelle, Paula and Gareth, and for Rowena and Valerie, professional values as articulated in their portfolios, are closely related to pedagogy which empowers learners and which promotes more equitable teacher–learner relationships. For Michelle, Paula and Gareth this is a response to the powerful influence of a 'results-driven' climate which validates prescription and spoon-feeding (Paula, extract from review of online learning; Michelle, extract from review of online learning; Gareth, interview) 'rather than actually engaging them (the students) in a process of learning which will eventually develop the transferable skills needed beyond school' (Michelle, selected extract, review of online learning).

For Freya and for Linda, considering the socio-political context is part of their definition of critical reflection. In her philosophical statement, Freya refers to the need to understand 'what else is impacting on what you've done' and defines critical reflection as 'looking at the broader picture and looking at what that is affecting and what you can do about it'. She acknowledges her understanding of the way that 'government-led policies affect schools and classrooms' and 'how children's home lives affect much of their learning'. Linda refers to 'thinking with wider perspectives…with political perspectives' and her selected extract from the philosophical statement acknowledges the power of 'league tables, trend lines and other statistical analyses' to undermine the 'needs and aspirations of individual pupils'. Ensuring the success of all pupils had required a change in her philosophy of teaching to a more holistic vision of herself as an educator rather than a subject specialist.

> I now see myself as more of a whole in that I'm a form teacher, I'm a geography teacher, a debate tutor and all these kinds of things. In the first Philosophical Statement I talked about these three roles, I talked about myself as a geography teacher, myself as a teacher professional with adults and these are separate…and I thought I don't feel like that any more. Everything's joined up. Being a geography teacher isn't as important as I thought it was. Being a teacher is much more significant.
>
> (Linda, interview)

Similar thinking about the teacher's role as an educator was found in David's philosophical statement, also selected as evidence of critical reflection:

> *For me, our role as teachers is more holistic than that for which we are trained and paid. I am not just a secondary science teacher or a Head of Year. Whilst these constitute the fundamentals of my job, they are not the nucleus around which my professional values are based.*
>
> (David, selected extract, philosophical statement)

This holistic role of the teacher is founded on the need to understand and develop learners as whole individuals:

> *An interest in their academic, pastoral and extra-curricular lives would be the ideal way in which I would wish to characterise my relationship with pupils. This is something that relates, fundamentally, to my sense of vocation as a teacher.*
>
> (David, selected extract, philosophical statement)

Understanding the individual as a whole is part of David's desire to nurture intrinsic motivation in his learners because it is the 'healthiest kind of motivation' – 'to perform an activity simply for the reward inherent in the participation' (David, selected extract, philosophical statement).

For Natasha (see section above, 'Engagement with the literature'), as for Linda, critical reflection encompasses deliberating about the moral and ethical dimensions of teaching in inner city environments of social and economic disadvantage where she sees herself as an agent of change.

Generally, the constraints imposed by the socio-political context in which the interviewees are working are implicitly acknowledged rather than overtly challenged in their portfolio extracts. Students' reflections do not extend to interrogating the validity and appropriateness of the values underpinning the dominant performance culture with its competitive league tables, even though the attendant adverse consequences for pupil learning are identified and questioned.

Discussion and conclusions

Our first interview study showed that our students considered the first portfolio to be a critical evaluation of their experiences and beliefs at a particular point in time, a sort of landmark as they set out on higher degree level study (Turner and Simon, 2007). In the second interview study we wanted to know about professional learning that had taken place in the course of higher degree studies as expressed in the second portfolio. In particular, we wanted to explore notions of critical reflection as understood and interpreted by the nine students in the study and as expressed in the portfolio itself. We considered the ability to interrogate and situate practical experiences and educational values, by referring to the work of others and locating these within the wider political context, to be fundamental to the furthering of professional knowledge.

We found that eight out of nine interviewees included the need to look beyond personal practice in their definitions of critical reflection or in their selected extracts. This involved engaging with the practices and beliefs of MTeach peers or with school colleagues. The collaborative nature of the Master of Teaching, with its underpinning co-constructivist philosophy of learning, supports this aspect of critical reflection. By the time the second portfolio is put together, MTeach peers are 'trusted others' (Hatton and Smith, 1995: 41) among whom ideas and beliefs can be safely interrogated and challenged. Moreover, the cross-phase, cross-subject nature of the MTeach tutor groups takes students out of their comfort zone to consider different perspectives. For six interviewees, definitions of critical reflection or extracts from their portfolio involved engaging with the academic literature. Encountering the ideas of writers and researchers in the field proved fundamental to seeing things differently and to challenging assumptions about teaching and learning. All interviewees articulated their educational values and some located these within the wider socio-political context. Generally, however, current educational policy and its underpinning ideological framework was not the subject of interrogation and we need to address this in our workshop sessions.

One interviewee defined critical reflection in a more technical, descriptive way:

> I guess it's me just, for example today, looking at – I don't know – not just about work but just looking back on things and thinking how did that go, what could I do better and what can I learn from it, what can I learn that is good from it, what is bad from it, would I do it differently next time.
>
> (David, definition of critical reflection)

This was perplexing and somewhat contradictory because it was articulated in the interview after David had talked at some length about the demands of writing the philosophical statement. He called it 'tricky writing', meaning it was not straightforward because it involved looking back over a number of years and was 'a much more general reflection, not just about academic literature and things like that, it was a much more real life – a reflection on real life':

> I think the Philosophical Statement was not just critically reviewing work and not just critically reviewing literature and so on; it's also critically reviewing my own beliefs and things and I found that quite hard to do…I guess I hadn't brought all these ideas together in my head and sat down and thought about them.
>
> (David, interview)

There is a disconnection here between the student's definition of reflection and the mental challenge of writing one of the portfolio components that required him to think more deeply and more comprehensively about his vocation as a teacher. Overall, David was not convinced that the portfolio as a whole had contributed to his professional learning.

In the interviews, students explained how the construction of the portfolio was in itself an act of reflection which helped them to assess their own learning over time. The portfolio was 'a great big reflection' and 'a bit of an eye-opener' (Rowena); 'a review and analysis over a long period' (Valerie); which allowed students to see progress and change (Freya, Michelle, Paula, Rowena and Valerie). The drafting and reflecting involved in putting the portfolio components together was itself 'a process of learning' (Linda), which pulled together what had been learned on the MTeach and at work (Valerie and Natasha). The evidence that had to be collected for the portfolio required students to return to the online module readings, to read more and to connect higher level studies with classroom practice which proved a stimulus to try out new approaches to teaching and learning.

It emerged from the interviews that the construction of the portfolio and the critical interrogation of practice and theory that it entailed supported learning which 'nourish(ed) a sense of professional dignity' (Ghaye and Ghaye, 1998: 23). In a socio-political context where teachers are positioned as technicians (Scott, 2000: 4), this is significant. The sense of professional dignity was manifested in expressions of increased professional confidence. Students talked about the confidence to question, to defend a position in the face of Ofsted questioning, to experiment and take risks, to take back control of their own classrooms (Rowena, Natasha, Freya, Paula and Linda). In some cases, this confidence was rooted in a growing academic assertiveness which Moon believes is concerned with academic self-esteem, with finding one's voice in one's specialist area in order to engage in critical thinking and debate so as to take a personal position and justify beliefs (Moon, 2008: 77–85). This included, for some students, the confidence to take a critical stance to the literature (Freya, Rowena, Natasha, Linda and Michelle).

In our second interview study, we set out to explore whether our students had broader notions of critical reflection than we found in our first study. Generally, we believe this to be the case. On the evidence of the interviews, we conclude that there is a strong interconnection between portfolio construction at Master's level and the development of critical reflection which supports professional learning. Nevertheless, powers of critical reflection have to be nurtured through explication and interaction with others.

Part 3

Case studies of professional learning and assessment

Chapter 7

Foreign language education: Preparing for diversity

Verna Brandford

This chapter aims to explore notions of culture and identity within a modern foreign language (MFL) context. The paradigm of teacher education that is adopted here is informed by an understanding of the centrality of culture to the experience of schooling and by an overarching commitment to an intercultural and inclusive approach that provides access for 'children from all groups and communities…to good education' (Gundara and Broadbent, 2009). In order for this to be realised, student teachers need to meet the complex challenges that they will encounter in diverse pupil populations and to develop the relevant knowledge, skills and understanding. Equally, they need to engage critically with current discourses around pupils' cultural identities. Paramount to this process is the student teacher's own principled understanding of intercultural issues which will form the basis of decisions concerning diversity and related practices, and interventions in the languages classroom.

Student teachers and cultural expectations

MFL student teachers necessarily tend to have an ability to function in more than one culture. If we start with Williams' definition of culture as 'a whole way of life' with common meanings, and the 'arts and learning' with its special processes of discovery and creative effort (in Ferguson, 2007), it would be fair to assume that we are all 'multicultured' (Moore, 2000) and that there are a number of meta-cultures (Gundara, 2000). This definition stands in opposition to more reductive and essentialist notions of cultural identity prevalent in some monocultural environments. The MFL classroom might helpfully be represented as the interaction of multiple cultural positions and histories: those of the learners, the student teacher and of the target language community (or communities). Indeed, the learners' culture and their relationship with the target language have a profound effect on classroom processes. It is a significant factor in both the learner's perception of language learning and how teachers and pupils alike evaluate their roles and performances in the classroom (see Jin and Cortazzi, 1993, 1996).

Student teachers also bring their different cultural experiences and expectations to the classroom. A professional challenge for the non-native speakers of the languages we teach on our PGCE MFL course is that the target language they are teaching not only reflects but also constitutes cultural aspects of the target language communities. Student teachers inevitably vary in the extent of their familiarity with – or up-to-date knowledge of – the target language. On the other hand, when the student teacher is a native speaker of the target language, their unfamiliarity with the learners' language and culture can make it difficult for them to use the pupils' own culture(s) as a basis and means of communication.

Cultures are dynamic and change over time. They are defined differently by different people and are often influenced by the individual's cultural reference points. It is important that the MFL student teacher is cognisant of this when presenting cultural and linguistic aspects of the target language and target language communities. Indeed, Lawes (2007) argues that MFL has the unique potential in the curriculum to overcome barriers between people and promote a universal outlook. She goes on to describe 'ethno culture' and 'enrichment culture'– the former emphasising commonalities and the latter, 'the best that humanity has achieved and aspired to, the best that is known and thought' (2007: 89). She sees these interpretations of culture as an opportunity for the learner to be exposed to more than just the 'functional and sometimes banal representations' that usually form part of their language learning experience.

Intercultural understanding is highlighted in the national curriculum (QCA, 2007) as a 'unique' opportunity for pupils to not only explore the notion of national identity but also to develop an awareness of the similarities and differences between the target language countries and their own. As part of its statement on the importance of languages, the programme of study for MFL (Key Stage 3) stresses that:

> Languages are part of the cultural richness of our society and the world…Pupils learn to appreciate different countries, cultures, communities and people…By making comparisons, they gain insight into their own culture and society.
>
> (QCA, 2007)

The question arises: How then might effective learning opportunities in MFL be realistically implemented for a diverse pupil population through a pedagogy which is firmly embedded in the principles of interculturalism and inclusion? Inclusion entails the teacher responding to individual needs, which include issues of ethnicity as well as those of special educational needs (SEN) and gender (Corbett, 2001). Student teachers need to recognise and be sensitive to the diverse needs of both the individual and groups of pupils in a responsive school environment where pupils feel valued. It is crucial that both individuals and groups of pupils do not see themselves as either being excluded or 'exclusive' in any subject domain or school generally. Through the PGCE lectures, course readings, assignments and discussions student teachers are helped to understand the principle of respect for differences and that these differences might range from SEN, gender, ethnicity, linguistics and religious affiliation to rates of progress, each of which have the potential to impact profoundly on pupils' eventual achievement in any subject.

Student teachers do sometimes find it hard to grasp that this notion of 'difference' goes beyond the superficiality of blurring and even denying the notion of 'otherness', in favour of ascribing sameness and taking a 'common humanity approach', which assumes that the basic construct of our identity is that of our humanity. However, the question of identity construction is more subtle and complex, and to think in terms of one overarching identity construct is misleading. For example, when considering issues of identity in education, Gundara suggests that young black people in Britain – visibly 'different'– are engaged in defining themselves in the context of both a dominant British identity as well as an identity as a black person in Britain. He makes the point that to assign a single black culture that covers all age groups would have 'exclusionary effects'. Second and third generation black people in Britain have 'no lived memories of the Caribbean'; they have different 'cultural moorings' and 'cultural reference points' within the same cultural map that their parents and grandparents have created. They will continue to create 'their own syncretic and multiple cultures' (Gundara, 2000: 42–7) while drawing on the cultural similarities of their white peers.

Through the MFL PGCE course we seek to develop a similarly nuanced view of cultural identity. We draw on the diversity of our student teacher cohort, and encourage the students to reflect at the start of the course on their own foreign language learning. This inevitably leads into discussions of the benefits of knowing, and feeling at home in, more than one language, and this in turn leads to the majority of the student teachers vigorously defending the opportunity to experience another culture that learning another language brings. The pieces that they write at this stage of the course testify to their understanding of the benefits of a cross-cultural and pluri-cultural vision. Readings at this stage support their reflections, such as Byram et al. (1995) and Lawes (2000, 2007). We introduce student teachers to the resources available to them through the World Languages Project (Garson et al., 1989.) and the work of Hawkins (1984) and others on language awareness. On visits and exchanges student teachers keep reflective logs to prompt their attention to cultural and intercultural issues. We also run workshops such as Storyline, an alternative approach in MFL (European Comenius project 2003–6), to introduce student teachers to ways of working with their pupils that draw on the multilingual and pluri-cultural resources that exist in many London classrooms.

In lesson planning too we emphasise how the multifaceted and different nature of the cultural capital brought to the classroom by the learners may be drawn on and extended. The student teachers' awareness of this diversity may be demonstrated by their ability to plan lessons and to organise classrooms where cultural distance is minimised and pupils are learning from each other while also focusing on the target language and culture. In terms of the 'enrichment culture' proposed by Lawes, there is a sense in which the student teacher of MFL needs not only to validate the pupils' preferred cultural forms and offer alternatives but also to consider the intrinsic justification (Moore, 2000) and possible arbitrary selection of the greatest and most creative works (Lawes, 2000) to present to pupils. Moore, drawing on Kress (1982), Brice Heath (1983) and Labov (1972), has shown that cultural bias as well as cultural and ethnic differences feature in 'favoured texts' that have a place in the school curriculum. It is important that student teachers and those involved in initial teacher education (ITE) develop a critical awareness of both this and of the implications for those pupils who are entering a school system not familiar with those particular cultural forms and preferences. Student teachers need to combat any deficit model in viewing such pupils as intellectually or creatively deficient.

It is the task of the MFL student teacher to provide opportunities which draw on the pupils' knowledge and experience base, to modify their own behaviour and attitudes where necessary when exploring the culture of the target language communities and to broaden their own perceptions of culture and its inherent complexities. Implicit in the National Strategy Key Stage 3 Framework for Languages is the suggestion that an intercultural pedagogic approach should be adopted if pupils are to be encouraged (without devaluing their own cultural backgrounds) to appreciate the cultural diversity of these communities and to recognise that there are different ways of seeing the world. The cultural backgrounds of the pupils represent specific strengths, experiences and valid histories which can contribute to and enrich the evolving cultural map that MFL seeks to develop. Cultural 'shocks' will inevitably be encountered by the pupils and student teachers alike, and should be discussed during the MFL teaching and learning process. The concept of 'bi-cultural' or cultural code switching is useful when considering the MFL context. It can be described as the ability and willingness to adopt some of the cultural aspects of the target language communities alongside one's home culture and, in some cases, that of the indigenous population.

Developing student teachers' understanding of cultural identity

A significant and increasing number of foreign nationals are now teaching MFL (and other subjects) in schools with diverse school populations. Many of the student teachers are from relatively monocultural and mono-ethnic communities in the target language countries, where they have had limited contact with people of colour or diverse sociocultural or socioeconomic backgrounds and where, in most cases, Europeans are still considered to be white. Most, though, have had experience as foreign language assistants which has afforded them some acculturation time to familiarise themselves with the new educational system and new pupil population. Nevertheless, native speakers who are MFL student teachers often experience particular challenges in adapting to the cultural diversity of pupils in their placement schools, and may be forced to develop broader and more inclusive understandings of knowledge and culture than they had previously considered. Questions arise for them as they engage with the course: what are their perceptions and knowledge of pupils from other ethnic groups and to what extent are they prepared to 'connect' with these pupils and make connections in the MFL classroom context and to the wider community, including Europe? And even when these teachers are from so-called 'multicultural communities' themselves, to what extent are they familiar with the British context and the more particular contexts of, for example, London schools?

These questions – which, of course, could be applied equally to some indigenous British student teachers – are central to teaching and learning in MFL. They are not reducible to matters of technique or skill. Language learners go beyond mere acquisition of a linguistic system. They are involved in a process of learning and discovering shared meanings, values and practices of groups as embodied in the meaning of language; negotiating and creating an alternative perspective while simultaneously sharing in a world interaction and experience. The process of acknowledging and encouraging learners to make comparisons with their own and other cultures also facilitates the student teachers' ability to perceive and cope with difficulties, as some of their pupils often instinctively do. When student teachers are able to gain a new perspective on their own language and culture they may question or challenge the socialised culture and be introduced to a new way of seeing or doing things. This understanding is key to MFL teaching and learning and is an underlying principle of the MFL PGCE course, discussed, for example, in a key lecture on barriers to learning.

Student teachers need to be encouraged to understand the multi-faceted nature of personal identity and that each person from different ethnic, sociocultural and socioeconomic groups may belong to a number of social identities and social groups, as well as having different cultures, cultural practices and beliefs. Rather than being ignored or seen as potentially divisive, difference in the classroom and in the target communities needs to be acknowledged and respected. The student teacher's task is to support pupils in their transition from one culture, including those of the target language community, to another in a mature and knowledgeable way. Pupils should be conscious of the value of their own identities as these are endorsed by the MFL student teacher – and the value of those of others, their peers in the classroom and the target language communities (Ferguson, 2007). Respect and enjoyment of difference are possible by-products of an intercultural understanding approach. Intercultural understanding is thus both the premise and the goal of MFL teaching.

Pupils enter the MFL learning arena with variations on what Gundara, following Bourdieu, refers to as 'cultural capital' – the conventions and discourses that they have been brought up with and have been initiated into (Gundara, 2000). The student teacher needs to be aware that what appears natural to one group may appear strange to another and vice versa, an occurrence that is not too uncommon in the MFL classroom. The level of cultural capital possessed by pupils will have a bearing on the extent to which they are prepared to embrace elements of the target language communities, and to accept that there are alternative ways of experiencing and viewing life. Student teachers also arrive on the PGCE course with their own cultural capital, and when they are unfamiliar with the expectations of a diverse/ indigenous pupil population in a placement school, there is a potential for conflict. Difficulties arise where the cultural capital of the pupil is perceived to be of little worth and is therefore not 'transferable'. Within an intercultural understanding approach, the MFL student teacher can seek to encourage the learner to engage with the identity of the target language communities as well as with their own identities (Ferguson, 2007).

However, while different cultural orientations to language learning can present barriers, the teacher who is a native speaker has a valuable role to play and can bring a useful cognitive dimension to the language learning classroom from which the pupils can benefit, for example, with up-to-date cultural and linguistic knowledge. Subject knowledge is an important aspect of any pedagogic approach adopted by the student teacher. First, the subject matter needs to be organised in a sufficiently coherent manner in the teacher's own mind to enable presentation of the material in ways that are accessible to the learners and the learning context. Secondly, this understanding will subsequently facilitate the sequencing of future lessons based on the teacher's knowledge of the diverse groups and the individuals within the groups. There clearly needs to be some mutual understanding of different cultures that can be more readily planned for and integrated in foreign language lessons than in some curriculum areas, given the nature of the subject and the statutory requirements of the national curriculum.

It is often the case that both the student teacher and pupils are from different ethnic, socioeconomic and cultural backgrounds. The student teacher should strive to create a classroom environment that engenders positive attitudes to learning among students in order to understand, respect and appreciate each other's culture without loss of status, role or cultural identity. Student teachers should be encouraged to think about what constitutes a good language learner more broadly than simply in terms of language acquisition alone. Questions such as these are a useful prompt for both pupils and teachers:

- How aware are the learners of their own identities and culture(s)?
- How is this perceived by others?
- Do the learners have some understanding of the identities and cultures of those with whom they are interacting?
- Are the learners able to establish relationships between their own and other cultures; mediate and explain differences as well as accept differences and see commonalities?

Expectations and relationships, mentioned in the final question above, are central to effective intercultural practices in the MFL classroom and may involve reviewing the stereotypes held by the pupils and student teachers when considering the culture and identities of the target language communities and challenging stereotypes in a national context. High expectations have to be based on the beliefs and aspirations of not only the teacher but also those of the pupils and their parents. These beliefs need to be communicated and scaffolded effectively into the learning process so that all pupils are viewed as potential high achievers despite their different learning styles and sociocultural/ethnic backgrounds.

Student teachers often question how high expectations might be realistically and consistently implemented in the classroom (DfES, 1998). An intercultural and inclusive pedagogical approach would seem appropriate in creating a learning environment conducive to high levels of attainment and confidence building. Praising and supporting pupils to take risks with and increase control of their own learning through making connections and transferring previous knowledge, learning strategies and generic skills in different language learning contexts is another approach. This will clearly be a gradual process based on coherent teaching objectives and learning outcomes which are both cognitively challenging and achievable. The student teacher needs to be encouraged to develop strategies to challenge any culturist, classist or racist criteria by which pupils are being assessed (Gundara, 2000) or that is being promulgated in a scheme of work/ curriculum. Student teachers need to be sensitive to and aware of the varying cultural endowments and cultural forms that pupils bring to the classroom and not only be ready to accept these interpretations but also to question the validity of their own (ibid.). During the MFL learning process, pupils will have the opportunity to reposition their own preferred cultural forms and practices, abandoning some and taking on board new ones.

In considering the four questions above, a depth and range of learning may be promoted. Classroom discourse presents opportunities for intercultural classroom learning for the student teacher and pupil alike. However, there may be a potential gap in their expectations, beliefs and classroom practices. Within the different ethnic groups there may be enormous socioeconomic and cultural variation. While most groups may share a common cultural background and language, for example Caribbean – with clear, long-standing cultural perceptions of what it means to be black and British and how to learn – different cultural orientations to language learning may throw up barriers. The classroom discourse is ultimately affected by the culture of both the teacher and the pupils. Is this easier to reconcile for a black teacher of black pupils? Although, initially, ethnicity might provide a basis for positive relationships, pupils have voiced the opinion that they want 'good teachers', not just those who are black (Callender, 1997). So what role might ITE play and how do student teachers arrive at a point where they are willing and competent to acknowledge and make appropriate connections with the pupils' culture?

Intercultural and inclusive pedagogy

In recognising the complex relationship between subcultures – class, ethnicity, religion, language, gender – and the dominant cultures, the school and training institution can raise awareness of potential barriers to learning and the pervasive nature of discrimination that is sometimes evident. Where student teachers are sensitive to the subcultures and the pupils feel valued and respected, they are more likely to create an inclusive community (Corbett, 2001) underpinned by a secure understanding of interculturality. The way in which a school community and training institution actively promote an ethos of inclusion has implications for all participants. Among characteristics to be encouraged are those where clear, consistent routines for acceptable conduct are established; the values of the institution itself are examined; and stereotypical views of pupils and staff are challenged. This includes attitudes to achievement and encompasses curriculum and organisational matters.

Inherent in an intercultural and inclusive pedagogical framework is an acknowledgement of the different pressures that pupils experience, which may be of a personal, cultural, racial and, sometimes, of a traumatic nature. Underpinning the approach is the aim to instil in individuals the confidence and linguistic competence that will enable them not only to challenge issues such as racism, where necessary, but also to look beyond their immediate circumstances to the 'bigger picture' and be part of (or even lead) a process which confronts and ultimately eradicates specific barriers to learning based on skin colour and ethnicity, for example. A pupil's self-confidence is crucial, and it is important that it is encouraged and not misconstrued by teachers as arrogance, as is often the case with some ethnic groups.

What becomes evident is that a framework is needed which is not only underpinned by a commitment to high expectations and the continuing cognitive development of the pupils but also integrates linguistic and cultural learning. Here the aim must be to facilitate communication and integration for pupils from different ethnic, sociocultural and economic groups and to provide the potential, ultimately, to prepare learners to meet and communicate in cultural contexts and societies other than the specific ones associated with the language that they are learning at the time. One approach lies in the possibility of exploring what a fusion of cultures might mean, for example, African Caribbean, British, French, Spanish, German. There can be opportunities for comparison and reflection, as well as a critical and questioning approach to the dominant culture(s) and its values into which the pupils are to be socialised. Student teachers should be encouraged to shift perspective where necessary. This would involve psychological processes and socialisation that make appropriate connections with the pupils' culture. An inclusive pedagogic approach in MFL actively builds upon the characteristics above, those skills from the other curriculum areas (such as literacy) and general 'learning capital' to enable pupils to know what action to take when faced with new situations or uncertainty. This is not unlike those encountered in the target language country or tackling an activity in the classroom.

From a community perspective, the pupils' prior knowledge of the target language communities and language and their own dialect, for example, patois, might be sources to draw on to make valid connections. Student teachers of MFL are accordingly encouraged to provide pupils with explicit opportunities to:

- articulate their thinking and their hypotheses in the target language or English;
- air difficulties that they or their peers may be experiencing in languages;
- clarify or confirm aspects of learning in MFL for themselves or for their peers.

An intercultural and inclusive pedagogy is therefore a non-discriminatory pedagogy that seeks to educate all learners in how to be more responsive and understanding of individual differences in the school community and society. It is a way of conceptualising how teaching is interrelated with aspects of the curriculum; that is, a lesson is only part of the learning process. In preparing student teachers for an inclusive pedagogy we have in mind the Professional Standards for Qualified Teacher Status, particularly Q18, for which student teachers need to 'understand how children and young people develop and that the progress and well-being of learners are affected by a range of developmental, social, religious, ethnic, cultural and linguistic influences' (TDA, 2007). Additionally, Q19 requires student teachers to 'know how to make effective personalised provision for those they teach, including those for whom English is an additional language or who have special educational needs or disabilities, and how to take practical account of diversity and promote equality and inclusion in their teaching' (ibid.).

Previously outlined activities and lectures in the MFL PGCE, such as those on cultural awareness and citizenship, invite student teachers to critically examine and discuss policies and practices in the classroom, including their own, with an intercultural and inclusive approach. However, it remains an area that requires significant development and commitment if it is to have real impact on the student teachers' attitudes, beliefs, pedagogy and pupil achievement.

An intercultural and inclusive pedagogy, while meeting the needs of a minority group, is concerned with meeting the needs of a majority through a differentiated curriculum and pedagogic practices where grouping and the placement of pupils are also seen to be important. Student teachers inevitably play a central role in the inclusive pedagogy process, one that requires empathy and commitment to understanding the range of learning styles and cultural backgrounds in their classes. Practice is characterised by deliberately introducing topics that will involve and interest those pupils who would otherwise feel alienated and demotivated. 'Connecting' with pupils may occur on an individual basis, such as when a student teacher is a form teacher who acts as a 'link' or a 'bridge' to the MFL classroom. 'Connecting' in this way entails recognising the pupils' experience of the world, an approach that validates the pupils' identities in the sense of their perception of themselves and others. As the connector, the student teacher should respond appropriately, sometimes challenging these perceptions but also acknowledging and respecting those of the pupils. The experience of being different may then become one in which the learner feels included and valued (Corbett, 2001). Teachers in all curriculum areas are continually having to draw on a number of pedagogic options based on their experience, the school context, values and policy (both of a national and local nature) to create learning environments which are conducive to high attainment for the maximum range of diverse learners. With societal changes, pedagogy should also be seeking to engage those learners who would otherwise be excluded (Corbett, 2001).

Racism, which hinders the life chances of any individual or group, is abhorrent and must be resisted and challenged consistently at every opportunity. An intercultural and inclusive pedagogic approach will not only value difference but will also encourage pupils – as future citizens – to recognise racism and discrimination in their multifarious and pervasive forms, to challenge the perpetrators and the ignorance that so often underlies them, in an appropriate and effective manner to diminish their impact and work towards their eventual eradication. It may be necessary for individual student teachers, ITE and partnership schools, pupils and parents to evaluate and transform their own attitudes, beliefs and racism towards other ethnic groups, an area which is not well documented. Teaching and learning a modern foreign language provides numerous opportunities for the student teacher to explore such issues. Those teachers seen to be actively countering the negative effects of discrimination in any form and who encourage such an approach with their pupils will clearly provide role models to be emulated in school and in the wider community.

An intercultural and inclusive pedagogy is also valuable in its promotion of ways in which learning can be generalised and transferred to other contexts, enabling learners to draw on previous learning and experiences that help to elucidate and consolidate knowledge. The challenge remains, however, where pupils sometimes have difficulties in making those links between formal learning in the classroom and real-life contexts. The onus is therefore on the student teachers' subject knowledge base and their understanding of the learning process, to extend the knowledge base of the pupils, to encourage transference and make connections in their learning.

A pedagogy based on intercultural understanding and inclusive principles evidently applies to all learners and involves striking a balance between cultural needs and specific learning needs, in order to help overcome potential barriers to learning and assessment for individuals and groups of pupils. Positive recognition of differences is an underlying notion. An intercultural and inclusive pedagogy therefore views the student teacher making 'connections' on several levels with the learners as a group and as individuals. Establishing positive relationships with learners is central. The process is one of building a 'community of learners' where the student teacher's knowledge is made explicit and accessible, while the pupils' knowledge and cultural background are also validated and promoted. The student teacher's prerequisite knowledge and understanding provides a sound basis for teaching and learning as well as the scope to focus on individual differences within an intercultural and inclusive pedagogic framework. The challenge for the MFL teacher is not only to draw on research and practice based on sound principles of learning in the subject but also to make explicit the distinct connections that can be made with experiences in the pupils' lives and beyond, their personal and social development, their age and interests and the rest of the curriculum. These connections will be made within the context of the target language and the target language countries.

The successful inclusion of pupils from different cultural groups continues to be cited by newly qualified teachers in surveys conducted by the TDA as an area in which they felt that they were inadequately prepared. While the expectation that all teachers are avid anthropologists is an unrealistic one, part of respecting individual differences is, at a very basic level, to know something about their pupils' ethnicity and culture and to develop this knowledge. Adopting a pedagogy that relates to the pupil as an individual helps to include the majority in classroom activities and involves teaching that promotes personal growth and raises high levels of empathetic awareness, through, for example, the Storyline approach which the student teachers are introduced to on the PGCE course. Assessment will clearly play a crucial role in the connective process in terms of knowing and responding effectively to pupils' needs.

One way of helping student teachers to evaluate their own practices in terms of inclusive pedagogy is to guide them with a series of questions for self-evaluation and reflection, for example:

1. Are we as teachers being unintentionally or unwittingly racist or discriminatory? How do we know? How secure are our judgements when reprimanding or sanctioning pupils from diverse backgrounds? Are the reprimands disproportionately made to particular groups?
2. Are all pupils' contributions valued? Are the same individuals encouraged to participate to the detriment and resentment of the others? How is praise used during lessons and in marking? Are there any rewards for effort, achievement and progress over time?
3. Is diversity generally acknowledged positively and viewed as part and parcel of the pupils' and teacher's individuality and personality?
4. Is there a working atmosphere of challenge, high expectations and mutual respect?
5. Is diversity reflected in the resources used and in displays? Are pupils encouraged to consider diversity positively? How?
6. How does teaching (in MFL) reinforce and promote diversity and intercultural understanding? What are the teacher's own attitudes and beliefs concerning diversity and intercultural understanding? Are the strategies deployed appropriate? How do you know?
7. When monitoring achievement, are groups of pupils as well as individuals identified, with subsequent interventions planned in order to raise/sustain achievement?

There are clearly no easy answers to some of the questions posed above. However, they should prompt the MFL student teacher to consider not only the achievement of specific groups of pupils but also their own attitudes and relationships with individuals, based on appropriate evidence. If accountability and preparing for diversity are to be taken seriously, then focusing on developing the student teacher's critical understanding of intercultural and inclusive practices must be made explicit. Such an approach should raise issues concerning providing for and the attainment of specific pupils, for example, white working-class boys (DfES, 2007) with the intention of raising the achievement of all groups.

Chapter 8

Playing a part: The case of theatre in education in the professional education of English with Drama teachers

Anton Franks

Towards the end of their year of initial teacher education (ITE), student teachers of English with Drama are released from their school placements for one day a week to work on a theatre in education (TIE) project. This is a project which they have about ten days to devise, followed by three days of presenting to pupils. Devising, presenting and reflecting on TIE constitute one of two subject-based, core modules on the English with Drama PGCE.

This chapter will explore how a project relying on collaborative practical and creative work can be seen to fit within the framework of a professional Master's level course such as a PGCE. Master's level criteria require that work presented by students has to demonstrate three broad intellectual and practice-based aspects of becoming a professional teacher: first, a sophisticated level of understanding of key aspects of the field of study and practice; second, the ability to reflect critically on practice; and third, the ability to present work by communicating clearly, coherently and with some degree of originality and flair. Traditionally, of course, the written assignment and the essay form have been accepted as the medium through which students are best able to demonstrate that they have attained a level of sophistication in each of the three areas.

An implicit proposition underlying the TIE project is that the development of sophisticated understandings, critical reflection and the ability to articulate and present ideas on teaching and learning English and Drama can be demonstrated by groups and individuals through devising, presenting and reflecting on a practical project such as this. One might go even further and suggest that an assignment such as TIE is a vehicle for integrating theory *into* practice, nurturing innovation in approaches to teaching and learning, while providing real audiences of pupils, teachers and student teachers for the circulation of such ideas. By comparison, the written essay might be seen to reinforce the separation of practical activity and critical reflection (or practice and theory) and provides rather limited audiences for the circulation of ideas – usually between students and their examiners.

Thinking of TIE as integrating intellectual and practical aspects of teaching and learning suggests three connected themes that are worth pursuing. The first is a consideration of the ways in which such a project might contribute to preparing teachers to be creative professionals. The second is to develop ideas about how such a project conceptualises and frames the relationship between teaching and learning. Finally, issues emerge about how subject teaching and learning, or the 'performance' of school teaching and its audiences, relate to wider culture and society, specifically how much learning and teaching are integrated with, or are encapsulated within, wider cultural concerns.

Framing and initiating the TIE project

When we meet on the first day of the TIE project, the atmosphere generated in the drama studio is always an alloy of excitement and trepidation. The English with Drama student teachers have been liberated from their classroom teaching to return to the relative security of their 'home base' and to meet with their peers; at the same time, they are not quite certain about what to expect. They know they will have to work in groups in which they will have to collaborate on devising a TIE presentation from scratch. They realise that they will have to cope with an adjustment in their roles and activities, but are not quite sure about what this new role will be, except that it will be somewhere on the spectrum between presenting as teachers and performing as actors. Having learned, to a greater or lesser extent, to meet the expectations of the pupils they teach and the subject mentors who supervise their practice, they will have to adjust their practice to meet other – for them – less clearly defined expectations. Some will have experienced TIE as pupils; others, as undergraduates studying Drama, will have had to devise presentations that go under the banner of TIE; and a few will have gained professional experience as actors in TIE companies. A few will have had no experience of theatre in education whatsoever.

On the first day of the project, I issue a handout to the group which states that the intention of the project is to use drama and theatre as a means of teaching and learning. Tony Jackson is a key figure in thinking about TIE, its history and its parameters of intent. Acknowledging the diversity of the field of practice, Jackson defines TIE in the following way (and, as he does it well and comprehensively, it is worth quoting at some length):

> *The TIE programme is not a performance in schools of a self-contained play, a 'one-off' event that is here today and gone tomorrow, but a co-ordinated and carefully structured pattern of activities, usually devised and researched by the company and involving the children directly in an experience of the situations and problems that the topic throws up. It generally utilizes elements, in a variety of permutations, of traditional theatre...educational drama (active participation of children, in and out of role, in improvised drama activities...); and simulation (highly structured role-play and decision-making exercises).*
>
> (Jackson, 1993: 4)

Because it is linked to the curriculum and to pupils' experience, the TIE presentation itself is not conceived of as an end in and of itself, not as 'art for art's sake', but is designed with accompanying teaching packs that include source materials and suggestions from lessons that can be picked up and used by teachers and pupils after the performance. Central to the purpose of TIE, therefore, is that it is conceived of as a teaching and learning event firmly situated in the context of schooling. At the outset of the project, student teachers are given a four-point rationale for the project which encompasses a broad definition of TIE and points explicitly towards an ethos for devising and presenting the piece.

Four aspects of the TIE project are central to its purpose as an educational project:

- *a topic or theme* that has clear links to local and national curriculum frameworks and that attends to the experience and interest of a particular year group in particular schools;
- *collaborative and creative work* that draws on the group's knowledge and skills in research and development, devising, teaching, performing, technical expertise and so forth;
- *a balance between teaching and performing;* that is, the potential to use drama and theatre as an *interactive* mode and form of teaching and learning;
- *an evaluative essay* of 2,000 words which provides evidence of what student teachers have learned, what pupils might have learned and how this learning might inform, or modify, student teachers' future practice.

The TIE project is launched a few weeks before the end of the second and final teaching placement of the PGCE course and student teachers return to the IOE for the last four Fridays of the block teaching practice. From various angles, both pragmatic and conceptual, timing and timetabling is significant. In the first place, in order to fit the exigencies of the PGCE year, including the requirements of formal examination and so forth, there needs to be time enough to devise the project from scratch, to present it to pupils at a convenient and appropriate point in the school year, to reflect on the processes of devising and presenting and then for it all to be assessed. Overall, from initial sessions on devising through to presenting the programme to pupils, the project covers from as few as 12 to, at most, 15 days. Issues of time, therefore, are interesting. Student teachers are often worried and tend to complain about the apparent lack of time for devising TIE before it has to be presented. On the other hand, from my perspective, the economy of time for this project appears to work in its favour.

The effect of particular pressures of time and limitations on the availability of material and technical resources is significant in terms of the effect this has on creative processes, and not necessarily in the direction that one might first imagine. Although a constrained economy of time and resourcing imposes foreseeable limitations on devising and production, it can also have liberating effects in terms of the inventiveness and creativity of the TIE group and its production. The timing of the project is important in that it provides impetus and salience, injecting particular forms of creativity into the TIE programme, which is connected to the fact that the project takes place at the end of the year but while student teachers are still on their practical teaching placements. They have the experience and acquired expertise from months of working in classrooms to sustain their sense of teaching and learning. Lessons, learners and schools are prominent in their thoughts and help to ensure that the project, its topic and themes articulate with learners, learning and the curriculum. At the same time, the Friday release from school provides a space for reflection, for reconnecting the tutor group as a community of learner-teachers and, consequently, for generating and consolidating ideas.

For the first meeting, student teachers are asked to bring a well-known story to share with the small group that they'll be working with for the duration of the project. The story may be a folk tale or fairy story or a myth. The focus on stories here draws forward and extends work done in sessions earlier in the PGCE year. In one session we work on organising active learning through storytelling, in which student teachers have to tell and retell well-known fairy stories and folk tales from different narrative points of view. In a later session, all student teachers of English and English with Drama have to read a selection from Ovid's *Metamorphoses* and then prepare lessons and sequences of lessons based on their readings and group discussions. Sometimes stories from conventional literary sources are chosen. Particular intentions stand behind the requirement for student teachers to begin with stories as source material for their TIE presentations. First, there is a tendency in TIE projects that I have experienced to start from an issue or concept, often worthy and generalised topics such as 'relationships', 'conflict', 'peer pressures' and so forth. Once a topic or theme is selected, groups then tend to cast around for a way of carrying the concept, finding a vehicle for the idea or issue. A story, particularly one such as a myth or folk tale that has been shaped and retold through time, often holds various and complex ideas and themes which can be tuned and turned to multiple purposes.

In one of the readings that support the TIE project, drama practitioner and academic Helen Nicholson highlights the importance of narrative and story for drama:

> *All stories are read and created through the lens of social and cultural experience, and this means that narratives are inevitably interpreted in many different ways. Recognising that stories have multiple interpretations involves identifying the limits of one's own horizons, and an interest in seeing alternative perspectives.*
>
> (Nicholson, 2005: 60)

A perspective on the essential mutability of stories in the telling or enactment is one of the foundations of the TIE project. It is a view that moves away from ideas of stories and narratives as belonging exclusively to literate and literary traditions towards oral and enactive traditions of storytelling. Drawing on Walter Benjamin's musing on storytelling, Nicholson emphasises how storytelling uses the expressiveness of the whole body and is intimately connected with the 'gift' of storytelling. In the spirit of gift-giving, storytelling is an intrinsically social activity and requires a sense of reciprocity and exchange.

The nature of the social and cultural settings together with the processes of dramatisation, mutability and exchange in the making and telling of stories are essential to the concept of the TIE project. As with teaching, a TIE presentation should not simply be conceived of as a performance by teachers to an audience of pupils. Neither should stories be seen as immutable and impenetrable, but rather as more open structures that might serve as bases for thematic improvisations. Alongside interactivity and openness to change, another main area of concern is the relationship between forms of telling and the content of what is told. Although learners might have great exposure to and experience of drama on television, film and through digital gaming, and despite the fact that drama continues to grow in popularity on the curriculum, learners are likely to have much less exposure to live drama and theatre. For the TIE project, therefore, it is important that learners' attention is drawn to forms of drama and theatre as well as to ideas and issues that are carried in the drama.

The pattern of devising

During the devising phase, days spent on TIE follow a similar pattern, as modes of collaborative work are established. The day begins with warm-up exercises designed to draw attention to and enhance collective work. More substantive work on stories follows quickly. On the first day, for example, I lead by telling a story that has its origins in Sufism, but which I came across embedded in a novel, *Obabakoak* by the Basque author Bernado Atxaga (1992). The mutability of stories and versions of storytelling are the main themes in the book. In practically applying the ways in which stories are generated in social and cultural life, it is important for me that the story is an ancient one, framed within a modern non-English novel and that, rather than reading, I tell the story from memory. This illustrates that stories are given life in the telling and that they change in the processes of being performed. Notions of mutability in performance are further reinforced when I ask student teachers first to select and retell significant moments of the story in a sequence of three tableaux or still images made with their bodies, and then to animate a short scene from the story, but seen from another narrative point of view.

The student teachers are then divided into groups, chosen on the basis of areas of London in which they live and/or have carried out their practical teaching. In part, this is to facilitate the short tour of schools they have to make at the end of the project. More significant, however, is that groups are not chosen on the basis of friendship, but are required to work productively and with maturity and professionalism within tight constraints of time and form. In their groups, the students are set the tasks for the day – notably that they share their stories, that they draw up a group contract that sets down particular roles within the group (including those responsible for coordinating the tour, marshalling props, etc.), ways of working (for example, rotating or assigning the roles of director/workshop leader) and modes of collaboration. TIE groups then spend three to four hours working independently and the whole group reconvenes at the end of each working day to share work in progress and comment on the work of other groups.

This pattern of work is set for the remaining 10 days or so allotted for devising TIE. At the end of each morning session it is usual for me as PGCE tutor to set a focus for work during the day and for sharing at the end of the day. These foci are subject to variation, contingent on the progress of the project, but typically at the end of the first day small groups are asked to present a scene or an image that asks a question of the audience. Subsequently, the focus for the day will include telling and showing stories from differing narrative viewpoints, working on contrasts (from movement to stasis, or sound to silence), working on interactive elements of the presentation and trying out workshop activities that will involve pupils in school.

Using drama and theatre as a means of teaching and learning

I shall stick to defining the project as theatre in education, even though the emphasis placed on using the project to teach *about* forms of theatre and drama as well as teaching particular content *through* theatre locates it somewhere on a continuum between the above definition of TIE and what is referred to as 'theatre for young people' (TYP). The banner heading of TYP is intended to do what its label suggests: to direct theatre towards a younger audience. As well as being a developed cultural form in its own right, it introduces young audiences to the conventions of theatrical production, accentuating the thrills and benefits to be had from being a spectator to 'live' theatrical events in which the bodies of actors and the body of the theatre troupe are relatively unmediated. To reprise briefly, part of the intention of our TIE project is precisely to introduce pupils to the unique experience of bodied space (Garner, 1994) and performance, and to draw attention to the various modes and conventions of modern theatre.

Under the banner of teaching and learning, other injunctions apply to TIE, and these are reinforced in various ways and at different times in the project. The first is that the theatrical aspects of the project should be genuinely interactive. The idea that the audience might be passive recipients and the performance is directed out into a black box auditorium is neither appropriate nor permissible. The concept of interactivity is mobilised in two main ways. On one side, the audience can participate in enhancing visual and aural aspects of the production – for example, by creating a 'soundscape' of a storm to accompany a representation of a sea journey in *The Odyssey* or by making 'human scenery' such as spooky woodland in a modernised version of *Red Riding Hood*. However, the group are under strict instructions that there must be time and space to allow pupils to prepare their contributions and there must be room in the scheme of the performance to allow for creative variations. In other words, the work of learners in school is not to be treated as passive 'set dressing', designed simply to enhance the performance elements. A second – and major aspect – of interactivity is the participatory workshop in which learners are encouraged to construct their own dramas, drawing on ideas presented to them as well as the narrative and dramatic resources exemplified in the student teachers' presentation. Workshop elements must be seen to be an integral part of the presentation and not simply 'bolted-on' afterwards as an afterthought to the dramatic presentation. This is to say that, although there need to be clearly delineated parameters for the workshop, these must again allow room for pupils to be genuinely creative, playing with the resources of thought and action that are presented and suggested to them in the TIE presentation.

Flexibility and accessibility constitute guiding concepts for the project. First and foremost, accessibility means that there has to be a fundamental reliance on the material and media of the human body as the way of communicating and making meaning in and through the drama. Partly out of the practicality of having to adapt to school spaces for the tour, the pieces have to be very light in terms of technical requirements and accoutrements –

minimum requirements for setting, lighting, sound and costume – and what there is has to be very portable. But mostly, in an age of technical wizardry and digital imagery, the power of live theatre rests in the adaptability and flexibility of the human body as material and means for communicating and creating meaning. This is to draw references to a style of what has become known (in my view, somewhat misleadingly) as 'physical theatre' (is not all theatre 'physical'?).

There are other, more practical, considerations and limitations, however, that set parameters for the project. One is that, because the presentations are toured in schools, they must fit within the confines of timetables, which is to say that a presentation will have to last somewhere between 50 minutes, a standard time-span for a single period, through an hour to an hour-and-40-minute double period. The effects of such temporal restriction is that the performance aspect of the programme should last between 20 to 30 minutes and the programme of workshop activities should be collapsible or expandable to fit available time. Another obvious variable is the available spaces for presentation – in some schools there might be a drama studio or a school hall available; in others, the presentation might be restricted to classroom spaces – and this reinforces the need for the presentation to be adaptable and based on the affordances and constraints of the performing body.

Restrictions of time and space have other implications for the TIE project. If the presentation is to fit Jackson's definition above, the TIE show should be seen as an element in a 'programme' and not a one-off performance, and to facilitate this, student teachers are required to produce a teaching pack to accompany the presentation, which they leave with teachers. The pack contains source materials (including versions of the story on which the presentation is based), plans for lessons that are based on the form and content of the presentation, plus resources linked with the lesson plans (all of this amply facilitated these days by digitising the pack and embedding internet links).

The role of TIE in teacher development and professional education

Near the beginning of this chapter, three areas connected with teacher development and professional educational development were outlined. I want to return to those in this concluding section. The areas outlined were, first, how TIE might be framed in terms of the development of teachers as creative professionals; second, how the project conceptualises the relationship between teaching and learning; and third, the ways in which the project is situated in the relation between schooling and wider cultural domains.

Concepts of creativity are now a commonplace in educational circles. It is not a history that I have room or desire to rehearse in its entirety here, but some references to recent preoccupations serve as a starting point. Readers may remember the publication of a trumpeted report into creativity and education at the end of the last decade (National Advisory Committee on Creative and Cultural Education (NACCCE) and Robinson, 1999). It splashed into the educational arena and then appeared to sink without much trace for a year or three, before resurfacing with some vigour on the establishment of Arts Council-controlled Creative Partnerships, which, among other projects, was prominent in bringing artists (both performing and visual) into schools. The committee that conducted the review into creativity and education and authored the report was emphatic, however, that although the arts are strongly associated with it, creativity is by no means the preserve of the arts and is an expedient factor in the development of science, technology and commerce too. Creative Partnerships had a strong commitment to 'brokering' relationships between schools and practitioners in these various domains. But neither the members of the committee, the words of the report, nor Creative Partnerships as an organisation, had much to say about the creativity of teachers. This is what the report had to say about such matters:

> *We define creative teaching in two ways: first, teaching creatively, and second, teaching for creativity…By teaching creatively we mean teachers using imaginative approaches to make learning more interesting, exciting and effective. Teachers can be highly creative in developing materials and approaches that fire children's interests and motivate their learning…By teaching for creativity we mean forms of teaching that are intended to develop young people's own creative thinking or behaviour.*
>
> (NACCCE and Robinson, 1999: 89)

The thrust of the argument here is that standardised national curricula have a deleterious, attenuating effect on teachers' creativity. Teachers *can* be creative, indeed they *might* be, but for the vice-like and stultifying grip of centralised educational policy on teachers' practice. Such views were elaborated in the wake of the NACCCE report, most prominently by writers such as Anna Craft (Craft, 2005: Craft *et al.*, 2001), whose emphasis is largely on teaching *for* creativity (see also Jones, 2009). Looking at the work of Alex Moore on conceptualisations of the 'good teacher', there is again an emphasis on how imposed curricula and teaching frameworks are 'debilitating the creative imagination' of teachers (Moore, 2004: 83) and on the 'marginalisation of creativity and innovation' in teaching (ibid.: 85).

At the same time, in recruiting new teachers, high value is attached to both subject knowledge and recent and relevant experience. It is a requirement in recruiting people to the English with Drama course, for example, that they have had prior experience of practical drama work with young people and this requirement is strictly adhered to when admitting people to the course. A variety of experience is presented, and it often includes professional experience of acting which frequently entails involvement in TIE or TYP. Others have been involved in youth theatre as performers and workshop leaders. Leaving aside the parallels (or lack of them) between teaching lessons and performing at a general level, commitment to and enjoyment of performance is often (but not always) a characteristic of the English with Drama teachers recruited to the course, so at a simple level, the TIE project allows them to reconnect to this experience. But there is more to it than reconnecting with previous experiences. The intention is that, after the year of getting to grips with the mechanics of classroom presentation and management, when planning has become less a voyage into the unknown and closer to habitual practice, the practice of teaching is informed and perhaps infused by some part of drama practice. It is to give the lie to the cynical (and offensive) Shavian dictum that 'he who can, does: he who cannot, teaches'.

Not only do English with Drama teachers *know* about drama, at some level or other, they can also *do* drama. A move that merges the role of the teacher with the actor is completely aligned with TIE practice in that its practitioners are referred to as actor-teachers (although in the case of the TIE project as a part of the PGCE programme, teacher-actor might be more appropriate). There is, furthermore, something liberating about shifting the centre of the role of teacher, something that draws attention to the nature of the role itself and folds back to enlarge and enhance the notion of what a teacher is, shifting others' perception of what a teacher does. In other words, for teachers and learners, and for teachers as learners, the shift into the fictional frame of the drama practitioner generates an active 'space' for reflecting on teaching and learning itself.

At the nexus of practice and theorised reflection is the domain of *praxis*, and this leads discussion towards considering the relationship between teaching and learning. The year of ITE demands that student teachers constantly have to shift perspective between that of the learner-teacher to that of the teacher who relates to pupils as learners. This is a hard process to sustain. When starting to teach, it is very common for new teachers to assume that there exists an equal and opposite relationship between teaching and learning – that teachers teach, and from their teaching, pupils learn. It is a view formed in and connected to the ways that beginning to teach draws attention to the self-as-teacher. The notion of interactive drama and theatre is, to my mind, intimately connected to the idea of teaching and learning as an interactive process. Teachers anticipate how learners might respond to particular stimuli and activities, but they never quite *know*. There has to be built-in flexibility, space for the unanticipated and, crucially, room for teachers to learn from their pupils.

Another view, and again not wishing to stretch the analogy between teaching and learning as forms of theatrical performance, is that classrooms are particular settings for very specific, generically ordered and routinised types of enactment. The centripetal forces of the institutions of schooling and education inhibit teachers' and learners' abilities to change or disrupt routine practices. It may well be that such routines, rituals and genres of classroom practice actually inhibit and exclude particular types of learning. Again, shifting the classroom, studio or hall space, making it a place where teachers and learners get up and 'do stuff' together, might pose different (perhaps new) relations between teaching and learning. In many respects, such a view picks up the arguments about the creativity of teachers and teaching with which I began this section.

Finally, and briefly, I come now to consider the ways that TIE throws light on the relationship between schooling and the wider cultural domains. The first move is to consider the relationship between the programme and the locations of ITE. It is notionally a 'partnership' between schools and higher education institutions but it is often perceived by each of the partners – student teachers, school teachers and education lecturers – as an uneasy partnership in which respective roles are divided and stratified in activity and status. Another perceived division, or polarisation, is between the intellectual and practical aspects of learning to become a teacher (tritely characterised as the theory–practice divide) referred to at the beginning of the chapter. What I want to return to here are the aspects of the TIE project that relate to Master's level criteria – how through the project, student teachers are able to demonstrate the development of understanding of the subjects of English and Drama and, through the processes of small and whole group work, how space is provided to develop critical reflections on approaches to practical teaching. Because it is presented to pupils and their teachers, not only is there a real sense of audience and purpose, it also provides a service to schools – giving something back to the teachers who have been responsible for day-to-day supervision of practical teaching experience, providing them with ideas for drama and stimulus for helping their pupils devise pieces of theatre. It provides another way of learning for these pupils, gives them direct and proximate experience of live theatre and, in so doing, stimulates and provides resources for making their own dramas. In the way that Nicholson describes storytelling as a way of exchanging gifts, it is important for me to regard the TIE experience as an enriching exchange of cultural goods between peers.

At a broader level, thinking about appropriate modes of teaching and learning and drawing on the writing of those involved in activity theory, I come to think about the encapsulation of school learning. From within this perspective a view is elaborated about the separation of school teaching and learning from 'real life' cultural and social domains (see Engeström, 1996). It is a view that Engeström, writing together with a theatre director, applies particularly to educational drama and its separation from theatre practice (Engeström and Kallinen, 1988). Well, yes, we cannot pretend that involvement in TIE projects is strongly connected with conventional theatre, the West End or national theatre practices. There is a wider view on drama in contemporary society, however, that is captured in Raymond Williams's well-known phrase the 'dramatized society' (Williams, 1983). The view put forward by Williams, which I support, is that with the advent of television, and now with digital technologies, drama is everywhere. Drama has become habitual experience, a way of representing and understanding the social and cultural world. Connecting with points about TIE's relation to issues of teaching and learning, the dramatic and dramatised have, more than ever before (and there is a long history to this phenomenon), become a means of teaching and learning. Now it is common in video-gaming, for example, for people to take roles inside digitally generated, 'simulated' worlds. There is, in other words, increasing reciprocity between dramatic and everyday modes of perceiving and understanding social and cultural environments, both immediate and seemingly remote. The TIE project provides opportunities for learners and teachers, and teachers as learners, to enter and explore alternative ways of doing things.

Chapter 9

Learning to teach Geography

Clare Brooks

The focus of this chapter is on how the Geography PGCE course at the IOE has sought to meet the challenges pertinent to initial teacher education (ITE) in Geography education. These challenges stem from changes in education alongside specific problems that face Geography education and have led some to describe it as being 'in crisis'. By focusing on professional practice, the PGCE course equips new teachers of Geography to generate their responses to these issues.

The key theme that underpins our definition of professional practice is the notion of balance between theory and practice both in ITE and in Geography education. Goodson (2003) has argued that theoretical knowledge and practical knowledge are out of balance in ITE. Similarly, Marsden (1997; 2005) has argued that the mission, matter and method of Geography education are out of balance. The Geography PGCE, mindful of its primary focus on Geography teacher *education* (and not training; see other chapters in this book), seeks to address both imbalances. Our main mechanism for doing so is to focus on professional practice.

Balance in Geography education

Marsden (1997, 2005) records how developments in Geography education have focused on either the 'mission' or the 'method' of teaching Geography, consequently taking the 'geography' out of Geography education. He explores how much of Geography education has been taken up by an emphasis on the goals of social education (the mission) or pedagogical approaches (the method). Marsden cites, for instance, how the emphasis on an issues-based approach was more concerned with the pedagogical challenge of engaging students than the learning of geographical content. Marsden's main argument was that this emphasis on mission or method was detracting from the 'matter' or the geographical content at the centre of the teaching and learning. Like Goodson, Marsden calls for this imbalance to be addressed.

Many have written in support of Marsden's analysis, and the trends he observed can be seen in other accounts of the recent history of Geography education (see Rawling, 2001; Morgan and Lambert, 2005; Standish, 2009). The popularity of the work of Alex Standish, who is critical of recent developments in Geography education, would suggest that there is a consensus of concern about the state of Geography education. In fact, such a concern has been expressed in strong terms by Ofsted, who suggest that Geography faces a number of challenges (Ofsted, 2005). These challenges include a predominance of strategy pedagogies used without deep understanding, an 'irrelevant' curriculum and a large number of non-subject specialists. Factor in the additional 'threats' to Geography education such as the growth of interdisciplinary approaches and the reduction of time allocated to Geography at KS3 in some schools (Lambert, 2009a; Butt, 2008) and this represents a significant challenge for Geography teachers and teacher educators.

This, then, is the context in which Geography teachers need to develop a theoretically informed practice and a sense of their role as Geography education professionals. They need to see themselves as subject experts and advocates who can describe and explain Geography's purpose, contribution and scope in a young person's education entitlement.

Challenges for Geography ITE

The list of priorities for the Geography PGCE is therefore a daunting one. While acknowledging that the PGCE is about enabling people to qualify as teachers, this is only one outcome of ITE. At the IOE, the Geography team's thinking and decision-making was informed by the development of the MA in Geography Education. This unique course, focusing on the field of Geography education, was established in 1968. A distance-learning version of the course was developed in 2000. Although different in style and scope to ITE or in-service training, the MA emphasises subject-specific professional development. The described outcomes of the course are indicative of what the course team understands a professional Geography educator to be (see Figure 9.1).

Figure 9.1

Course outcomes of the MA in Geography Education

A graduate with an MA in Geography Education will:
- ask critical questions about policy and about practices which are often taken for granted
- be well equipped to understand professional challenges and professional encounters and how to respond to them

---

- have a wide range of intellectual resources to draw upon (particularly from the field of Geography education)
- be analytical and be able to understand and use different approaches and traditions in Geography education
- be discriminating and evaluative about their professional actions
- understand current practices and appreciate the broader contexts of their professional practice
- have a broad range of strategic perspectives
- be actively involved in contributing to the field of Geography education
- be active and creative in curriculum development at a local level
- develop their capacity to make good judgements, concerning content, balance, choice of pedagogy, and the role of assessment in the field of Geography education
- understand the value of the contribution of research in Geography education and what constitutes quality in research.

The emphasis in the list of outcomes detailed in Figure 9.1 is on the Geography teacher's understanding of theory and practice, and developing the skills necessary to be an autonomous but collegiate professional. The framework acknowledges the importance of practice, alongside the ability to reflect critically on that practice and to develop a degree of research literacy to support and lead change. We feel that the professional skills and values described in the MA outcomes are also what a Geography PGCE student should be working towards. This orientation is also reflected in the fact that we encourage all our PGCE students to consider the PGCE year as the first year of their Master's degree and to pursue their subject studies with us. Taking these goals into account, three key strands guided the development of the PGCE course:

- enabling students to synthesise their understanding of theory with their understanding of practice;
- developing students' professional judgement and expertise particularly in relation to their individual context;
- using that understanding and professional judgement in new contexts.

In the rest of this chapter I will explore each of these strands and illustrate how they have been developed within the PGCE course. The development of the PGCE was a combined effort of the Geography team, and the ideas that follow are a result of that teamwork.

Synthesis of theory and practice

Practice is an important emphasis on the PGCE, but should not be considered in isolation. As previously outlined, there are particular issues that face Geography education which new teachers need to be able to respond to. Analysis of this is necessary to understand the theory/practice nexus in Geography education.

Lambert (2009a) recounts many critics who challenge the place of traditional subject disciplines in a postmodern education and describes the positioning of Geography as 'lost'. He cites the pursuit of 'excellence' in the current political vernacular as having a detrimental effect on the quality of subject teaching:

> The ideology of excellence has undermined teachers because subject knowledge is reduced to 'delivering' the specification. Their educational role is proscribed, being reduced to a technical one, assessed by what is measured and measurable in term[s] of value-added output.
>
> (Lambert, 2009a: 10–11)

He continues: 'Thus one of the contemporary challenges for Geography teachers, as curriculum makers, is to work out the nature of their relationship with the discipline of Geography' (ibid.: 12). However, Lambert also highlights that this does not mean merely re-creating academic Geography in the classroom or viewing the subject as slabs of content, but that this engagement will result in 'inducting young people into geographical enquiry and how to "think geographically"' (ibid.: 13).

This is a challenge for ITE as most graduates understand their subject unproblematically. Many new teachers have been inspired by excellent teachers during their own education. In the interviews for the PGCE, many candidates describe their motivation to inspire others about the subject. Their conception of good Geography teaching is determined, to a large extent, by their own experience. An aim of the PGCE course is therefore to enable the student teachers to question their subject knowledge critically and to explore what Geography may mean to others, including their learners.

Our approach has been influenced by research on how 'expert' Geography teachers use their subject knowledge (Brooks, 2007). In Geography education, the term 'synoptic capacity' has been used to describe how these expert teachers draw upon their understanding of the subject and make it applicable to young people (Brooks, 2009; Lambert, 2008). Synoptic capacity captures how a teacher makes decisions about the content of their lesson that reflects both their own subject expertise and the needs of their students: in other words, how they choose to connect the knower with what they wish to be known. The challenge for the PGCE was how to model this interaction and to encourage student teachers to reflect critically on the Geography they are teaching and its relationship to the young people they are teaching it to. This became the major emphasis in our first module which focuses on developing an understanding of Geography in curriculum planning.

Developing an understanding of Geography in curriculum planning

This module develops student teachers' understanding of lesson planning in Geography. The course is structured so that they spend their first academic term focusing on lesson planning. They are introduced to planning lesson episodes and then to planning full lessons. Within that framework they explore different approaches to lesson planning, and key movements in Geography education (such as enquiry-based learning). They are encouraged to be critical of lessons taught by others and of commercially or locally generated resources. By November, most student teachers will already have taught several lessons and are developing their skills in planning lessons and generating resources. The student teachers are ready to start thinking beyond single lessons and to begin thinking about how to plan sequences of lessons, and how to ensure progression in learning from one lesson to the next, across a scheme of work.

The assignment focuses on progression in geographical learning which is explored in two ways: first, by linking the learning in the lesson sequence with geographical concepts and ideas, and enabling students to develop their understanding of these concepts, and secondly, by evaluating how pupils' learning has progressed through the sequence of lessons. Progression in Geography is particularly complex. The nature of the subject is such that achievement in a scheme of work on say, settlement, may not translate to the next scheme on rivers. This is particularly the case when the subject is viewed thematically and not conceptually. Geographical themes (such as those specified in the 2000 Geography national curriculum: tectonic processes, geomorphological processes, weather and climate, ecosystems, population distribution and change, settlements, economic activity, development, environmental issues, resources issues and country studies) are commonly used to structure learning in schools, but they do not automatically follow sequentially or incrementally in the development of their conceptual understanding. For instance, rivers are not more difficult to understand than coasts, but it is through the study of both (or either) that a young person may develop their conceptual understanding of physical processes or interconnectivity.

The assignment for this module is designed in two parts. First, the teachers are required to plan and teach a sequence of lessons. What they select to teach and to whom is left to the student teacher to negotiate with their school-based colleagues. The lesson sequence is normally between six to eight hours of teaching, but this can vary widely according to differences in schools' curriculum structures. The second part of the assessment is a reflection on the sequence of lessons in two ways: on the progression in Geography, and also the learning developed. There is no explicit requirement to reflect on pedagogy because that is embedded in the other two criteria. Student teachers are recommended to identify pertinent themes and to structure their assessments around these themes.

The assessment is a challenging one. Our student teachers report that they find the planning and teaching fairly straightforward, but have more difficulty with the critical reflection. A requirement of the course is for the student teachers to critically evaluate their lessons regularly, but this assignment requires a different type of thinking about learning. In order to consider progression, the student teacher has to determine the geographical learning they intended to occur and how it is linked to geographical concepts, and what learning actually did occur and whether any of it was indeed geographical.

Often our student teachers will focus on a geographical concept such as one of those listed in the 2008 Geography national curriculum (place, space, scale, interdependence, physical and human processes, environmental interaction and sustainable development, cultural understanding and diversity). The definitions of these concepts are contested in the academic field and are poorly understood by many Geography teachers. Surveys of our student body (some of whom did their Geography degree some time ago) shows that they may feel confident with one or two of these concepts, but rarely all of them. The assignment therefore requires the student teachers to explore their geographical understanding and how they have made it applicable to their learners. During this process, the student teacher needs to articulate their understanding of subject knowledge, and to reflect on the representation of these complex ideas about Geography in the classroom. For many this is the start of developing their pedagogical content knowledge or synoptic capacity: in other words, how they make their subject's big ideas accessible to uninitiated learners. The assessment therefore encourages the student teacher to make clear links between theory and practice. Using their practice as 'evidence' they describe and explain what they intended to achieve, what they did achieve and, as such, how they think about theory and practice becomes iterative.

Developing professional judgement and expertise

The second strand that influenced our course is also geared towards developing student teachers' understanding of professional practice. The second assignment goes beyond the idea of using practice as evidence, but requires the student teacher to make judgements within the context of the school where they undertake their second practical teaching experience.

In this assignment we emphasise research literacy, particularly in the field of education and Geography education. Research literacy enables the student to learn how to conduct research in educational contexts, but also how to read and be critical of educational research. Research literacy plays a strong role on the Master's, featuring in all the four compulsory modules; one module – Reading research in Geography education – is dedicated to it entirely. As education professionals, new teachers need to explore what is meant by research literacy.

This assignment adopts a broader definition of how we understand professional practice. The traditional values attached to professionalism no longer apply to teaching (if they ever did), and debates in the sociology of education have tried to define what the new professionalism means (Whitty, 2000; Sachs, 2003). The preferred approach adopted by the Geography PGCE is that described by Judyth Sachs as 'activist' professionalism (ibid.). David Lambert (2009b) has transferred her ideas to Geography education. For him, being a professional Geography teacher means being:

- *inclusive rather than exclusive*: this means at the very least to combine primary and secondary educational perspectives and to cross the academic communities of school and higher education where the discipline is 'made' and developed;
- *collective and collaborative*: this implies membership of the subject association, if only to share in the making and the promotion of a broader view;
- *able to communicate aims clearly*: the Geography team need to have a clear sense of purpose which parents and pupils can understand;
- *able to create trust and mutual respect*: students are respected as learners and teachers are respected as colleagues…the formation of productive relationships lies at the core of teaching, and Geography is the medium in which this happens – worth learning for itself but also because it contributes to the formation of the educated person;
- *passionate*: this takes different forms of course, and does not need to invoke images from the *Dead Poets Society*. However, the professional teacher is relentless, determined and usually committed to nurturing achievement in others.

Sachs also highlights the importance of research in teacher development. This is especially significant in Geography education, as Butt (2006) has identified that Geography education research is in a poor state. This is reflected in the international picture (see Kent, 2000). There is a significant body of small-scale research in Geography education, but larger scale, funded research is limited. An active research community is vital for a sustainable field of enquiry and, therefore, this lack of funding has an impact on the growth of the field.

Research in education is also important in enabling teachers to understand and address problems pertinent to their local context. I have argued elsewhere that valuing the outcomes of practitioner research is important for the continued development of the field (Brooks, forthcoming). In addition, developing research literacy enables a Geography education professional to fully participate in the debates pertinent to them.

Becoming this kind of professional necessitates a particular approach in ITE, one that encourages teachers to be research active, and to generate their own response to initiatives and perspectives. Such an approach requires that teachers are able to identify issues and problems in the local context, to understand why that problem has arisen, the significance of the local context and to seek systematic action to improve the situation. Critical reflection is key. These features influence the second assignment, which focuses on developing research literacy and practitioner research.

Developing research literacy and modelling practitioner research

The second assignment aims to encourage the student teacher to engage with three specific focuses in Geography education: assessment for learning, teaching with geographical information systems (GIS), and education for sustainable development and global citizenship (ESDGC). Although these three areas are different, each is complex and requires sustained engagement, thought and reflection. To understand them fully requires teachers to engage in reading, theory and practice. They are also aspects of geographical education that it is possible to encounter on a superficial level on the PGCE and in schools.

The challenging nature of the three areas is influential in deciding when this assessment takes place during the academic year. To fully understand their complexity, teachers need to engage with the literature, consider their classroom practice and how the two are related. Therefore exploration of these areas needs to take place alongside practical teaching experience.

The student teachers are required to conduct a small-scale practitioner research project into each of the three themes. The students are introduced to the cyclical process of action research and are encouraged to adopt a similar strategy (although somewhat truncated due to the time constraints). The first step is for the student teachers to identify where the school is positioned in the three themes identified, and then to plan an intervention that would move the school forward in some way. They are required to explain both the problem and their intervention alongside a critical evaluation of the results. Students are encouraged to think beyond their own practice, and to reflect on whole school development. For instance, the work on ESDGC may take them beyond the Geography Department to considering the school's policies on sustainability, the EcoSchools movement or, in one case, students' engagement in the political process.

Again, this is a challenging assignment. Feedback from students and analysis of their work suggest that it has several key features. Primarily, the emphasis in each of the three areas requires them to read and consider these areas in an informed way, further developing their understanding of theory and practice. For instance, they report to us that 'doing assessment for learning' is not enough – it is through having to think about where the school is positioned and what they can contribute to bring it forward, that they are able to think about the school's actions, policy and practice in a critical way. Many students become critical of the school's adoption of the assessment for learning strand of the KS3 Strategy and seek ways to improve children's learning. Similarly, if their experience of assessment for learning is positive, then they are able to consider why it has been so and its salient features. This seems to resonate with the difference between understanding assessment for learning and using some of the techniques associated with it (see Stobart, 2008).

The assignment's importance is based on its emphasis on systematic enquiry into practice. It empowers the student teachers to see how they can be agents of change in schools. It also challenges them to consider issues within their local context, exercising nuanced professional judgement. Taking these two factors together is significant in Geography education, particularly when we recall Marsden's criticism of how Geography education is out of balance. Learners, classes and schools have different needs and present a range of challenges. From the perspective of Geography, learners in different contexts will have different understandings and views of the world. Knowing what the students already know or have experienced is key knowledge for the Geography teacher, as it is from this that they can decide how to plan for future development. One of the aims of this assignment is to get student teachers to think critically about their local context and how it affects the development of geographical learning. It requires them to think about what they have read, what their experience has been and possible reasons for why there may be a difference between the two. The assignment thereby models some of the features of professional practice that Lambert highlights, particularly an inclusive understanding and working collectively and collaboratively.

Professional practice: Applying understanding in new contexts

The final assessment in the PGCE has a different emphasis. It focuses on an important dimension in Geography education, that of learning outside the classroom. It builds on what the students have already learned on both of their practical school experiences and their previous modules. It challenges this knowledge by placing it in another context, that of fieldwork or learning outside the classroom.

Fieldwork has always had a strong emphasis on the Geography PGCE. The final four weeks of the PGCE, in June, feature a residential field trip during which the students plan and develop fieldwork for post-16 courses. In recent years, this fieldwork has been based in the Lake District, where students spend two days with Brockhole Lake District Authority where they are taken on some typical Geography post-16 courses. Using this experience, as well as all they have gained so far on their teaching experiences and practice, the students are required to plan a fieldwork day for post-16 students and to consider what is important about planning for learning outside the classroom.

Fieldwork is not just about learning in a different context, but also represents a new set of challenges and opportunities for Geography teachers. Identifying risk and planning an effective risk assessment is a vital part to leading learning outside the classroom and, indeed, its importance runs through the module. But, in addition, teaching young people in the field provides a unique learning opportunity. It challenges all dimensions of a teaching repertoire, including behaviour management, planning and resourcing. The experience can be stimulating for both the teacher and the students as they generate new understandings about the Geography of the environment in situ. The ability to create such learning experiences outside the classroom is, arguably, one of the most challenging dimensions of a Geography teacher's work.

Traditionally, assessment of a 30-credit Master's module is through a 5,000-word essay. In this assignment, the assessment product comprises a poster, a presentation and a viva, reflecting the team's understanding that the essay is not the only appropriate way to assess the understanding of professional practice. This is particularly pertinent for a topic like learning outside the classroom. On the PGCE, teaching practice is assessed through lesson observations and examining teaching practice files and documentation. Practice is the focus of the assessment. The emphasis on the written modules is on understanding of practice. With learning outside the classroom, the assessment needs to focus on both practice *and* the teacher's understanding of it. This is much more challenging to do as, by definition, learning outside the classroom can take place anywhere. However, with the availability of electronic media it is possible to 'capture' learning outside the classroom (through video clips or still photography or video-diaries). The challenge is how these can be used to demonstrate student teachers' grasp of the field and understanding of how it works in practice. The poster and presentation enables student teachers to do that.

A further issue is how to ensure that these presentations were academically rigorous. A viva examination enables a probing of teachers' understanding of learning outside the classroom, alongside their grasp of the field and their consideration of their practical experience. In addition, a presentation enables student teachers to demonstrate their skills of exposition. The emphasis on developing effective learning outside the classroom means that the work builds on all that they have already achieved in learning about teaching.

The assignment focuses on the question 'What is a necessary component for planning for effective learning outside the classroom?', and the students have a strict time slot for their presentation. This means that they need to focus on one dimension and to consider its importance. This then has to be substantiated by readings and through their own experience. As such, students have to demonstrate how their understanding of what they have experienced relates to what they have read. Importantly, this assignment takes the development of professional practice further. Not only do the student teachers have to apply their professional understanding in a new context, but they have to consider which aspects of it are important and why. This challenges their understanding of both educational theory and geographical content.

Final words

This chapter began by arguing that balance was important in education and particularly so for Geography education. The approach adopted on the Geography PGCE focuses on professional practice and bringing theory and practice together. The advantage of this approach is its grounding in professional practice, but it is not unique or particularly pertinent to Geography education. The emphasis on professional practice enables teachers to develop their understanding of both theory and practice iteratively and in a way that is mutually supportive to the development of both. During their time in schools, it is easy for teachers to focus on the day-to-day of practice. It is the responsibility of the PGCE, as the first year of a teacher's development, to encourage their engagement with theory and to enable them to explore how theory can complement and inform professional practice. We have designed our assessment pieces to meet this end.

The emphasis on professional practice also enables student teachers to consider the central place of the geographical content of their lessons alongside the social and educational goals of Geography education. This approach is not prescriptive but promotes teachers developing their own perspective on the Geography they want to teach and how local factors can influence that perspective.

Chapter 10

Music, musicians and learning modes

Pauline Adams and Kate Laurence

Applicants for PGCE secondary music courses are currently drawn, in the main, from two kinds of institutions: the universities and specialist colleges of music. Traditionally, each of the two routes leading to degree status places a different emphasis in its approach to music training: the universities on theoretical studies and the music colleges on practical musicianship and performance.

A report published over 50 years ago by the Standing Conference of Music Committees for England (1954), entitled *The Training of Music Teachers*, indicated that degree courses across universities were varied, but that the majority had introduced some practical work and instrumental teaching as components. This was considered to be a move in the right direction as there was a shortage of music teachers, and such changes in degree structures would give students a better background knowledge for teaching the subject. In contrast, the performance and one-to-one instrumental teaching was at the heart of conservatoire practice and, although the Burnham Committee (responsible for pay and conditions for teachers from 1918 to 1987) recognised graduates of the Royal Schools of Music Diploma (GRSM) as a teaching qualification, the training was deemed on the whole to be unsatisfactory, with too little time spent in schools and lacking appropriate staffing. One of the recommendations of the Standing Conference was that 'university degrees in music to be further strengthened with post Graduate Training should provide first class preparation' (1954: 18). This was fully realised in the 1980s as the PGCE became the route favoured by the incumbent government for all those opting to enter the teaching profession.

In 1998 the Higher Education Council for England (HEFCE) commissioned a review of conservatoire training. The Conservatoires Advisory Group highlighted the continuing differences between the courses offered at music colleges and universities: 'academic pathways in conservatoires do not duplicate the work of university departments' (HEFCE, 1998: 6). However, it was observed that university syllabuses for music involved performance, and that more academic strands had been added to programmes of studies in conservatoires, including expansion into Master's and PhD courses. University validation has impacted on conservatoires but it is still the case that their emphasis, time and resources are directed towards their main aim, that of training high-level performers. However, for some music colleges, shifts from the apprenticeship model of instrumental training towards a more reflective practice agenda is promoting a growing awareness of how musicians engage with and communicate their art (Odam and Bannon, 2005). An increasing emphasis on research is informing practice and encouraging musicians to consider their wider role within society since 'the career patterns of musicians involve multiple sources of employment and changing mixes of activity' (HEFCE, 1998: 6).

In the universities, options choices have broadened considerably and offer both academic and more practical ways of gaining a degree qualification. These include the study of jazz, music technology as well as popular and contemporary styles of music. In addition, courses that reflect local traditions have given credence to particular forms of music-making such as brass band studies in the north of England and folk and traditional music in the north east. Intercultural aspects of music embedded within specialist courses in ethnomusicology, and with practical experience of learning an instrument other than a Western one, are reflecting growing global perspectives on musical styles, genres and traditions, including cross-over. The music colleges too have responded by creating courses such as jazz, music technology and film composition.

The majority of music teachers in the country are drawn from the universities. The results of a survey of the long-term occupations of alumni at Kings College, London revealed that 53 per cent had entered the teaching profession with 8 per cent taking the performance route (HEFCE, 1998). However, there are conservatoire musicians who wish to develop a broader portfolio that includes teaching as an option, and the IOE has witnessed a steady stream of student teachers from the four main music colleges based in London and beyond. Also within the PGCE intake are student teachers who have gained significant experience in their own music careers, through engagements as professional and semi-professional performers, as instrumental and vocal teachers, or by working in some capacity within the music industry. The reasons for such applicants entering a PGCE course are many and include:

- a growing interest in teaching promoted by instrumental teaching work, usually initially undertaken with little knowledge of educational pedagogy and practice;

- the desire for a career change but one that would still involve work within the field of music;
- a recognition of the demands of whole-class instrumental teaching under a government-led Wider Opportunities remit that is providing new challenges and requires better training and understanding of the principles and practice of working with large groups of pupils;
- an interest in teaching promoted by involvement in community music and professional partnerships.

It is encouraging that musicians with such varied interests and experiences are keen to undertake a teaching route, and express a desire and motivation to deepen their understanding within the field of music education. Many of these applicants bring with them an invaluable wealth of experience, and a number have already gained a Master's or PhD.

Such an eclectic mix of musicians brings richness to any PGCE route, but also highlights the need to consider a range of implications when constructing a rigorous and meaningful course which embraces challenges that are both musical and academic. Here there are opportunities too for creating peer learning contexts and for providing a platform for discussion and sharing through the use of a virtual learning environment.

Teacher education for the modern classroom

It is now accepted that school music benefits from a department that can offer a wide range of musical experiences provided by specialists within their field. This is good news for music education and for the modern music department, where curriculum teaching, including the employment of advances in music technology, and extracurricular activity should reflect and broaden the interests of pupils. It is time to dispel the long-held view of the position of school music being unrelated to pupils' musical interests beyond school. The challenge for those in teacher education is to be aware of and to respond to both undergraduate and postgraduate developments in music training within universities and colleges, and to connect with the growing awareness of informal and formal practices within music-making in the diverse intercultural context of British society.

Student teachers arrive on the PGCE course with a range of specialisms, and with their own identity as musicians. Course content and assessed components, therefore, need to harness and develop both musical and academic skills. The Master's level module assignments are designed to accommodate and build on this vast range of expertise across the course. At the interview stage, when applicants are asked why they want to become a teacher, they often cite a desire to transmit to pupils their own passion for music. Cox (2002), in conversation with secondary music teachers, verifies this intention, particularly in relation to enjoyment of the subject and the opportunities it provides to communicate with others.

The role of IOE tutors in introducing idealistic musicians/student teachers to the world of music education is to engage them in examining prevailing orthodoxies through a true synthesis of theory and practice within the field. In writing about teacher research in the conservatoire, Sonia Purcell proposes that it should 'make the musical experience paramount, involving a co-ordinated and balanced or more "whole-brain" approach rather than the cognitive approach so prevalent in most other curriculum subjects and teaching style' (2005: 225). These words appositely summarise the aims of IOE music tutors when designing their particular Master's level module requirements and assessment procedures.

Assessment strategies used on the PGCE secondary music programme

Incongruence between the identities of musician and music teacher arises regularly in discussion with student teachers on the PGCE music course: many are keen to maintain the socially constructed view of themselves as *musicians who teach*. The increase in personality and identity research into musicians and teachers (Hargreaves and Marshall, 2003; Cox, 2002; Dolloff, 1999; Kemp, 1996) has begun to illuminate 'some insights into the likely internal conflicts that a musician may suffer when finding him or herself mismatched to the demands of classroom life' (Kemp, 1996: 232). The PGCE music programme at the IOE responds to such a tension by providing part-time training routes and distance learning modules, which encourage student teachers to maintain and develop their independence and skills as musicians as they embark on their teacher education.

It is important that assessment strategies for student music teachers are not completely 'alien' as these may serve to broaden the divide between their experiences as musicians and those in initial teacher education (ITE). Assessment strategies from music undergraduate programmes influence the PGCE course design in order to promote continuity in the development of skills and experiences. Boud's memories of being assessed as a student are founded in frustration, resulting in his preoccupation with a 'code of assessment to be learned' (Boud and Falchikov, 2007: 6), and subsequently cracked, on his course of study. It would not be helpful for music student teachers to be preoccupied in this way and assessment practices are designed to avoid this. However, it must also be stated that assessment strategies on the PGCE music course are not only designed with student teachers' existing strengths and prior assessment experiences in mind; a number of assessment strategies seek to develop less honed skills as well.

Critical reflection and analysis, the ability to engage and critique music education theory and research, and the synthesis of theory and professional practice are common currency at Master's level. Though there is commonality in the required skills, ITE music providers in the UK approach their programmes and their assessment practices very differently. Some PGCE music programmes, for example, approach modular assessment by means of a single written task which might include a review of relevant literature, critical reflection on professional practice and the development of curriculum materials. Other programmes include non-written alternatives, with oral presentations a popular and common alternative to written assignments. The music PGCE model presented here seeks to develop a range of assessment practices, including those which are more ephemeral in nature but which build upon approaches from undergraduate music programmes. Practical musicianship tasks, oral and multimedia presentations, music technology portfolios, as well as more traditional, written forms of assessment, support and develop student music teachers' skills, knowledge and understanding of teaching and learning issues.

Practical musicianship assessment strategies

Kemp suggests that traditionally trained musicians might respond to the tension between musician/music teacher identity by 're-directing much of their energies to extracurricular choirs and orchestras. In this way they manage to retain a sense of their musical persona through the overt direction of concert performances' (1996: 229). The PGCE music course at the IOE focuses on the development and assessment of practical musicianship, placing student teachers' existing and often highly developed skills as composers, performers and improvisers within pedagogical frameworks.

The Rehearsal and Performance Assessment requires student teachers to compose or arrange a piece of music for a group of school pupils who differ in their instrumental and vocal abilities. It seeks to advocate the 'practicum model' of music education (Elliott, 1991), summarised by Dunn as 'the curriculum and assessment of musical achievement [placed] within its authentic professional environment' (Dunn et al., 2004: 147). Student teachers must rehearse the piece with the pupils and subsequently reflect on the event.

Student music teachers must research and consider a number of factors in order to succeed in this assignment, including how well pupils are able to sight-read, physiological instrument-playing issues relating to pupils' ages, gender and stages of development, a detailed knowledge of instrument- and voice-specific issues such as compass range, tone and technique as well as other performance and ensemble challenges. Though music graduates might have some experience in conducting and rehearsing with proficient musicians, they are faced with a different challenge when presented with young musicians of varying levels of instrumental and vocal skill.

Student music teachers do have some control over the task in terms of instrumental choices and repertoire. However, they cannot know the exact level of each pupil's instrumental competence and they will not be able to predict how the rehearsal might unfold. Very often, student teachers must respond to pupils whose graded performance and sight-reading abilities are mismatched. Student music teachers must find ways, under the pressure of an observed rehearsal, to adapt parts, offer alternate teaching strategies and respond to the very individual situation in which they find themselves. Response to unscripted situations in such a rehearsal provides opportunities for self-assessment. Though the score provides specific directions of pitch, rhythm and playing directions, student music teachers must invite and facilitate musical interpretation from each of the young performers. John reflects on how he realises this in the rehearsal:

> I decided to approach a difficult rhythmic passage by asking the pupils to clap it before they transferred it onto their instruments. I'd planned this in advance because I'd experienced this difficult passage before and knew that it would present problems. Although the pupils clapped the rhythm accurately as written in the score, I noticed that they interpreted the accenting differently from one another, something which changed the colour of the performance when played on instruments. I did not consider this in my planning and I very quickly re-evaluated my role to be more of a facilitator and coach. I realised that it was far more important to avoid an overly didactic approach so that pupils' own musical interpretations were developed, rather than imposing my own.
>
> (John, student teacher, 2009)

'Real time' self-reflection is observed and there are strong parallels between the improvisation of teaching strategies and student teachers' practised skills in creativity and adaptation as musicians.

The assessment strategies are varied for this particular assignment and the reflection process is ongoing. These strategies follow the cyclical model of reflection and reflective practice (Boud *et al.*, 1985; Boud, 1995) in which the constructed task allows choice and ownership by the student learner. The rehearsal or 'learning event' (Boud, 1995) is not predictable and subsequently illuminates unexpected outcomes for the student teachers as they must make immediate choices. Additional feedback takes the form of verbal dialogue between observer and student immediately after the rehearsal and subsequent written feedback is offered in a number of areas, including conducting, rehearsing, arranging/composing and communication skills. This leads student teachers to further reassess their experience. A final written reflection is completed by the student after the event, which focuses on how the arrangement and planning unfolded in the actual rehearsal. Student teachers are encouraged to make connections and challenge new and existing 'frameworks of understanding' (Boud, 1995), and ensure that they have a solid theoretical foundation for their practice.

This extract, taken from the reflective written assessment task, is representative of music student teachers' responses to the task, where the experiential nature of learning is explicit:

> As I observed the pupils' musical responses, not only demonstrated by their ability as musicians to sight-read, listen, improvise and perform, it also reminded me that everyone learns differently and that it was my job to recognise this and to encourage each player's own personal interpretation of the music. You could argue, then, that whilst the pupils' different instrumental grades were an indication of the preparation needed to create a challenging score, the most important and powerful differentiation happened on the rehearsal day through the recognition of each individual's way of learning and by how I was able to exercise and utilise my subject knowledge and skills...This immediate response was challenging – the experiences that arose in the rehearsal were familiar, but also entirely new.
>
> (Vanessa, student teacher, 2009)

Student evaluations of this assessment reveal that although they are able to draw heavily upon pre-existing musicianship skills, the challenge of arranging and composing for and rehearsing with young musicians, often for the first time, results in significant re-assessment of existing skills and knowledge and authentic, theorised reflections on practice.

Music technology portfolio assessment

The application and critical evaluation of music technology presents student music teachers with multiple challenges, not only to their subject knowledge and skills but also in how they reconcile the many tensions and contradictions between traditional music-making and music technology. At the interview for the PGCE music course, a number of applicants identify that they have limited music technology skills, with many only having experience of notation-based software as a way to publish their work. It is important that approaches to the assessment of music technology skills are in the vernacular, as it might be deemed somewhat contradictory to assess the skills, understanding and evaluation of technology through a traditional written portfolio.

As part of a distance learning module, student music teachers complete a range of weekly tasks using music technology. The portfolio assessment seeks to address this with ongoing assessment taking place in online weekly sessions. Progressive tasks seek to illuminate an understanding of the principles of sound, the theory which underpins the application of music technology as well as the practice of audio editing and music sequencer skills. Dunn *et al.* (2004) use a music composition portfolio example to illustrate the strengths of this type of assessment as it supports the process and development of student teachers' knowledge and understanding, providing opportunities for ongoing assessment and formative feedback. As the music technology tasks are released weekly, they encourage reflection and analysis to be progressive and to be approached as a draft, avoiding a collection of work put together for summative assessment. It is also a model of assessment which student teachers have, in turn, developed and applied for composition teaching and learning in their own professional practice.

Online discussion plays a large part of the web-based portfolio assessment, including problem-solving and critical analysis of the technology used in relation to student teachers' professional practice. This promotes a model of collaborative, critical thinking (Dunn *et al.*, 2004) which helps student teachers to examine dissension and debate in music technology education, comparing experiences and subsequently broadening their thinking about teaching and learning.

Research and written assessment

Case studies require music student teachers to observe and monitor two pupils who demonstrate differing needs; one who has been assessed as needing extra support in a range of subjects, and another who is musically very able and requires a different kind of support to reach their full musical potential. The rationale for using a case study research strategy is to encourage student teachers to consider why they have selected specific pupils and to defend their suitability (Denscombe, 2003). It is a focused research strategy intended to support often-fledgling skills in analysing and evaluating their pupils' musical responses, seeking to illuminate the intricacies and subtleties in each 'case' (Denscombe, 2003; Blaxter *et al.*, 2001). This is not a task that necessarily requires generalisations from the student teacher; it is more that they learn to think critically about issues surrounding generalisations, and are often helped to examine, sensitively, the issues of unhelpful labelling of pupils with differing needs. It is the first research task that student music teachers undertake on the course and serves as a useful introduction to understanding research methods and ethical considerations, something that is largely absent in undergraduate music programmes.

The action research project is intended to broaden and develop student teachers' critical and analysis skills from those of the initial case study assessment. This evaluative task seeks to convey insightful understanding of the relationship between student teachers' subject knowledge and subject pedagogy, taking into account current issues and developments in music education. Finney explains that though 'case study is about understanding the ways things are, action research is characterised by an intervention of some kind, an attempt to bring about change, to test alternatives and to begin a cycle of experiment' (2009: 4). Maintaining a critical perspective of research findings is essential for student teachers, with reflection encouraged both during the research process and in a final oral presentation to peers. Student teachers are encouraged to think beyond their school experience and to enter into wider educational debate in music education such as instrumental teaching, collaborative partnerships between professional musicians and schools, gender issues or informal pedagogies. Regular group inquiry is encouraged through online and face-to-face discourse with peers and tutors, and is essential in promoting continued *open awareness, phenomenological discrimination* and *active choosing* (Boud *et al.*, 1985) throughout the research process.

Learning and assessment opportunities beyond the classroom: Musicians in education

Two recent government-backed initiatives have provided opportunities for a renewed focus on music education. The first has been in response to *All Our Futures* (NACCCE and Robinson, 1999). This resulted in the setting up of 'creative partnerships' between schools and other stakeholders in order to support creative learning across a range of domains, including music. The second significant development resulting from two further government reports – the *Music Manifesto 1* (2005) and *Music Manifesto 2* (2006) – has been a funding commitment to musical learning, particularly in the area of singing and instrumental teaching opportunities. These initiatives have raised issues connected to the training of instrumental and vocal tutors and the quality of experience they are able to provide, and to the setting up and evaluation of musical learning within collaborative projects.

Partnerships between professional orchestras and ensembles are well established, and there has been a growing interest in developing the workshop and leadership skills of those musicians involved in their communities. Since the 1980s the London Guildhall School of Music and Drama has maintained its long tradition of contact with schools and communities, with student training focusing on devising and leading projects. Students on the brass band studies course at the University of Huddersfield are positively encouraged to become members of the local musical community: 'many students are members of both the University of Huddersfield band and an additional band in the area

(Huddersfield Brass Band Studies, 2009: 2). Such shifts in emphasis within the music colleges and universities signal a desire to blur musical boundaries and reach out beyond the institution.

With a burgeoning of collaborative opportunities it is essential that PGCE student teachers are aware of the challenges and possibilities within such wide-ranging options. Within this context what needs to be avoided is workshops and projects being viewed as 'little more than an artistic, educational and cultural meltdown, reducing collaboration through facilitation to little more than a warm-up activity' (Gregory, 2005: 181). Therefore the setting up, monitoring and evaluation of any form of collaborative venture is crucial to ensuring that quality is maintained, and the encounter is both musically effective and affective for all those involved.

The Learning and Assessment Opportunities Beyond the Classroom module has been devised with this in mind, and is intended to provide student teachers with a module that promotes investigative research, based on interaction with other practitioners within the field of music education. Goodson and Sikes (2001) suggest that engaging with others can identify values and motivations through observing professional practice, thus deepening insights into teaching styles and educational approaches. The requirements for the module are threefold:

- A written report that draws on relevant reading and research literature and refers to experiential research, and which conveys the ability to critically evaluate, through sustained analysis and argument, the challenges and benefits of bringing school music into partnership with the wider arts community.
- A portfolio which is collated in response to practical experience within collaborative ventures and which provides an evidence base of research undertaken.
- Oral presentation that allows for dissemination of findings and encourages the articulation and exchange of ideas between student teachers.

Research is encouraged that employs questionnaire and interview skills, in themselves a testing methodology. The relationship between the individual and music is a personal one and does not lend itself to measurement by a positivist approach. The challenge for the student teacher is to unpick the different voices of participants, from which some conclusions can be drawn and from which further questions can be formulated, some of which may even be contradictory (McNiff et al., 2002). The outreach work that this module promotes enables student teachers to look beyond the classroom and to engage with educational research which is both socially and politically embedded and which is real, located within the here and now.

Student teachers are advised to decide on their own particular focus for the written report, which will be influenced by a number of factors. One student teacher had secured a teaching post and had decided to research opportunities within the local education authority that had engaged her as a newly qualified teacher, thus linking her active research to a specific locality. Another focused more globally on the socially focused work of the Venezuelan 'El Sistema' project, attending a conference and workshops at London's South Bank Centre. Discussions about the purpose of this project led to useful comparisons between past and present initiatives in music education in this country. Both student teachers were proactive in setting up visits, observations and participation. Freedom of choice and ownership of the research allowed for personal exploration of ideas. It is envisaged that such assessment structures will promote a more reflective and 'creative' teacher who can think beyond the boundaries of the classroom and interpret the requirements of the National Curriculum for Music (2007) in an inventive and exciting way.

Below are two examples of rationales produced by the student teachers for the written report, which demonstrate a similar focus, that of 'authentic experience' but with each employing their own distinct approach. Josh writes:

This report will explore wider issues around positioning learning outside the classroom, and reflect on recent examples that have involved pupils and teachers in real encounters with their community, and within contexts of professional arts settings. The report will show that these opportunities not only help provide authentic experiences, thought to be our first and foremost objective as music teachers, but also create contextual links with other areas of learning, such as with PHSE and Citizenship.

(Josh, student teacher, 2009)

This report intends to explore contemporary attitudes to culture, music and education. After coming to definitions of culture, and music's relation to this, it looks into the nature of 'authentic' musical experiences and the benefits and challenges of approaching music in this way. What opportunities are there outside the classroom that could support the teacher in providing these 'authentic experiences', and what recommendations can be made to the newly qualified teacher?

(Vanessa, student teacher, 2009)

In addition to the report and portfolio of experience, oral presentation of the research through the use of PowerPoint is intended to promote confidence in engaging in professional debate, and in realising the importance of being engaged with the music education research community.

The three aims of the module attract a range of assessment procedures but, overall, student teachers are expected to become familiar with and be able to present a written critique of related literature, including government-produced documents, to undertake independent investigation and draw some conclusions by employing appropriate research tools and, finally, to disseminate findings to a critical audience.

If the idea of 'lifelong learner' (Fichtman and Yenol-Hoppey, 2009) is to be embedded within a continuum of personal development, the Master's level components of a music PGCE should prepare student teachers for advanced studies in their chosen field. With the emphasis on musician as educator it is also important for music teachers to continue to engage in musical activity of their own.

In ITE there is a danger that the competency-led model for teaching the standards required for QTS might be applied to Master's level assignments. Purcell (2005) implies that research and scholarship demand 'deeper learning', and can counterbalance a competency framework. Paynter, in a documented discussion about the origins and influences of the *British Journal of Music Education*, expresses a preference for the 'speculative' articles 'that provide stimulating questions rather than predictable answers' (Paynter and Salaman, 2008: 235). The reflective practitioner model allows student teachers to engage unashamedly in this form of scholarship. Paynter, a distinguished and influential music educator, believes that teachers need to develop styles of teaching that are 'innovative, imaginative and, above all, musical' (ibid.: 235). This is also the challenge for the teacher educator when devising modules and assignments.

Conteh proposes that 'writing is a way of shaping and testing emergent ideas' and 'aids reflection' (in Conteh *et al.*, 2005: 46). In addition to written expectations within the PGCE music course, oral presentation is designed to enable the sharing of research methodologies and findings with student teacher colleagues, thus confirming personal identity, attitudes and personal relationship to the work. Jorgenson (2008) posits the view that there is not enough representation from teachers in music journals, and Fichtman and Yenol-Hoppey (2009) also raise the issue of the absence of teachers' voices, proposing that teachers need to be armed with the tools of inquiry and be committed to change, and well enough informed to shape and re-shape their ideas.

Swanwick, reflecting on the twenty-fifth anniversary of the publication of the *British Journal of Music Education,* highlights significant changes that have influenced developments: 'our original concept of mainstream music has already given way to recognition of a plurality of settings, a network of tributaries rather than a single river' (2008: 231).

The following statement, which appears in the summary paragraph of one student teacher's assignment, neatly echoes the words of Swanwick:

This is a very exciting time to be involved in music education. There are so many initiatives at the moment that the most difficult problem for the music educator is being able to select what is most appropriate for their school and what will be most beneficial for the students involved.

(Fran, student teacher, 2009)

The inception of Master's level work within a PGCE course, although challenging within current ITE frameworks, can ensure that student teachers are armed with professional insights, knowledge of scholarship in the field and the confidence to participate in the discourse, thus being able to contribute to the future shaping of music education.

Chapter 11

Performativity versus engagement in a Social Science PGCE

Jane Perryman

This chapter will discuss the tensions and dilemmas in relation to assessment that are experienced by students on a professional course. Our student teachers are expected to produce assignments at Master's level, at a time when many are more focused on the rigours of completing their school experience. This occurs in an atmosphere of performativity – the culture of outcomes, efficiency and accountability that has swept through education in England and Wales since the 1988 Education Reform Act.

Performativity is a technology of power and normalisation. Avis says that 'performativity becomes embodied in a regime of truth that refuses other conceptualisations of good practice, which therefore become silenced and are denied legitimacy' (2005: 211). Performativity is a regime of rituals such as inspection, audits, interviews and routines such as meetings and record-keeping (Ball, 2001). Teachers and teaching are saturated in discourses of performativity. Teacher education is increasingly permeated with standards, performance and assignment criteria. One possible effect of the move to Master's level accreditation is that student teachers might be confronted with yet another arena of performativity. This chapter will suggest that student teachers' best defence against an entirely performative approach to their assignments will be if they can see the benefits of engagement with theory and perceive the theory–practice relationship as close and dialectical.

The Social Science PGCE cohort under discussion here was of a high academic calibre, with some already holding Master's or postgraduate qualifications, and while some enjoyed the challenge, others adopted a more performative approach, performing engagement and reflection with efficiency rather than with genuine enthusiasm.

As well as reflecting on the tutor's experience of running a Master's level PGCE for the first time, this chapter will explore themes which were reflected in responses to a questionnaire circulated to the cohort in their first year of teaching, as well as in the students' end-of-course evaluations. These themes are: the usefulness of the assignments for the students' teaching; the intrinsic interest of the assignments; the tension between completing assignments to Master's level and being a good classroom teacher; and the impact of doing a Master's level PGCE on future study.

Performativity

As suggested above, performativity is a complex and contested term. I define it as a disciplinary technology (Foucault, 1977) that uses judgements and comparisons against what is seen as efficient as a means of control. A culture of performativity leads to performances that measure efficiency. For student teachers the measurements are the standards for qualified teacher status (QTS), and the grade boundaries for their academic work. I argue that there is a tension inherent in meeting both and, for some, this is manifested in them adopting a performative approach to their assignments, jumping through the required hoops rather than genuinely engaging.

The term 'performative' was introduced by J.L. Austin (1962) when he talked of 'performative utterances', words which describe an action as the action is happening or 'saying as doing'. Examples of performative utterances are 'I promise', 'I dare' and 'I bequeath'. Perhaps, in this context, I should add 'I reflect'. Performative utterances in education can be seen in terms of labelling theory, such as labelling certain students as 'A' grade, or, in the arena of this book, labelling PGCE students as 'outstanding' or 'cause for concern'. Marshall, writing about teacher appraisal, says that performative language acts in appraisals to normalise individuals and 'the appraisals themselves, masquerading as descriptors, in turn mask the underlying power-knowledge in the force of performative utterances' (1999: 316). During a PGCE course, when we award a student Master's level grades for their assignments, and H-level and Ofsted grades for their performances in school, we are often recognising their ability to demonstrate how they have met the standards for QTS and followed the assignment criteria. But in satisfying these requirements can they fully engage with the theory and glimpse a future life as a public intellectual – or are they merely being performative?

From 'performative' comes the word 'performativity'. There are many, often confusing, uses of the term 'performativity'. In the field of performance studies it is used as a definition of the theory of performance or analysing performance. Indeed, when reading about performance studies, it is quite hard to differentiate where the boundaries are between performance and performativity. Goffman defines performance as 'all the activity of a given participant on a given occasion which serves to influence in any way any of the other participants' (1959: 15). This is such a broad definition that it must include performativity. Schechner uses performative as an adjective which 'inflects what it modifies with performance-like qualities' (2002: 110) and says that performativity is the extension of performance into all areas of everyday life. Hence performativity is 'like a performance without actually being a performance in the orthodox or formal sense' (ibid.). So, in other words, when an action or situation is performative, it is not about performance as we traditionally understand it. Instead, according to Alexander, Anderson and Gallegos (2005), the concept of performance implies an audience; that which is performative is performance taken beyond its formal setting. They maintain that 'teaching is a performance event as well as being a performative event' (Alexander *et al.*, 2005: 4). Nowhere is this more apparent than when a student teacher is being formally observed, and special resources are created which exceed the student teacher's normal efforts. Teachers are constantly required to perform, especially student teachers who are under constant surveillance. Their lessons are observed in a formal setting, but their ongoing professionalism and capacity for reflection is under constant scrutiny.

Lyotard (1984) uses 'performative' to refer to a method of maximising efficiency through a culture of controlled outcomes and accountability. He argues that power depends on the optimisation of performance. Lyotard's version of performativity obscures differences, by requiring everything to be measurable and to be accountable against the same standards. Thus 'an equation between wealth, efficiency and truth is established' (Lyotard, 1984: 46). Clearly, for student teachers the QTS standards and the Master's level criteria are the measures against which their performance is judged. However, if they are able to recognise the links between theory and practice on a Master's level course, they may be able to move beyond the merely performative.

In the performative accountability culture of education in the first decade of the twenty-first century, 'concepts like efficiency are treated as though they were neutral and technical matters, rather than being tied to particular interests' (Ball, 1990: 154). In other words, the hegemonic belief is that efficiency is seen as 'a good thing' irrespective of the cost to people – intensification, loss of autonomy, monitoring and appraisal, lack of decision-making and lack of personal development are not considered. Gewirtz says that the language used to describe and promote change and innovation in teaching is not neutral, but 'forms part of discourses which function as powerful disciplinary mechanisms for transforming teacher subjectivities and the culture and values of classroom practices' (1997: 219). Thus, teaching and learning must be determined in accordance with learning outcomes and objectives. Student teachers are typically required to document their practice with detailed lesson plans; this preparation, it is implied, is the key to good teaching itself. Teaching and learning in this manner matches inspection and accounting and the efficient use of resources. The teacher becomes a learning resource, a facilitator, and teaching is theorised as a set of fixed recipes. The variety of good practice can be suppressed, and according to Alexander, Anderson and Gallegos 'new practices based on surveillance and performativity encourage the targets of power to collude in their own disempowerment' (2005: 211). Perhaps an engagement with theory can enable students to move beyond this.

The performance context is also relevant, as it is repeated and stylised actions that enable teachers to perform this efficiently. Performativity is about performing efficiently in a publicly accountable way. To use the analogy of the driving test, in order to pass the driving test the driver not only needs to look in her mirror, but to make sure the instructor sees this happen. I am not, of course, suggesting that drivers only look in the mirror when they are being tested, but a quick flick of the eyelids necessary to look in the mirror is not sufficient when one is being watched, and is replaced by an exaggerated stylised gesture.

Power argues that performativity 'signifies a displacement of trust from one part of the economic system to another, from operatives to auditors' (1994: 7). This issue of trust is important. Mahony and Hextall characterise the education system as a 'high surveillance/low trust' regime (2000: 102). The performance is not as important as the mechanisms to ensure the quality of performance. It is not just about public, external discipline, but about a teacher being in a constant state of readiness and meticulous preparation. In Ball's words:

> It is the database, the appraisal meeting, the annual review, report writing and promotion applications, inspections, peer reviews that are to the fore. There is not so much, or not only, a structure of surveillance, as a flow of performativities both continuous and eventful that is spectacular. It is not the possible certainty of always being seen that is the issue, as in the Panopticon. Instead it is the uncertainty and instability of being judged in different ways, by different means, through different agents, the 'bringing off' of performance.
>
> (Ball, 2001: 102)

It could be argued that in order to perform well in a PGCE, a student teacher must find a way to resolve the tension between concentrating their efforts into meeting the standards for QTS and the requirements for Master's level assignments. In configuring the course and the assessment with a theoretical Master's component, space can be created in which student teachers glimpse another teacher identity. The next section discusses the extent to which students were engaged or merely performing engagement.

Redesigning the assessment

I took over as course leader in the April of the year before the structure of the Master's level PGCE was finalised, so to a certain extent was constrained by the planning that had gone on before my arrival. However, I was fortunate to be able to work alongside my predecessor for a month, and was in full agreement with the redesign of the assignments. We started from the notion that the written work produced by students on the PGCE Social Science was already often at Master's level. Accordingly there was not a great need to rewrite assignments, just to reorder them to fit into the new modular structure of the course, and ensure that they were demanding enough to fit the Master's level criteria. The existing assignments were:

- an assignment in which the students had to design and evaluate a scheme of work, including a critical consideration of learning theory and/or other theoretical stances;
- a portfolio of assessed work with an analysis of how the work was assessed, using both formative and summative methods;
- an essay to consider the assumption that ICT enhances students' learning in Social Science, including an exploration of the contribution of the literature on the use of ICT and a critical appraisal of the different types of ICT used.

Some redesign was needed, but it was felt that the Master's assignments should continue to reflect the practical work in which students were engaged, help to enhance practice and, most crucially, stimulate engagement for further study. Hence any theory needed to be linked to the implications for practice, but it was clear that in order to avoid an over-performative approach, the assignments needed to be more immersed in critical engagement with research.

Master's assessment on the PGCE Social Science

Like all the other courses on the IOE Master's level PGCE, there are two core modules and one optional module. The optional assignment is the Professional Learning Portfolio (PLP) (discussed in detail elsewhere in this book), so I will focus on discussing the two core assignments. The first subject-based assignment – the curriculum and pedagogy assignment (CPA) – is entitled 'Good practice in Social Science – critically evaluating a scheme of work'. Evaluating a scheme of work enables the students to synthesise theories and themes taught on the PGCE course with their own practice of drawing up and using a scheme of work in their specialist subject of sociology, psychology or politics for AS/A2. They are required to use the principles of good planning and the factors affecting this, and to integrate into the scheme of work a range of teaching and learning methods. The usefulness of learning theories and concepts is reflected upon and evaluated, and a critical consideration of the role of ICT in supporting teaching and learning is undertaken. The assignment consists of the following:

- an analysis of the impact that recent educational reform has had on curriculum planning within Social Sciences;
- the context of the school with type and size of school and the demographic and social profile of students;
- an account of the factors affecting the scheme of work, with reference to examination requirements, resources available, teaching and learning methods and the different needs of students;
- a critical consideration of the role of learning theories and concepts in the planning and teaching of the scheme of work, justifying their selection of activities and resources;
- a critical appraisal of the role of ICT in supporting teaching and learning, discussing the different types of ICT used, with an indication of how far these were successful in terms of student learning, and with an evaluation of what has been learned;
- a reflective commentary on how the scheme of work worked in practice, through the lesson plans, learning materials, teaching strategies and students' responses;
- an evaluation of the strengths and weaknesses of the scheme, with targets for improvement.

The students are required to include in an appendix the relevant scheme of work and all the lesson plans taken from the scheme of work, with an evaluation of each and the accompanying teaching and learning materials. As previously discussed, this assignment is not radically different from the assignment on the pre-Master's level course. There is a greater expectation that the students will discuss theory, and understand and grapple with policy.

The second core assignment relates to Social Science in the wider educational context (WCA). The first part is an essay which reflects on Social Science teaching and the issues raised in the cross-curricular lecture programme. Students focus on the following two questions for their research:

- What does the reading of general texts tell us about 'good practice' in relation to a chosen issue, for example, inclusion, equal opportunities, differentiation, personal and social development, thinking skills?
- How can these ideas be related to good practice in Social Science? What place does Social Science have in the wider educational context? What implications do these theories have for planning?

The assignment should include reading and reflecting on educational theory and recent research on the chosen issue, reference to relevant practitioners' texts, understandings arrived at through the whole school/cross-curricular and subject studies, observations in school and their own teaching, and how enhanced understanding of the chosen issue relates to good practice in Social Science teaching.

The second part of this assignment is a portfolio of assessed work (WCA2). Having explored the wider context in the first assignment, in part two the student teachers provide evidence that they have assessed students' learning effectively using assessment for learning strategies. The assignment should consist of the following:

- a critical and reflective account of the relationship between the different forms of assessment and raising attainment (students need to refer to the research on assessment, assessment *for* learning and its critics);
- how the chosen educational focus (from part 1) has affected the progress of students;
- how students' learning was assessed, and should include use of both formative and summative methods, with specific reference to students' work and the tracking of their performance in class;
- what was learned about the process of assessment from this experience: how far does the literature on assessment and assessment *for* learning correspond with their experience, and how did learning about students' progress influence their classroom practice?

For this assignment, students are required to include a portfolio of assessed work in an appendix. Again, the aim of this assignment is to encourage critical reflection and engagement with theory as well as sophisticated links across the two halves of the assignment.

Master's in practice

In previous years, my experience as a PGCE course leader had been that assignments appeared to be something that students completed as an ongoing task, more like practical coursework than theoretical essays. Apart from guidance in the handbook and that provided at the start of the course, and the occasional individual informal tutorial, students completed the work and handed in final versions which were summatively marked.

With the move to Master's level accreditation, one of the main things I noticed was students' increased stress levels about assignments. Because of the minimal redesign of our assignments as detailed above, I do not believe that students had to work much harder, but I think that they perceived they did. This was partly due to the new emphasis placed on the fact that they were engaged in Master's level study and – ironically – because of the level of support we integrated into the course.

Assignment support was made a more explicit and integral part of the course. On top of the handbook guidance, students had two workshop days while at college, assignment-focused tutorials and were expected to hand in a draft version of their assignment to be formatively marked. During the workshop days students would interrogate the Master's level criteria, peer review progress made on assignments, have any questions answered by their tutors, and get individual support, if required. They would also have looked at past examples of assignments and graded them in order to get to know the expectations and criteria in more detail, but of course in this first year there were no past examples for them to work with. In tutorials students were invited to discuss work in progress. During practical teaching experience visits assignment support was also offered. Most of the students availed themselves of the opportunity to have draft versions of their work formatively marked.

So far, so supportive. However, I would argue that this constant focus on assignments ratcheted up student anxiety to a degree I had not noted before. With seven pieces of coursework to write (the CPA, two for WCA and then four for the PLP, which most had opted for), the students had draft hand-in deadlines in December, January, March (two), April (two) and May, and final deadlines in January, May and June (five). This seems a heavy workload in itself, notwithstanding that the students were also engaged in a full-time professional course.

End-of-course evaluations

The end-of-course evaluations were conducted for course purposes, not for the purposes of this chapter, and asked various questions about the course in general, which are not particularly relevant here. However, the section on assignments was phrased as follows:

This year you completed three written assignments. Comment on them, considering:

- what you learnt from them;
- Their usefulness in developing your skills as a teacher;
- the clarity of assessment criteria being used to judge them;
- the usefulness of draft feedback;
- the timing of deadlines;
- how they could be improved or added to.

The open nature of the question allowed two main themes to emerge: first, the extent to which the assignments were useful for teaching and, secondly, their intrinsic usefulness.

Usefulness for teaching

Students agreed that they did learn from the assignments in terms of developing their skills as a teacher, especially from the assignment on assessment for learning:

> I learnt so much! Completing both assignments meant that I now have a clear idea of the difference between summative and formative assessment as well as a good insight into practitioners' theories about classroom management.

> WCA2 for me was very useful especially as a teacher, as it helped me understand the importance of assessment – and tracking students and reflecting on your assessment methods allowed you to see how assessment impacts on your teaching.

> I really enjoyed researching and writing WCA1 and it definitely helped me evaluate my teaching and wider school practices.

They also appreciated the opportunity to learn about pedagogy, behaviour management and other cross-curricular issues:

> Learning about theory of teaching methods was very helpful. Useful when cross-referencing examples from my own experience and observations.

> I was able to see the importance of it and it was useful as it helped put learning theories into context and visibly see how they apply in our teaching!

> Useful in helping me to appreciate the bigger picture when planning to teach a topic. It also helped me to make sure that I was varying the learning experiences over a number of weeks rather than just worrying about a one hour lesson.

> Learnt a lot about what to do in classroom situations.

> I found all the PLP assignments useful – as they related to teaching practice and practical implications of using ICT, or understanding the importance of training days.

Students also commented that the assignments were useful and manageable:

> good preparation for teaching as they gave us extra insight into specific educational areas.

Intrinsically useful

Unsurprisingly, the students chose to focus on the usefulness of the assignments to their teaching, but some also commented on their intrinsic usefulness, not a question that was specifically asked. Some typical responses were:

> A good introductory assignment into the theory of education.

> Good to look in depth at SEN/differentiation and gained understanding of AFL strategies and monitoring progress.

> I learnt a lot about topical tensions in education and found this awareness useful in teaching as it encouraged me to try strategies and form my own opinions about these debates.

> It also gave me the opportunity to engage with theory into the use of ICT in education.

> The part of it I found interesting was the effect of educational reform on planning.

> The PLPs were useful reflective pieces.

> By looking at a range of different components this provided me with a well rounded set of research and information. This was my favourite assignment as it allows more freedom in subject matter. I enjoyed reflecting on how theory does not work in practice and I discovered areas of being a teacher that I wish to develop e.g. how to take the emotional needs of students into account when planning.

So, in the context of a course evaluation, students were able to appreciate the assignments' usefulness not just in terms of enhancing classroom practice but more generally. Perhaps they had moved beyond the performative and were experiencing genuine engagement with theory. However, this evaluation was completed while the students were still on the course, and thus subject to the power dynamics therein. They may have felt unable to criticise the worth of the assignments before they received their final grades on their ability to perform as a reflective practitioner. I was interested to know how Master's level affected them, one year on.

One year on

When asked to contribute to this book I took the opportunity to survey the cohort on their reflections on the Master's level assignments one year on. I emailed them a brief questionnaire, the first part of which was a simple tick box chart (reproduced with results in Figure 11.1); the second part comprised a very open question asking them to comment on their experience. I emailed the cohort of 27, and received 17 responses. The respondents were a representative mixture of disciplines, qualifications and grades. The results of the survey are summarised in Figure 11.1.

Figure 11.1

Tick as appropriate: 1 = strongly disagree, 5 = strongly agree

	1	2	3	4	5
I worked harder because of the M level accreditation	5	4	3	3	2
I was very eager to get a good grade	1	1	4	4	6
The assignments helped my professional practice	1	4	4	3	4
The assignments took time away from teaching/planning	0	6	3	1	6
I just wanted to pass and did just enough	4	4	5	1	0
The grade I got for the first assignment influenced the effort I put into subsequent assignments	0	3	8	3	2
I worked hard on targets set in the draft feedback	0	4	5	3	4

A number of themes are apparent. Students' responses are evenly spread on the issue of whether or not they worked harder on their assignments because of the Master's level accreditation. Most claimed to be eager to achieve a good grade. Although most thought that the assignments helped with their professional practice, they also felt that the assignments took time away from planning and teaching. Most did not just want to pass and worked hard on targets set in draft feedback.

The most interesting responses came in the open response section of the survey, where main themes emerged: these were the extent to which Master's level work was useful in the development of professional practice; the performative nature of attaining Master's level on a professional course; and Master's level work as intrinsically useful. I will examine these themes in turn.

Helped with teaching

Several respondents argued that the work they had done on their assignments had helped their teaching in their NQT year. Jack argued that this had been his motivation to do well:

> I didn't ever really worry about the Master's level qualification specifically – I wanted to do well and engage as fully as I could with the topics we looked at because I hoped it would help my teaching. I didn't, however, care that the essays we were set were Master's level – my only interest in writing those essays was that it might make me a better teacher.

With hindsight Paul claimed that 'a lot of that information still influences my practice now' and Helen agreed, writing:

> Whether the assignments were Master's level or not I would have spent the same amount of time on them as I enjoyed writing them and also I felt they had huge benefit professionally. The assignments aided my professional practice as I purposefully chose topic areas that I felt were my weakness e.g. differentiation. Writing assignments in these areas improved my confidence practically.

It is interesting that Helen used the assignments as a way of strengthening her own understanding of areas in which she felt less confident. Mary had a similar experience in terms of clarifying her own thoughts: 'I also thought that the essay on assessment for learning was a good way of understanding the topic and then applying it, having to write about the topic makes you think about how you would use it in practice, from previous examples provided in the books, and makes it a lot clearer'.

However, in the open response section, more student teachers expressed their frustration at the tension created by having to simultaneously concentrate on learning to teach and pass assignments at Master's level, as discussed in the following section.

Passing and performativity

Daniel has a rather cynical point of view:

> Personally, I think that the PGCE year should be vocational and separate from Master's level study. Let's be honest, the Master's level PGCE assignments are a pain and I managed to get a reasonable result without being asked to produce anything particularly rigorous from an academic point of view. I think most of us just treated them as another hoop to jump through.

Others agree that, for them, the practical teaching experience came first, and for some prioritising teaching was a deliberate decision. Linda responded, 'I wanted to focus more on my training in terms of planning and teaching much more than the MA credits.' This even led Linda to choose modules according to workload: 'I did choose a module which would be [the] less time consuming, consequently not achieving the same status as most of the other modules. This just emphasised my main aims of what I wanted to achieve from my PGCE.' Natalie agreed, arguing that the time spent on assignments was an irritant: 'I came on the course to learn how to teach effectively – anything I was expected to do in order to pass the course which did not have a direct link to the aim was a bit of a nuisance…!' She goes on to suggest that she:

> did what I did in order to get good grades – I would argue that I was skilled at following essay criteria as opposed to engaging with the topics in the essay, which had no lasting impact on my teaching. What has had a lasting impact was my practical teaching experience on my placements.

This is a clear example of performativity – an intelligent student knowing what to do to meet criteria, and prioritising effort and workload accordingly. Joan even calculated how much effort would need to go into getting an acceptable grade:

> I didn't want to fail my assignments and I didn't really want a D/E but I knew that I wouldn't be putting the work in to get an A. It was hard enough to learn a new way of thinking, trying to decide the best way to try and alleviate the hatred of your Year 8 class, figure out exactly what band an essay would fall into, and get your head around various subject material, without the extra hassle of Master's level based assignments.

Caroline adopted the same approach: 'Tried my best with the assignments at the beginning of the course. Then it was a case of meeting [targets,] planning and aiming for a pass.' Farhana also adopted a performative strategy:

> I feel that the assignments were done for the sake of doing them, as I had to do them, no real deep thought was gone into my assignments, as to me it was more important developing my professional practice. Majority of my assignments lacked engagement from my part, as I want to focus on planning better lessons, and meeting targets set on my teaching placements. The assignments just added extra pressure to a year which is very difficult.

Farida perhaps sums up the performative viewpoint:

> *My feelings were that as long as I passed and could qualify as a teacher at the end of the course I wasn't really concerned about the Master's level accreditation. I saw the assignments as something that had to be done to pass rather than a learning experience.*

Future

Another frequently discussed aspect was how the Master's level credits could or would be used in the future. This is important as perhaps those students who resented the perceived extra workload and do not recognise the intrinsic value of the engagement and reflection will be able to use the credits in the future, and this might provide the motivation necessary to move beyond the performative. Many of the student teachers expressed a desire to continue with their studies:

> *I didn't choose the PGCE in order to get MA credits but since passing the assignments and achieving the credits I am seriously considering completing the course.*
>
> (Linda)

> *However, I do think it's a good idea introducing master credits especially having the opportunity to complete the rest of the units in due course to obtain a full MA.*
>
> (Rachel)

> *However, it is good to know that I have got at least some 'credits in the bank', so that when I do decide to do my Master's I can put them towards it*
>
> (Thomas)

Thomas also recognised the usefulness of the qualification in the context of the government's aim to make teaching a Master's level profession.

> *The government's stated intent is to make teaching a Master's level profession in the near future. Considering this fact, it is nothing but sensible for the IOE to be introducing the element of assignment writing now, in order to start to embed the Master's element into their courses.*

However, this is not relevant to those who already have a Master's when they embark on a PGCE.

Intrinsically useful

Many students argued that the assignments were intrinsically useful. Mary stated that the 'reflective accounts are a good way of thinking about your development as a teacher and progress throughout the year'. Obviously an element of reflection is essential and forms part of the standards, evidenced by lesson evaluations. However, rewarding critical reflection within Master's level qualifications can be crucial in honing this crucial skill. Linda agreed, commenting that 'the assignments helped me to process and evaluate my training experience'.

Mary also commented that the assignments helped her to understand what it took to be a teacher. Thomas agreed, arguing that 'the assignment was an indication of a wider juggling act that all good teachers need to do – that is, the dual process of active and practical teaching contrasted with the more reflective practice that should occur to constantly evolve and improve'.

Others thought that they had been given a more authoritative grip on some pedagogical concepts. Jack reported:

> Only today I looked back at WCA2 to check what AFL actually is. My school have their own version of the concept which is somewhat different to the original ideas behind AFL and I wanted to check that I wasn't going mad. Having actually conducted some research on the subject allowed me to speak and critique a crucial aspect of teaching with some confidence which was quite empowering. In retrospect I would say that the assignments were indeed useful and being able to either champion an academic theory because you believe it enhances teaching and learning or reject something is a lot easier and more justifiable when you've actually conducted some research.

However, it is interesting to note the comment of one of the cohort who already had a Master's qualification. Joan expressed frustration that although 'the subject areas that were given for the assignments were interesting and I did find the reading material for the first assignment especially interesting [I] just did not feel that [I had] as much time to spend on these assignments as I did for my Master's degree'. It is this tension that perhaps leads some students to adopt a more practical instrumental or performative approach, and it is for this reason that it is useful if the assignments are perceived as contributing to teaching, in order to encourage genuine engagement with theory.

The nature of a PGCE course, with its focus on becoming a teacher, and the ensuing conflicting demands with written assessment requirements, means that if we want students to engage critically with academic work, it needs to be perceived as useful to their development as teachers. Then students will engage critically and move beyond the performative. Thus assignments should be designed which, though drawing on theory and reflective critical engagement with research, are fundamentally based in practical work. Students on my course would have to design and evaluate a scheme of work and assess pupil progress anyway, so this was the practical basis of the assignments. How far the students then choose to critically engage with the theory is up to the individual, and is recognised in their final grades. In addition, at least the prospect of future Master's study can increase students' motivation here, as well as, for some, opening up a new way of thinking. On PGCE courses there will always be those who express their frustration with assignments and 'just want to teach', but if teaching is to become a fully Master's level profession, then offering Master's level qualifications alongside a PGCE is essential, as is encouraging an approach which goes beyond performativity. This is best achieved when the theory–practice relationship is close and dialectical.

Chapter 12

The principled practitioner: A model of knowledge acquisition

Shirley Lawes

This chapter will consider the relative importance of professional and theoretical knowledge in the shaping of principled practitioners and explore the role of higher education in the initial education of teachers. The chapter is informed by research undertaken prior to the introduction of Master's level PGCE courses, and particularly by tutors' perceptions of their roles and the experience and expectations of student teachers. Earlier chapters outlined the thrust of educational policy since the 1980s: the reduction in the role and influence of higher education in initial teacher education (ITE) in England; the prescription of a framework of mandatory competence-based standards, largely of a practical orientation, which placed theoretical knowledge on the margins of the student teacher's professional knowledge; and the implementation of predominantly school-based training. Where policy has dictated that two-thirds of the PGCE course must take place in a school, the underlying assumption appears to be that effective practice is mainly developed *through* practice and that academic considerations are secondary. While ITE programmes retain theoretical perspectives in their subject studies programmes, the time allowed for each topic is such that only a limited engagement with the theoretical field is possible. Equally, the abandonment of the so-called 'foundation disciplines' of Philosophy, Psychology, Sociology and History of Education in favour of more practically oriented 'Professional Studies' has arguably left student teachers bereft of a broader understanding of the aims and purposes of education that inform subject pedagogy.

The accreditation at Master's level of elements of the PGCE course, recently introduced in a large number of higher education institutions (HEIs) around the country, may be seen as an attempt to address the perceived narrowness of the standards-oriented, partnership model of ITE. It also raises a number of interesting questions regarding the nature of the initial experience. Are we moving 'back' towards an educational rather than training model and, if so, is 'Master's level' compatible with the existing training model based on the standards prescribed by the Training and Development Agency for Schools (TDA)? Might we assume that courses are becoming more theoretically oriented in order to comply with Master's level criteria? Does the shift imply a reconceptualisation of what preparing to teach means, or is it just a 'repackaging' exercise? Indeed, at a time when educational policy in general appears to favour functional and instrumental knowledge and skills over theoretical insights and conceptual understanding, is there likely to be any significant shift in thinking in what is perceived to be of the most long-term professional and intellectual benefit to teachers starting out in their careers? The recent Master of Teaching and Learning initiative (DCSF, 2008), which aims to encourage teachers to gain a higher level qualification, might seem to contradict this, but it is far from clear how this qualification will compare with traditional Master's courses.

There appears to be some scepticism among teacher educators, in particular, as to whether it is possible for accreditation at Master's level within ITE to represent a significant departure from the largely skills-based training currently in operation or, indeed, whether it is an appropriate development. There is also some concern as to whether it will be possible to attract the calibre of graduates capable of achieving a Master's level qualification, and there are indications that some student teachers struggle to achieve the academic standard in writing at the same time as the standards required for qualified teacher status (QTS).

However, it will be argued here that teachers who start their careers with a strong sense of professional identity, founded on a critical intellectual engagement with teaching and learning, and education in general, will not only wish to improve their practical teaching skills collaboratively with their colleagues, but – more importantly – will also want to continue to develop their theoretical and professional knowledge, and that ultimately this will do more to enhance their capabilities as classroom practitioners.

The research study

Research carried out in 2002 to 2003 sought to explore the views, attitudes and beliefs of university PGCE tutors and student teachers in relation to the place of professional and theoretical knowledge in the ITE process. Student teachers in the research saw their PGCE courses as coherent and generally meeting their needs, as they perceived them (Lawes, 2004), but the courses also appeared to limit the development of broader perspectives on education (Whitty, 2002: 76). The research shed light on a number of problems, challenges and dilemmas that teacher educators faced in their work, and also on the potential of student teachers to go far beyond the baseline of

QTS competence to become principled practitioners. The study compared a number of PGCE Modern Foreign Languages (MFL) courses with a dual certification programme, the PGCE and *the Maîtrise Français Langue Etrangère* (FLE). The PGCE/*Maîtrise* FLE was an 11-month course in which student teachers spent a semester in France studying for a French *Maîtrise*, as well as completing the PGCE at an English university, leading to QTS. Although the research focused on the PGCE in MFL, Professional Studies tutors were also interviewed, and the results may be seen to reflect the concerns of PGCE tutors and student teachers more broadly.

The relevance of the study to Master's level PGCE lies in the findings regarding the attitudes, aspirations and knowledge base of dual certification students compared with their PGCE counterparts, and also in the comparative expectations and attitudes of HEI tutors in relation to a more academically oriented ITE course. The study's findings are, on the whole, encouraging for the future of the Master's level PGCE, particularly in relation to student teachers' aspirations and expectations of what it means to learn to teach and the nature of professional knowledge in education.

The expectations and aspirations of student teachers are formed in a number of ways, and it is natural that they have considerable concern about learning the 'craft' of teaching. But at the beginning of their initiation into teaching, instrumental and functional expectations are susceptible to challenge and change. Accreditation at Master's level may offer such challenges and affirm the value of an *educational* initiation into teaching that is more open-ended, where the outcomes are more variable and uncertain, but potentially more creative and likely to foster a more 'thinking' teacher.

Beliefs about teacher education: Student teachers

The study enabled comparisons to be made between PGCE and dual certification student teachers and revealed some interesting contrasts in terms of their aspirations and expectations of their ITE courses, and how they perceived the links between the various aspects of the course. The PGCE student teachers interviewed did not expect their course to be entirely focused on classroom practice. At the outset some student teachers expected and wanted there to be some 'theory', although their ideas about the nature of theory were shaped by their experience of the course: that is, what can be called 'principled guidance on practice' – a mediated presentation of aspects of theory, as well as how to do things like plan lessons, assess learning and draw effectively on teaching and learning resources. Their subsequent experience of spending the majority of their time in school led them to become more focused on the development of effective classroom management, of their teaching skills and on promoting effective learning in the classroom, which is mainly achieved through practical experience. Time spent in school was seen by student teachers as the most challenging part of their course. The role of teacher educators was seen to contribute a broader perspective to the development of classroom expertise, but the essential focus was to support practice. This assessment is supported by student teachers' approach to the academic side of their courses, notably the reading they undertook, which was almost exclusively related to the assignments they had to write and to obtaining ideas or tips for classroom use. As one interviewee confirmed:

> *The assignments are beneficial because you do have to think, you have to reflect, you have to do research and I found out stuff when I was doing my assignment but at the same time I felt it was more added pressure. Four thousand words. It is quite a bit when you are doing other things as well. For the assignment I read Kyriacou, so that is quite a helpful one and I have also been reading How to Teach Modern Foreign Languages in the Secondary Classroom. To be honest the only time I have read anything is for the assignments.*
>
> (Student teacher interviewee)

PGCE student teachers interviewed for the study reported that they had no time to read once they were immersed in the school experience. They were more likely to seek practical advice from experienced teachers or tutors than to research issues in books or journals. What is more, course assignments were largely oriented to reflecting on practical experience, rather than requiring more than a superficial knowledge of the principles that guide practice. This experience seems to be one that will limit the future intellectual aspirations of student teachers and further reinforce the notion that teaching is a practical occupation.

In contrast, the PGCE/*Maîtrise FLE* dual certification course introduced student teachers to aspects of the applied theory of MFL that were not offered to PGCE MFL student teachers. Interviews with PGCE/*Maîtrise FLE* course members suggested that when student teachers are required to read substantial works of a theoretical and academic nature, they achieve a greater appreciation of the value of reading as an integral part of professional development. This would seem to challenge the notion that student teachers' functional expectations and aspirations cannot be challenged and, furthermore, presents a more positive and optimistic view of the potential of ITE. Although evidence thus far from current Master's level PGCE is anecdotal, it seems to bear out this observation.

The extent to which PGCE/*Maîtrise FLE* student teachers drew maximum benefit from the *Maîtrise FLE* course was in part dependent on the individual's disposition towards theoretical study and an understanding of its value. But, more importantly, the HEI where the PGCE course was undertaken was of specific significance. The PGCE course tutor had a pivotal role to play in maximising the benefits of the dual certification programme by providing systematic discussion and reflection on their *Maîtrise FLE* studies. This is what made explicit the complementarity of the two courses. What the research shows is that tutors varied in their understanding of, commitment to and ability to achieve complementarity. For some, there was a tendency for the requirements of the English national curriculum for teacher education and the development of classroom skills to be their overriding concern. However, other tutors had been very successful in developing complementarity and in helping student teachers to make links between the theory of the *Maîtrise FLE*, and the 'principled guidance on practice' of the PGCE. Even where PGCE tutors were less committed or less successful in this, there was evidence that a significant number of the student teachers interviewed had reflected and drawn on the knowledge they had gained on the *Maîtrise FLE*, particularly in PGCE coursework. Moreover, even if some student teachers were not conscious at that time of how this course of study had changed their understanding of teaching and learning, it is likely that, as they develop as professionals, they will become more conscious of the value of the theoretical knowledge that they have acquired.

The PGCE/*Maîtrise FLE* interview data showed that the majority of student teachers on the various joint programmes read significantly more than those on PGCE MFL courses. The ability of PGCE/*Maîtrise FLE* student teachers to engage with the teaching and learning of MFL at a more abstract level than PGCE MFL student teachers was confirmed by most tutors and was reflected both in what students said in interviews and in their coursework. However, it was also the case that for student teachers to gain maximum benefit from the two courses in terms of their professional knowledge and development, their complementarity and the importance of the academically oriented aspect of their study needed to be made more explicit. This conclusion is supported by the fact that a number of student teachers interviewed appeared to have largely rejected the knowledge gained on the French university course as being important to their professional development because it could not be directly applied to their teaching. The fact that the course has not met their immediate professional needs does not necessarily mean that it was not of value to them in the longer term. Other PGCE/*Maîtrise FLE* student teachers interviewed did not expect much in the way of immediate usefulness from the course; for them, exposure to much broader perspectives on teaching and learning, both in terms of methodology and range of learners, was interesting and challenging in and of itself.

One interviewee was finding the PGCE/*Maîtrise FLE* intensive in terms of workload: for her, as an English national, studying in a French university had been a very challenging, but fulfilling experience in which she had been well supported by her tutors on both sides of the Channel. When asked to comment on the complementarity of the two courses, she said she had not really had time to reflect and think about the connections between the two courses, but then went on to say:

> *But I guess that generally speaking it's to have a broader view of teaching because we're learning about teaching. For example, we were learning about teaching French to adults, things we can use, and these are universal skills in a way. Perhaps the audience there was different, from that in PGCE where we teach secondary school children, but I think that the skills that I developed in France I am continuing to develop now. So that's how I see it – complementarity. It might not seem so obvious at the beginning because they've got a different way of seeing things or because the audience was different, so it might seem that these are like chalk and cheese and it doesn't go well together. But I disagree, because I think that the underlying thing about it, the skills that you pick up from there…the things we had to do there…we had to do presentations and research for them, we had to discuss things, we had to meet different people from different cultures and that sort of environment is one that you find in the classroom and that has been good experience for placement B [PGCE school experience] where the first language is not necessarily English.*
> (Student teacher interviewee)

Her use of the word 'universal skills' is interesting in that it shows an insight that had eluded some of the other interviewees as far as understanding the links between school experience and university teaching. She also drew a parallel between her own experience as a student in a class with students from a variety of ethnic backgrounds and those of the pupils she taught in school in England, which indicates a reflective approach to her professional development. The knowledge gained on the *Maîtrise FLE* was informing her work on the PGCE and, indirectly, her classroom practice. She observed that the required course reading in England was not as 'scientific' or in depth as that in France, but that she continued to read whenever she could. She considered that theory had an important role to play in developing a teacher's personal values and principles. Despite the fact that her school placement was in a very tough inner-city school, she maintained that this was the other 'highlight' of the course because she learned a great deal, particularly about discipline. She had not adopted a 'survivalist' approach (though she had encountered this in others) and, rather than expecting to be given solutions for solving problems, as some PGCE student teachers did, she seemed to be confident in her own ability to work at finding her own solutions, although she added that there was sometimes a discrepancy between the expectations of her HEI and what was possible in her particular school placement. She said that reading about issues had helped her to solve classroom problems.

The PGCE/*Maîtrise FLE* joint certification course might be viewed as a precursor to the Master's level PGCE. The evidence of this study suggests that a more substantial initiation into professional and theoretical knowledge at the initial stage is possible and desirable. Master's level PGCEs may be seen to incorporate the academic and professional principles that drive the joint certification course, without encountering some of the inherent difficulties and pitfalls. The PGCE/*Maîtrise FLE* dual certification course, by initiating student teachers into theory, elevated their expectations of what it means to be a teacher beyond being competent in the classroom and engendered a set of aspirations and an elevated sense of professional identity that provide a more firm foundation for future development. This is exactly what accreditation at Master's level should be taking forward.

Beliefs about teacher education: The teacher educators

Interviews with PGCE tutors revealed a high degree of critical awareness of the strengths and shortcomings of the model of ITE which they had to implement, and of the suggestion that the level of prescription and bureaucratisation was burdensome both for tutors and student teachers. There was some sense of disillusionment with the system in that while HEI tutors are responsible for the quality of their courses, at the same time their role has been reduced in favour of school-based training. Nevertheless, the overriding message from the tutor interviews was the desire to foster the development of imaginative, knowledgeable teachers. This, however, was seen to be curtailed by the pervasive preoccupation with the achievement of the QTS standards.

The overall consensus among tutors was that the contribution that higher education makes to the initial education of teachers is essential and could not be reproduced elsewhere. There was a strong sense, however, that policy-makers did not value the work of higher education and that it had been 'downgraded'. One tutor expressed the view that, although *he* thought higher education has an important role, the 'present administration' does not. Evidence for this, he suggested, was not only to be found in the focus on the QTS standards, but also in the increasing emphasis on alternative, school-based routes into teaching which 'see it as a technical, operational job'.

Most interviewees emphasised in various ways that the higher education component offered student teachers a broader overview of professional practice, the opportunity to take a step back and look objectively at practice, to gain a principled and deeper understanding and to promote reflection. One tutor expressed explicitly the firm belief, reflected by all tutors interviewed, that their job was vital to teachers' professional development. The following comment suggests loyalty to a principled view that sees beyond the development of practical skills:

Of course it has a distinctive role to play. And practice alone, experience alone, doesn't make an effective practitioner. We do have a role to play in terms of where theory and practice play off each other and can influence each other…and I think it is important to be scholarly in our education system…there is such a wealth of information there, of research that's already happened…and we certainly have a role to open our student teachers' eyes to that.

(HEI tutor interview)

The higher education part of the PGCE experience was also seen as a sort of haven for student teachers to meet, discuss and explore new ideas and to talk about their practice – a key element in the development of reflective practice which echoes comments made above about how this part of their professionalism is developed. Tutors spoke confidently and offered insights into what goes on in the classroom and how student teachers are best supported in their development. Tutors visit schools regularly, observe student teachers regularly and are often engaged in either classroom-based research or aspects of teaching and learning. This would appear to be a great strength in terms of relating theory and practice, as the following section suggests. A number of tutors emphasised the relationship of higher education to practice, suggesting that it is at the 'cutting edge' of good practice, that it should 'blaze the trail a little bit, lead the way in terms of what good practice is'. While recognising that this might be seen as an arrogant view, she felt it was nevertheless the duty of the PGCE tutor to be at the forefront of 'good practice'. This view was taken further by another interviewee who felt that part of what higher education did was to 'plug the gaps' in school experience. Others, while not wishing to downplay the role of school experience, were clear that there were differences. One observation encapsulates these:

I think we have different purposes, there are things that we can do, obviously what we look at are things in a decontextualised way. We can't provide the actual context that schools can, but we can take an overview of things. We have the time, expertise, perhaps, to draw a variety of sources together to present a point of view or a different perspective. We have more access to theory and theoretical perspectives than the teacher and I think it's taking a more objective view, of being able to be a little more analytical than there is scope to be in schools. While it would be easy to give lots of handy hints, I don't think that's our job. That's the school mentor's role and the teachers in the school – they are there to give all the contextualised help and support, the hint and tips and stuff, but we are there to give more of an overview.

(HEI tutor interview)

As tutors recognised, it is not only important for them to be engaging in their own research, but that their contribution to the PGCE should always be informed by research findings, so that, for example, '[the students] don't come to see that what goes on in that particular school is the whole picture', as one tutor commented.

Some tutors' responses to the question of what professional theoretical knowledge PGCE courses should provide, however, indicated more of a rhetorical commitment than an actual one. There seemed to be an assumption that an inexplicit theoretical underpinning – what could be called 'principled guidance for practice' – was sufficient to ensure the effective development of future teachers. The preoccupation with preparing student teachers to perform in the classroom and to reach the standards required for QTS is, to some extent, legitimate, given the level of accountability that teacher educators are subject to and the low level of trust conferred upon them, but it is narrow and limited in aspiration. This belief has the effect of eroding the distinctive role of higher education by placing practice at the centre of ITE and making teacher educators the inspiration for practice rather than the intellect. On the other hand, dual certification tutors reported that PGCE/*Maîtrise FLE* student teachers achieved a higher academic level in their coursework. One tutor spoke of actively encouraging student teachers to draw on knowledge gained on the *Maîtrise FLE* course and to cite French texts in PGCE assignments. Others encouraged student teachers to make presentations of the *dossiers* (course assignments) that they had produced in France. Tutors, in particular, commented on the deeper cultural knowledge in an academic, as well as a social and cultural, sense gained by the student teachers. This not only provided them with a rich source of knowledge that they could draw on directly in the classroom, but also gave them confidence in their subject knowledge and expertise.

One tutor made a number of comments on how the initial professional development of student teachers on the dual certification programme had been enhanced. She began by observing that because of the university-based, academic content of the *Maîtrise FLE*, student teachers were required to undertake in-depth reading in a number of areas. As a result they developed 'high levels of abstract thinking' and were familiar with 'technical vocabulary', by which she meant linguistic terms. She went on to infer that their greater academic knowledge contributed to these student teachers' ability to reflect analytically on their teaching:

> *Again, obviously, the good teacher is one that can pull it off in the classroom, but the best teacher is one who can reflect – thinking about why is this working. So it's not a load of tricks that happen to work. They 're thinking about why did that work, why didn't that work, does it mean that I'll never do it again, or does it mean that I'll*

do it differently? And I think they're very good at working that out and it's really quite astonishing, that in quite a short time they seem to internalise and have an understanding about pupils' learning. It astonishes me. After my PGCE, I wasn't at that level.

(HEI tutor interview)

What this tutor is discussing are the ways in which this student teacher was able to draw on knowledge gained during academic study at a French university, mediated by the 'principled guidance for practice' offered by the PGCE component in England, linked to practical teaching experience. Although this example may be exceptional, perhaps this particular combination of knowledge and experience is what is essential to the development of the reflective practitioner?

The place of reflective practice in a Master's level PGCE

'Reflective practice' has become the guiding principle of the majority of PGCE courses (Furlong and Smith, 1996). Teacher educators and academics now see 'reflective practice' as *the* medium through which theory can now be approached, thereby conceiving of the problem of theory as the traditional gap between theory and practice. Since reflective practice is oriented entirely around practice, it requires a subjective definition of knowledge and theoretical understanding. How then, does it sit within a framework of ITE that is reoriented towards a more objective and scholarly knowledge base? While it is sometimes argued that 'reflective practice' does not preclude knowledge of theoretical perspectives, nevertheless, the underpinning ethos of 'reflective practice' points to a redefinition of 'theory' in education – that *practice* has become theory. Such a redefinition could mean that professional and theoretical knowledge is undermined and pushed back to the margins of ITE in favour of a more subjective consideration of practical experience. Since the process of reflection as a psychological phenomenon is necessarily subjective, placing the responsibility to improve professional practice firmly on the individual may have the effect of discouraging a broader critical understanding. Chapter 3 suggests that the promotion of what is there termed 'well grounded reflection' may be needed to overcome this danger.

Tutors interviewed in my study saw reflective practice as a desirable, but unrealistic, goal within the initial period. As one tutor put it, 'sophisticated levels of reflection are something that you can't possibly expect student teachers to achieve'. In some instances, what tutors referred to as reflective practice might more accurately be described as simply the basis of good professional practice, such as 'look(ing) at the learners rather than their own teaching', 'the beginnings of the sort of philosophical foundation for yourself as a teacher' and 'looking at whether the pupils' needs are actually being met'. In this sense, the term was little more than a label used to give credence to the induction into classroom practice. Equally, the emphasis placed on getting student teachers to engage critically with reading and research to inform their reflection could imply a functional approach in which reading and research are selected only on the basis that they shed light on issues or problems that a student teacher may be experiencing. However, this may be more a feature of the attempt by higher education tutors to assert a conceptual underpinning to the education programme and hold on to philosophical principles that the QTS standards are considered to ignore. In this sense, reflective practice may have become what passes for theory. The development of the reflective practitioner has been absorbed into the culture of higher education in ITE and has become an essential feature of our work, but there is a danger that it may provide a professional 'comfort zone' for teacher educators, legitimising our concern for the professional development of the individual, rather than raising difficult social and political issues. Taking a 'reflexive turn' (Moore, 2004), and ensuring that reflection is conceived of in a 'well grounded' way, is essential to the development of principled practitioners and critical educators.

Master's level PGCE: The legacy of the past and future possibilities

For the accreditation of PGCE at Master's level to be more than a 'repackaging' exercise, the issue will have to be settled as to whether practice is developed best through practice or whether, in the light of recent experience in refining the approach to developing practical skills, it is now possible to return to a more principled approach and to find a way of placing professional and theoretical knowledge at the heart of practice. The importance of PGCE tutors in rising to the challenge of reorienting courses towards more scholarly, although with professionally oriented content and approaches, cannot be underestimated. This is an intellectual project which those who express a commitment to professional and theoretical knowledge need to espouse, both in terms of their own engagement with theory and research and in the ways in which this might be reflected in their courses. As we have seen, this is not a given, as tutors have their own sets of values and beliefs, and a variety of views about how teachers best learn to teach.

In the past two decades, in parallel with the introduction of a partnership model of teacher education and QTS, there have been enormous changes in education and schools themselves, marked by vastly increased government intervention into many aspects of school life and the curriculum. This intervention is seen by some as unprecedented regulation and micro-management of education that undermines the autonomy and authority of the teacher. It is also argued that a broader crisis of adult authority impacts on education through the greater responsibility placed on education to solve the problems of society, which may be seen as the outsourcing of authority and the abdication of responsibility by government (Furedi, 2009). These are strong words, but it is nevertheless true that in recent years we have seen far higher levels of accountability placed on schools and teachers as well as the growth of a managerial culture that make learning to teach less straightforward than it was in the past. Less straightforward for teacher educators too, who struggle with knowing how to present policy initiatives and curriculum developments to student teachers in a way that enables them to develop an independent critical view, while at the same time recognising that guidance on implementation may also be needed.

This new school culture is what student teachers are required to make sense of and engage with, become a part of and, hopefully, view with a critical eye, which is what Master's level PGCEs could and should aim to develop. Student teachers seem to spend much more time than in the past becoming familiar with and implementing the plethora of policies that are either imposed on or created by schools, and there is less room for the individual student teacher to experiment and take risks. It might be argued that student teachers developing the confidence to teach is eroded by the increasing formalisation of practices and relationships that now exist in schools and that they have a diminished freedom to develop their professional imaginations and own individual style.

It may be true that the initial preparation of teachers has become more coherent and 'professional' than in the past, but the level of prescription in meeting the requirements of the TDA has arguably led to a 'technicist' approach and a culture of compliance and conformity in teacher education that is hard to challenge. As has been previously discussed, the balance of the PGCE course favours school practice over higher education study, and it is thus the case that school experience is what counts the most with student teachers. However, if they do not have the opportunity that higher education offers to develop the objective knowledge and understanding of practice that should accompany subjective experience, how else are they going to make critical sense of the bewildering array of sometimes alien demands made on them, such as the requirement to teach the 'three-part lesson', to implement regimented behaviour management policies or to make almost exclusive use of Powerpoint in lessons?

If Master's level is to be truly achieved, there needs to be a reconsideration of the higher education/school balance, a fundamental re-evaluation of the content of higher education courses, and an active commitment to theory and professional knowledge at institutional level, and – more importantly – among teacher educators. Without this, it is difficult to see how Master's level accreditation can have any real substance. The reconceptualisation of PGCE that Master's level accreditation offers is an intellectual project that must be led by those who express a commitment to a more academically oriented PGCE, both in terms of their own engagement with theory and research and in the ways in which this might be reflected in their courses. In this way, student teachers' expectations and aspirations of their initial professional development can be raised and reoriented towards educational thinking and the development of their professional autonomy, and rewarded through credits at Master's level. Teachers who tread this path from the beginning of their careers may have a vision of education, more commitment to the profession and greater certainty about the value of their professional knowledge as well as their practical skills and really have the confidence to teach. This should be what drives Master's level PGCE.

References

Alexander, B.K., Anderson, G.L. and Gallegos, B.P. (2005) *Performance Theories in Education: Power, pedagogy and the politics of identity*. New Jersey: Lawrence Erlbaum Associates.

Alexander, R. (2004) 'Still no pedagogy? Principle, pragmatism and compliance in primary education'. *Cambridge Journal of Education*, 34 (1), 285–98.

Apple, M.W. (2001) 'Markets, standards, teaching, and teacher education'. *Journal of Teacher Education*, 52 (3), 182–96.

Askew, S., Carnell, E. and Klenowski, V. (2005) 'Students' conceptions of critical writing in higher education: From being critical to critical being?'. Paper presented at the Institute of Education, University of London, 17 November.

Attard, K. and Armour, K. (2005) 'Learning to become a learning professional: Reflections on one year of teaching'. *European Journal of Teacher Education*, 28 (2), 195–207.

Atxaga, B. (1992) *Obubakoak*. London: Hutchinson/Vintage.

Austin, J.L. (1962) *How to Do Things with Words*. Oxford: Oxford University Press.

Avis, J. (2005) 'Beyond performativity: Reflections on activist professionalism and the labour process in further education'. *Journal of Education Policy*, 20 (2), 209–22.

Ayers, W. (2006) 'The hope and practice of teaching'. *Journal of Teacher Education*, 57 (3), 269–77.

Bakhtin, M.M. (1981) *The Dialogic Imagination*. Austin, Texas: University of Texas Press.

Ball, S. (1990) 'Introducing Monsieur Foucault'. In S. Ball (ed.), *Foucault and Education: Disciplines and knowledge*. London: Routledge.

-- (2001) 'Performativities and fabrications in the education economy: Towards the performative society'. In D. Gleeson and C. Husbands (eds), *The Performing School: Managing teaching and learning in a performance culture*. London: RoutledgeFalmer.

Barnett, R. (1997) *Higher Education: A critical business*. Buckingham: SRHE/ Open University Press.

Barrs, M. and Cork, V. (2001) *The Reader in the Writer*. London: CLPE.

Barthes, R. (1974) *S/Z*. Translated by R. Miller. New York: Hill and Wang.

Benn, C. and Simon, B. (1972) *Half Way There: Report on the British comprehensive school reform*. Harmondsworth: Penguin Books.

Benton, P. (1990) 'The internship model'. In P. Benton (ed.), *The Oxford Internship Scheme: Integration and partnership in initial teacher education*. London: Calouste Gulbenkian Foundation.

Blaxter, L., Hughes, C. and Tight, M. (2001) *How to Research*. Maidenhead: Open University Press.

Bold, C. (2008) 'Peer support groups: Fostering a deeper approach to learning through critical reflection on practice'. *Reflective Practice*, 9 (3), 257–67.

Boud, D. (1995) *Enhancing Learning through Self-Assessment*. London: Kogan Page.

Boud, D. and Falchikov, N. (eds) (2007) *Rethinking Assessment in Higher Education*. Abingdon: Routledge.

Boud, D., Cressey, P. and Doherty, P. (2006) *Productive Reflection at Work*. Abingdon: Routledge.

Boud, D., Keogh, R. and Walker, D. (1985) *Reflection: Turning experience into learning*. London; New York: Kogan Page and Nicols.

Brice Heath, S. (1983) *Ways with Words: Language, life and work in communities and classrooms*. New York; Cambridge: Cambridge University Press.

Britzman, D.P. (1986) 'Cultural myths in the making of a teacher: Biography and social structure in teacher education'. *Harvard Educational Review*, 56 (4), 442–56.

-- (2003) *Practice makes Practice: A critical study of learning to teach*. Albany: State University of New York Press.

Brooks, C. (2007) 'Towards understanding the influence of subject knowledge in the practice of "expert" Geography teachers'. Unpublished PhD thesis, Institute of Education, University of London.

-- (2009) 'Teaching living geography – Making a Geography curriculum'. In D. Mitchell (ed.), *Living Geography: Exciting futures for teachers and students*. London: Chris Kington Publishing.

-- (forthcoming, 2010) 'How does one become a researcher in Geography education?'. *International Research in Geographical and Environmental Education*.

Burbules, N. and Hansen, D. (1997) *Teaching and its Predicaments*. Boulder, Colorado; Oxford: Westview Press.

Burkard, T. and Talbot Rice, S. (2009) *School Quangos: An agenda for abolition and reform*. London: Centre for Policy Studies.

Burke, J. (2008) 'Writing, power and voice: Access to and participation in higher education'. *Changing English*, 15 (2), 199–210.

Butt, G. (2006) 'How should we determine research quality in Geography education?' Paper presented at the Changes in Geographical Education: Past, Present and Future Symposium of the International Geographical Union – Commission on Geography Education, Brisbane.

-- (2008) 'Is the future secure for Geography education?'. *Geography*, 93 (3), 158-65.

Byram, M., Lloyd, K. and Schneider, R. (1995) 'Defining and describing "cultural awareness"'. *Language Learning Journal*, 12, 5–8.

Calderhead, J. (1987) 'The quality of reflection in student teachers' professional learning'. *European Journal of Teacher Education*, 10 (3), 269–78.

Callender, C. (1997) *Education for Empowerment – The practice and philosophies of black teachers*. Stoke on Trent: Trentham.

Carnell, E., MacDonald, J., McCallum, B. and Scott, M. (2008) *Passion and Politics: Academics reflect on writing for publication*. London: Institute of Education, University of London.

Carr, D. (1993) 'Questions of competence'. *British Journal of Educational Studies*, 41, 253–71.

-- (2003) 'Rival conceptions of practice in education and teaching'. *Journal of Philosophy of Education*, 37 (2), 253–66.

Carr, W. (2006) 'Education without theory'. *British Journal of Educational Studies*, 54 (2), 136–59.

Chitty, C. (1990) 'Central control of the school curriculum, 1944–1987'. In B. Moon (ed.), *New Curriculum National Curriculum*. London: Hodder and Stoughton, in association with The Open University.

Clark, C.M. (ed.) (2001) *Talking Shop. Authentic conversation and teacher learning*. New York: Teachers College Press.

Clarke, L. and Winch, C. (2004) 'Apprenticeship and applied theoretical knowledge'. *Educational Philosophy and Theory*, 36 (5), 509–21.

Cochrane-Smith, M. and Lytle, S. (1993) *Inside/Outside: Teacher research and knowledge*. New York: Teachers College Press.

Conteh, J., Gregory, E., Kearney, C. and Mor-Sommerfeld, A. (2005) *On Writing Educational Ethnographies: The art of collusion*. Stoke-on-Trent: Trentham.

Corbett, A. (1968) *Much to Do about Education*. London: Council for Educational Advance.

Corbett, J. (2001) *Supporting Inclusive Education: A connective pedagogy*. London: RoutledgeFalmer.

Cox, G. (2002) *Living Music in Schools 1923–1999*. Aldershot: Ashgate.

Craft, A. (2005) *Creativity in Schools: Tensions and dilemmas*. London: Routledge

Craft, A., Cremin, T., Burnard, R. and Chappell, K. (2007) 'Teacher stance in creative learning: A study of progression'. *Thinking Skills and Creativity*, 2(2), 136–47.

Craft, A., Jeffrey, B. and Leibling, M. (2001) *Creativity in Education*. London: Continuum.

Crick, R.D. and Wilson, K. (2005) 'Being a learner: A virtue for the 21st century'. *British Journal of Educational Studies*, 53 (3), 359–74.

Dadds, M. (2001) 'The politics of pedagogy'. *Teachers and Teaching: Theory and Practice*, 7 (1), 43–58.

Daly, C., Pachler, N. and Lambert, D. (2004) 'Teacher learning: Towards a professional academy'. *Teaching in Higher Education*, 9 (1), 99–111.

Davis, A. (1998) *The Limits of Educational Assessment*. Oxford: Blackwell.

Davis-Case, D. (2001) *The Reflective Practitioner: Learning and teaching in community-based forest management*. Online <http://www.consecol.org/vol5/iss2/art15/> (accessed 7 August 2009).

Denscombe, M. (2003) *The Good Research Guide*. Maidenhead: Open University Press.

Department for Education (DfE) (1993) *The Initial Training of Primary School Teachers, New Criteria for Courses*. Circular 14/93. London: HMSO.

DfE and the Welsh Office (1992) *Initial Teacher Training (Secondary Phase)*. Circular 9/92. London: HMSO.

-- (1993) *Initial Teacher Training (Secondary Phase)*. Circular 14/93. London: HMSO.

Department for Education and Employment (DfEE) (1997) *Excellence in Schools*. London: HMSO.

Department for Education and Skills (DfES) (1998) *Making the Difference: Teaching and learning strategies in successful multi-ethnic schools*. Research Report RB 68. London: DfES.

-- (2003) *Excellence and Enjoyment: A strategy for primary schools*. London: DfES.

-- (2007) *Diversity and Citizenship Curriculum Review*. The Ajegbo Report, S0 0045. London: DfES.

DfES and TTA (2002) *Qualifying to Teach: Standards for the award of QTS*. London: TTA.

Department of Children, Schools and Families (DCSF) (2008) *Being the Best for Our Children*. Nottingham: DCSF. Online <http://www.teachernet.gov.uk/_doc/13488/Being%20the%20Best%20for%20our%20Children.pdf> (accessed 1 January 2010).

Department of Education and Science (DES) (1984) *Initial Teacher Training: Approval of courses*. Circular 3/84. London: DES.

Dewey, J. (1966) *Logic: The theory of inquiry*. New York: Holt, Rinehart and Winston.

-- (1990) 'Educational lectures, 10: Some elements of character'. In J. Boydston, (ed.), *John Dewey: The Later Works, 1925–1953*, Volume 17. Carbondale; Edwardsville; London; Amsterdam: Southern Illinois University Press with Feffer and Simons.

Dick, B. (2003) *Papers on Action Research and Related Topics*. Online <http://www.scu.edu.au/schools/gcm/ar/arp/arphome.html> (accessed 29 January 2006).

Dinham, S. and Scott, C. (2003) 'Benefits to teachers of the Professional Learning Portfolio: A case study'. *Teacher Development*, 7 (2), 229–44.

Dinkelman, T. (2000) 'An inquiry into the development of critical reflection in secondary student teachers'. *Teaching and Teacher Education*, 16, 195–222.

Doecke, B. and McKnight, L. (2003) 'Handling irony: Forming a professional identity as an English teacher'. In B. Doecke, D. Horner and H. Nixon (eds), *English Teachers at Work: Narratives, counter narratives and arguments*. Kent Town, South Australia: Wakefield Press/AATE.

Dolloff, L. (1999) 'Imagining ourselves as teachers: The development of teacher identity in music teacher education'. *Music Education Research*, 1 (2), 191–208.

Drever, E. and Cope, P. (1999) 'Students' use of theory in an initial teacher education programme'. *Journal of Education for Teaching*, 25 (2), 97–109.

Dreyfus, H. and Dreyfus, S. (1986) *Mind Over Machine: The power of human intuition and expertise in the era of the computer*. Oxford: Basil Blackwell.

DSEA (2005) *Teacher as Researcher*. Online <http://www.dsea.org/teachingtips/researcher.asp> (accessed 1 February 2006).

Dunn, I., Morgan, C., O'Reilly, M. and Parry, S. (2004) *The Student Assessment Handbook: New directions in traditional and online assessment.* London: RoutledgeFalmer.

Dunne, J. (1993) *Back to the Rough Ground.* Notre Dame, Indiana: University of Notre Dame Press.

-- (2003) 'Arguing for teaching as a practice: A reply to Alasdair MacIntyre'. *Journal of Philosophy of Education*, 37 (2), 353–71.

Edwards, A. (1997) 'Guests bearing gifts: The position of student teachers in primary school classrooms'. *British Education Research Journal*, 23 (1), 27–37.

Elliott, J. (1991) *Action Research for Educational Change.* Buckingham: Open University Press.

Ellis, V., Fox, C. and Street, B. (eds) (2007) *Rethinking English in Schools: Towards a new and constructive stage.* London; New York: Continuum.

Engeström, Y. (1996) 'Non scolae sed vitae discimus: Toward overcoming the encapsulation of school learning'. In H. Daniels (ed.), *An Introduction to Vygotsky.* London: Routledge.

Engeström, Y. and Kallinen, T. (1988) 'Theatre as a model system for learning to create'. *The Quarterly Newsletter of the Laboratory of Comparative Human Cognition*, 10, 54–67.

Eraut, M. (1995), 'Schön shock'. *Teachers and Teaching: Theory and Practice*, 1, 9–22.

Ewbank, A. (2004) *The Teacher as Researcher.* Online <http://www.teacherasresearcher.org> (accessed 1 February 2006).

Ferguson, R. (2007) Multimedia programme for 'Integrated Training System for Training in Intercultural Education'. Developed for the EU Leonardo da Vinci Community Vocational Training Action Programme.

Fichtman, D. and Yenol-Hoppey, D. (2009) *The Reflective Educator's Guide to Classroom Research.* California: Corwin Press.

Finney, J. (2009) 'Beginning Music teachers researching their own practice'. *NAME Magazine*, 26, 2–5.

Fitz, J., Davies, B. and Evans, J. (2005) *Educational Policy and Social Reproduction.* London; New York: Routledge.

Foucault, M. (1977) *Discipline and Punish: The birth of the prison.* Harmondsworth: Penguin.

Freebody, P. (2003) *Qualitative Research in Education: Interaction and practice.* London; Thousand Oaks; New Delhi: Sage.

Freire, P. (1972a) *Pedagogy of the Oppressed*. Harmondsworth: Penguin Books.

-- (1972b) *Cultural Action for Freedom*. Harmondsworth: Penguin Books.

Furedi, F. (2009) *Wasted: Why education isn't educating*. London: Continuum.

Furlong, J. and Smith, R. (1996) *The Role of Higher Education in Initial Teacher Education*. London: Kogan Page.

Furlong, J., Barton, L., Miles, S., Whiting, C. and Whitty, G. (2000) *Teacher Education in Transition: Re-forming professionalism?* Philadelphia; Buckingham: Open University Press.

Furlong, V.J., Hirst, P.H., Pocklington, K. and Miles, S. (1988) *Initial Teacher Training and the Role of the School*. Milton Keynes; Philadelphia: Open University Press.

Galton, M. (2007) *Learning and Teaching in the Primary Classroom*. London: Sage.

Garner, S.B. Jr. (1994) *Bodied Space: Phenomenology and performance in contemporary drama*. Ithaca, NY: Cornell University Press.

Garson, S., Heilbronn, R., Hill, B., Pomphrey, C., Willis, J. and Valentine, A. (1989) *World Languages Project*. London: Hodder and Stoughton.

Gewirtz, S. (1997) 'Post-Welfarism and the reconstruction of teachers' work in the UK'. *Journal of Education Policy*, 12 (4), 217–31.

Ghaye, A. and Ghaye, K. (1998) *Teaching and Learning through Critical Reflective Practice*. London: David Fulton.

Giddens, A. (1991) *Modernity and Self Identity*. Stanford: Stanford University Press.

Gilroy, P. (1993) 'Reflections on Schön: An epistemological critique and a practical alternative'. In P. Gilroy and M. Smith (eds), *International Analyses of Teacher Education*. Abingdon: Carfax Publishing Company.

Gitlin, A. (2004) 'The double bind of teacher education'. *Teaching Education*, 11 (1), 25–30.

Goffman, E. (1959) *The Presentation of Self in Everyday Life*. London: Penguin.

Goodson, I. (2003) *Professional Knowledge, Professional Lives: Studies in education and change*. Maidenhead: Open University Press.

Goodson, I. and Sikes, P. (2001) *Life History Research in Educational Settings*. Buckingham: Oxford University Press.

Gove, M. (2009) *A Comprehensive Programme for State Education*. Online <http://www.conservatives.com/News/Speeches/2009/11/Michael_Gove_A_comprehensive_programme_for_state_education.aspx> (accessed 8 February 2010).

Gramsci, A. (1971) *Selections from the Prison Notebooks*. London: Lawrence and Wishart.

Grant, G.E. and Huebner, T.A. (1998) 'The portfolio question: The power of self-directed inquiry'. In N. Lyons (ed.), *With Portfolio in Hand: Validating the new teacher professionalism*. New York: Teachers College Press.

Gregory, E. (1996) *Making Sense of a New World: Learning to read in a second language*. London: Paul Chapman.

Gregory, E. and Williams, A. (2000) *City Literacies: Learning to read across generations and cultures*. London and New York: Routledge.

Gregory, S. (2005) 'The creative music workshop: A contextual study its origin and position'. In G. Odam and N. Bannon (eds), *The Reflective Conservatoire – Studies in Music education*. Aldershot: Ashgate Publishing and Guildhall School of Music and Drama.

Grossman, P. and McDonald, M. (2008) 'Back to the future: Directions for research in teaching and teacher education'. *American Educational Research Journal*, 45 (1), 184–205.

Gundara, J.S. (2000) *Interculturalism, Education and Inclusion*. London: Sage.

Gundara, J.S. and Broadbent, J.E. (2009) 'Viable School Responses In Dynamic Linguistic Contexts: An invitation to the membership of IAIE to join in further exploration of issues raised in language education'. Text published to the membership of the International Association of Intercultural Education (IAIE).

Hackman, S. (2006) 'Competence'. In QCA *Taking English Forward: The four Cs*. London: QCA. Online <http://www.qcda.gov.uk/libraryAssets/media/qca-06-23-23-the-four-cs.pdf> (accessed 21 July 2009).

Hager, P. (2000) 'Know-how and workplace practical judgement'. *Journal of Philosophy of Education*, 34 (2), 281–96.

Hagger, H. and McIntyre, D. (2000) 'What can research tell us about teacher education?'. *Oxford Review of Education*, 26 (3-4), 483–94.

Handal, G. and Lauvas, P. (1987) *Promoting Reflective Teaching*. Milton Keynes: Open University Press.

Hardcastle, J. (2002) 'Carlos' task: Pictures of language and English teaching'. *Changing English*, 9 (1), 7–22.

Hargreaves, D. and Marshall, N. (2003) 'Developing identities in music education'. *Music Education Research*, 5 (3), 263–73.

Hatton, N. and Smith, D. (1995) 'Reflection in teacher education: Towards definition and implementation'. *Teaching and Teacher Education*, 11 (1), 33–49.

Hawkins, E. (1984) *Awareness of Language: An introduction*. Cambridge: Cambridge University Press.

Haynes, B. (2004) *Is Teaching a Practice?*. Online <http://k1.ioe.ac.uk/pesgb/z/Haynes.pdf> (accessed 10 January 2006).

Hazzan, O. (2002) 'The reflective practitioner perspective in software engineering education'. *Journal of Systems and Software Archive*, 63 (3), 161–71. Online <http://portal.acm.org/citation.cfm?id=771440> (accessed 10 August 2009).

HEFCE (1998) *Review of Music Conservatoires – Report of the HEFCE Conservatoires Advisory Group*. Bristol: Higher Education Funding Council for England.

Heilbronn, R. (2008) *Teacher Education and the Development of Practical Judgement*. London: Continuum.

Heilbronn, R., Lawes, S. and Yandell, J. (2009) 'Developing articulation of critical reflection in ITE: Writing at Masters level for a Professional Learning Portfolio'. In A. Jackson (ed.), *Innovation and Development in Initial Teacher Education: A selection of conference papers presented at the 4th ESCalate ITE conference, University of Cumbria, 16 May 2008*. Bristol: Higher Education Academy Education Subject Centre.

Hillgate Group (1989) *Learning to Teach*. London: Claridge Press.

Hirst, P. (1974) *Knowledge and the Curriculum*. London; Boston; Henley: Routledge and Kegan Paul.

Hirst, P.H. (1996) 'The demands of a professional practice and preparation for teaching'. In J. Furlong (ed.), *The Role of Higher Education in Initial Teacher Training*. London: Philadelphia: Kogan Page.

-- (ed.) (1975) 'The Curriculum: The Doris Lee lectures 1975'. *Studies in Education 2*. London: Institute of Education, University of London.

Hodkinson, H. and Hodkinson, P. (2005) 'Improving school teachers' workplace learning'. *Research Papers in Education*, 20 (2), 109–31.

Hoffman-Kipp, P., Artiles, A. and Lopez-Torres, L. (2003) 'Beyond reflection: Teacher learning as praxis'. *Theory into Practice*, 42 (3), 248–54.

Hogan, P. (2003) 'Teaching and learning as a way of life'. *Journal of Philosophy of Education*, 37 (2), 207–24.

Hoyrup, S. and Elkjaer, B. (2006) 'Taking it beyond the individual'. In D. Boud, P. Cressey and P. Doherty (eds), *Productive Reflection at Work*. Abingdon: Routledge.

Huddersfield Brass Band Studies (2009). Online <http://www2.hud.ac.uk/mhm/mmt/music/programmes/brass-band-studies.php> (accessed 20 December 2009).

Institute of Education, University of London (2009) *Grade Related Criteria for Master's Degrees.* London: Institute of Education, University of London.

Hyland, T. (1994) *Competence, Education and NVQs: Dissenting perspectives.* London: Cassell.

Jackson, T. (1993) *Learning Through Theatre: New perspectives on theatre in education.* London: Routledge.

Jin, L. and Cortazzi, M. (1993) 'Cultural orientation and academic language use'. In D. Gradol, L. Thompson and M. Byram (eds), *Language and Culture.* Clevedon, Avon: BAAL and Multilingual Matters.

-- (1996). '"This way is very different from Chinese ways": EAP needs and academic culture'. In M. Hewings and T. Dudley-Evans (eds), *Evaluation and Course Design in EAP.* Hemel Hempstead: Phoenix.

Johns, C. (2004) *Becoming a Reflective Practitioner.* London: Blackwell.

Jones, C. (1997) 'Beginning teachers as researchers'. In R. Heilbronn and C. Jones (eds), *New Teachers in an Urban Comprehensive School: Learning in partnership.* Stoke on Trent: Trentham.

Jones, K. (1989) *Right Turn: The Conservative revolution in education.* London: Hutchinson.

-- (2003) *Education in Britain: 1944 to the present.* Cambridge: Polity.

-- (2009) *Culture and Creative Learning: A literature review.* London: Creativity, Culture and Education. Online <http://www.creativitycultureeducation.org/research-impact/literature-reviews/> (accessed 19 January 2010).

Jones, K., Cunchillos, C., Hatcher, R., Hirtt, N., Innes, R., Johsua, S. and Klausenitzer, J. (2008) *Schooling in Western Europe: The new order and its adversaries.* Basingstoke; New York: Palgrave MacMillan.

Jorgenson, E.R. (2008) *The Art of Teaching Music.* Indiana: Indiana University Press.

Kemmis, S. (1993) 'Action research and social movement: A challenge for policy research'. *Education Policy Analysis Archives 1.* Online <http://epaa.asu.edu/epaa/v1n1.html> (accessed 30 January 2006).

Kemp, A. (1996) *The Musical Temperament.* Oxford: Oxford University Press.

Kent, A. (2000) 'Geography's changing image and status – Some international perspectives'. *International Research in Geographical and Environmental Education,* 9(2), 157–59.

King, S. (2009) 'Reflecting critically on practice'. In C. Brooks (ed.), *Studying PGCE Geography at M level.* London: Routledge.

Klenowski, V. (2002) *Developing Portfolios for Learning and Assessment: Processes and principles*. Abingdon: RoutledgeFalmer.

Kress, G. (1982) *Learning to Write*. London: Routledge and Kegan Paul.

-- (2008) Interview transcript. In E. Carnell, J. MacDonald, B. McCallum and M. Scott (eds), *Passion and Politics: Academics reflect on writing for publication*. London: Institute of Education, University of London.

Kress, G., Jewitt, C., Bourne, J., Franks, A., Hardcastle, J., Jones, K. and Reid, E. (2005) *English in Urban Classrooms: A multimodal perspective on teaching and learning*. London: RoutledgeFalmer.

Labov, W. (1972) *Language in the Inner City: Studies in the black English vernacular*. Philadelphia: Pennsylvania Press.

Lambert, D. (2008) 'Review Article: The corruption of the curriculum'. *Geography*, 93(3), 183–5.

-- (2009a) 'Geography in Education: Lost in the post?'. An Inaugural Lecture delivered at Institute of Education, University of London.

-- (2009b) 'Reflecting on Geography teaching in practice'. In C. Brooks (ed.), *Studying PGCE Geography at M Level*. London: Routledge.

Lave, J. and Wenger, E. (1991) *Situated Learning: Legitimate peripheral participation*. New York: Cambridge University Press.

Lawes, S. (2000) 'The unique contribution of Modern Foreign Languages teaching'. In K. Field (ed.), *Issues in Modern Foreign Languages*. London: RoutledgeFalmer.

-- (2004) 'The end of theory? A comparative study of the decline of educational theory and professional knowledge in Modern Foreign Languages teacher training in England and France'. Unpublished PhD thesis, Institute of Education, University of London.

-- (2007) 'Cultural awareness and visits abroad'. In N. Pachler and A. Redondo (eds), *A Practical Guide to Teaching Modern Foreign Languages in the Secondary School*. Abingdon: Routledge.

Lawlor, S. (1990) *Teachers Mistaught: Training in theories or education in subjects?* London: Centre for Policy Studies.

Lillis, T.M. (2001) *Student Writing: Access, regulation and desire*. London: Routledge.

Lovatt, S. and Gilmore, A. (2003) 'Teachers' learning journeys: The quality learning circle as a model of professional development'. *School Effectiveness and School Improvement*, 14 (2), 189–211.

Lum, G. (1999) 'Where's the competence in competence-based education and training?'. *Journal of Philosophy of Education*, 33 (3), 403–18.

-- (2003) 'Towards a richer conception of vocational preparation'. *Journal of Philosophy of Education*, 37(1), 1–12.

Lyle, S. and Handley, D. (2007) 'Can portfolios support critical reflection? Assessing the portfolios of Schools Liaison Police Officers'. *Journal of In-service Education*, 33 (2), 189–207.

Lyons, N. (1998) 'Portfolio possibilities: Validating a new teacher professionalism'. In N. Lyons (ed.), *With Portfolio in Hand: Validating the new teacher professionalism*. New York: Teachers College Press.

-- (2002) 'The personal self in a public story: The portfolio presentation narrative'. In N. Lyons and V. A. LaBoskey (eds), *Narrative Inquiry in Practice: Advancing the knowledge of teaching*. New York: Teachers College Press.

Lyotard, J. (1984). *The Postmodern Condition: A report on knowledge*. Translated by G. Bennington and B. Massumi. Manchester: Manchester University Press.

Macdonald, R., Hargreaves, D. and Miell, D. (eds) (2002) *Musical Identities*. Oxford: Oxford University Press.

MacIntyre, A. and Dunne, J. (2002) 'Alasdair MacIntyre on education: In dialogue with Joseph Dunne'. *Journal of Philosophy of Education*, 36 (1), 1–20.

Maclure, J. S. (1969) *Educational Documents: England and Wales 1816–1968*. London: Methuen.

Maguire, M. (2000) 'Inside/outside the ivory tower: Teacher education in the English academy'. *Teaching in Higher Education*, 2 (2).

Mahony, P. and Hextall, I. (2000) *Reconstructing Teaching: Standards, performance and accountability*. London: RoutledgeFalmer.

Marsden, W.E. (1997) 'On taking the geography out of geographical education'. *Geography*, 82 (3), 241–52.

-- (2005) 'Reflections on Geography: The worst taught subject'. *International Research in Geographical and Environmental Education,* 14 (1), 1–4.

Marshall, J.D. (1999) 'Performativity: Lyotard and Foucault through Searle and Austin'. *Studies in Philosophy and Education*, 18 (5), 309–17.

Maynard, T. (2001) 'The student teacher and the school community of practice: A consideration of learning as participation'. *Cambridge Journal of Education*, 31 (1), 39–52.

McLaughlin, T. (1999) 'Beyond the reflective teacher'. *Educational Philosophy and Theory*, 31 (1), 9–25.

-- (2003) 'Teaching as a practice and a community of practice: The limits of commonality and the demands of diversity'. *Journal of Philosophy of Education*, 37 (2), 339–52.

-- (2004) 'Philosophy, values and schooling: Principles and predicaments of teacher example'. In W. Aiken and J. Haldane (eds), *Philosophy and its Public Role. Essays in ethics, politics, society and culture*. Exeter; Charlottesville: Imprint Academic.

McNiff, J., Whitehead, J. and London, J. (2002; 2nd edition) *Action Research and Practice*. London: RoutledgeFalmer.

McShane, R. (1999) *S1306 Sports Pedagogy and the Reflective Practitioner*. Online <http://www.glos.ac.uk/subjectsandcourses/undergraduatefields/si/descriptors/si306.cfm> (accessed 7 May 2005).

Minns, H. (1997) *Read it to Me Now! Learning at home and at school*. Buckingham: Open University Press.

Moon, J. (2008) *Critical Thinking: An exploration of theory and practice*. London: Routledge.

Moore, A. (2000) *Teaching and Learning. Pedagogy, curriculum and culture*. London: RoutledgeFalmer.

-- (2004) *The Good Teacher: Dominant discourses in teaching and teacher education*. London: RoutledgeFalmer.

Moore, A. and Ash, A. (2002) 'Reflective practice in beginning teachers: Helps, hindrances and the role of the critical other'. Paper presented at the British Educational Research Association Conference, University of Exeter. Online <http://www.leeds.ac.uk/educol/http://www.leeds.ac.uk/educol/> (accessed 3 February 2006).

Morgan, J. and Lambert, D. (2005) *Geography: Teaching school subjects 11–19*. London: Routledge.

Nash, R.J. (2004) *Liberating Scholarly Writing: The power of personal narrative*. New York: Teachers College Press.

National Advisory Committee on Creative and Cultural Education (NACCCE) and Robinson, K. (1999) *All Our Futures: Creativity, culture and education. Report to the Secretary of State for Education and Employment [and] the Secretary of State for Culture, Media and Sport*. London: DfEE.

Newman, J. (2003) *Educating as Inquiry; A teacher action research site*. Online <http://www.lupinworks.com/ar/index.html> (accessed 1 February 2006).

Nias, J. (1992) 'Self or others? Conflicting tendencies in the occupational culture of English primary school teachers'. *Primary Education*, 2(2), 1–9.

Nicholson, H. (2005) *Applied Drama: The gift of theatre*. Basingstoke: Palgrave Macmillan.

Noddings, N. (2003) 'Is teaching a practice?'. *Journal of Philosophy of Education*, 37 (2), 241–52.

Noel, J. (1999) 'On the varieties of phronesis'. *Educational Philosophy and Theory*, 31(3), 273–89.

Noel, K. (2000) 'Experiencing the theory: Constructivism in a pre-service teacher preparation programme'. *Teachers and Teaching: Theory and Practice*, 6 (2), 183–96.

Odam, G. and N. Bannon (eds) (2005) *The Reflective Conservatoire – Studies in Music education*. Aldershot: Ashgate Publishing and Guildhall School of Music and Drama.

Ofsted (2005) *Geography in Secondary Schools: Annual report 2005*. Online <http://www.ofsted.gov.uk/publications/annualreport0405/4.2.6.html>.

O'Hear, A. (1988) *Who Teaches the Teachers?*. London: Social Affairs Unit.

Orland-Barak, L. (2005) 'Portfolios as evidence of reflective practice: what remains "untold"'. *Educational Research*, 47 (1), 25–44.

Paynter, J. and Salaman, W. (2008) 'Reflections on progress in musical education'. *British Journal of Music Education*, 25 (3), 233–5.

Pearce, S. (2004) 'The development of one teacher's understanding of practitioner research in a multi-ethnic primary school'. *Educational Action Research*, 12 (1), 7–14.

Pedro, J. (2005) 'Reflection in teacher education: Exploring pre-service teachers' meaning of reflective practice'. *Reflective Practice*, 6 (1), 49–66.

Peters, R. and White J. (1969) 'The philosopher's contribution to educational research'. *Educational Philosophy and Theory,* 1, 1–15.

Peters, R.S. (1965) 'Education as initiation'. In R.D. Archambbault (ed.), *Philosophical Analysis and Education*. London: Routledge and Kegan Paul.

Power, M. (1994) *The Audit Explosion*. London: Demos.

Pring, R. (2000) 'The false dualisms of educational research'. *Journal of Philosophy of Education,* 34(2), 247–60.

-- (2007) 'Reclaiming philosophy for educational research'. *Educational Review*, 59 (3), 315–30.

Purcell, S. (2005) 'Teacher research in a conservatoire'. In G. Odam and N. Bannon (eds), *The Reflective Conservatoire – Studies in Music education*. Aldershot: Ashgate Publishing and Guildhall School of Music and Drama.

QAA (2008) *The Framework for Higher Education Qualifications in England, Wales and Northern Ireland*. London: The Quality Assurance Agency for Higher Education. Online <http://www.qaa.ac.uk/academicinfrastructure/FHEQ/EWNI08/FHEQ08.pdf>.

QCA (2007) *National Curriculum for Modern Foreign Languages*. Online. <http://curriculum.qcda.gov.uk/key-stages-3-and-4/subjects/key-stage-3/modern-foreign-languages/index.aspx> (accessed 12 February 2010).

Rawling, E. (2001) *Changing the Subject: The impact of national policy on school Geography 1980–2000*. Sheffield: Geographical Association.

Reynolds, B. (1965) *Learning and Teaching in the Practice of Social Work*. New York: Russell and Russell.

Ritter, J.K. (2007) 'Forging a pedagogy of teacher education: The challenges of moving from classroom teacher to teacher educator'. *Studying Teacher Education*, 3(1), 5–22.

Robinson, K., Aspin, D., Allen, J., Underwood, N. and Brinson, P. (1982) *The Arts in Schools*. London: Calouste Gulbenkian Foundation.

Roth, R. (1989) 'Preparing the reflective practitioner: Transforming the apprentice through the dialectic'. *Journal of Teacher Education*, 40(2), 31–5.

Ryle, G. (1963) *The Concept of Mind*. Harmondsworth: Penguin Books.

Sachs, J. (2003) *The Activist Teaching Profession*. Maidenhead: Open University Press.

Schall, E. (1997) 'Notes from a reflective practitioner of innovation'. In A.A. Altshuler and R.D. Behn (eds), *Innovation in American Government: Challenges, opportunities, and dilemmas*. Washington, DC: Brookings Institution Press. Online <http://govleaders.org/schall.htm> (accessed 10 August 2009).

Schechner, R. (2002) *Performance Studies: An introduction*. London: Routledge.

Scheffler, I. (1974) *Four Pragmatists*. New York: Routledge and Kegan Paul.

Schön, D. (1971) 'Implementing programs of social and technological change'. *Technological Review*, 73(4), 47–51.

-- (1983) *The Reflective Practitioner: How professionals think in action*. New York: Basic Books.

-- (1987) *Educating the Reflective Practitioner*. San Francisco, CA: Jossey-Bass.

-- (1992) 'The theory of inquiry: Dewey's legacy to education'. *Curriculum Inquiry*, 22 (2), 119–30.

Schulman, L. (1986) 'Those who understand: Knowledge growth in teaching'. *Educational Researcher*, 15(2), 4–14.

Scott, D. (2000) *Reading Educational Research and Policy*. London: RoutledgeFalmer.

Shulman, L.S. (1999) 'Knowledge and teaching: Foundations of the new reform'. In J. Leach and R. Moon (eds), *Learners and Pedagogy*. London: Paul Chapman/Open University Press.

Siraj-Blatchford, I. and Sylva, K. (2004) 'Researching pedagogy in English pre-schools'. *British Educational Research Journal*, 30 (5), 713–30.

Smith, R. (1992) 'Theory as an entitlement to understanding'. *Cambridge Journal of Education*, 22 (3), 387–98.

-- (2003) 'Unfinished business: Education without necessity'. *Teaching in Higher Education*, 8 (4), 477–91.

Standing Conference of Music Committees (1954) *The Training of Music Teachers: A report by the Standing Conference of Music Committees*. London: Standing Conference of Music Committees.

Standish, A. (2009) *Global Perspectives in the Geography Curriculum: Reviewing the moral case for Geography*. Abingdon: Routledge.

Stobart, G. (2008) *Testing Times: The uses and abuses of assessment*. Abingdon: Routledge.

Swanwick, K. (2008) 'Reflection, theory and practice'. *British Journal of Music Education*, 25 (3), 223–32.

Swenson, D. (1999) *The Reflective Practitioner*. Online <http://faculty.css.edu/dswenson/web/reflectivepractitioner2.html> (accessed 7 August 2009).

TDA (2007) *Professional Standards for Teachers: Why sit still in your career?* London: TDA. Online http://www.tda.gov.uk/teachers/professionalstandards/ (accessed 11 April 2010).

Teachers TV (2008) *Changing Teachers – Finland comes to England – Secondary*. Online <http://www.teachers.tv/video/24484> (accessed 21 July 2009).

Turner, K. and Simon, S. (2007) 'Portfolios for learning: Teachers' professional development through M-level portfolios'. In J. Pickering, C. Daly and N. Pachler (eds), *New Designs for Teachers' Professional Learning*. London: Institute of Education, University of London (Bedford Way Papers).

Turvey, A., Brady, M., Carpenter, A. and Yandell, J. (2006) 'The many voices of the English classroom'. *English in Education*, 40(1), 51-63.

Van Manen, M. (1991) *The Tact of Teaching*. Alberta: The Althouse Press.

-- (1995) 'On the epistemology of reflective practice'. *Teachers and Teaching: Theory and Practice,* 1 (1), 33–50.

Van Merriënboer, J.J. and Kirschner, P.A. (2001) 'Three worlds of instructional design: State of the art and future directions.' *Instructional Science*, 29, 429–41.

Watkins, C. (2006) 'When teachers reclaim learning'. *Forum*, 48 (2), 121–29.

Wenger, E. (1998) *Communities of Practice*. Cambridge; New York: Cambridge University Press.

Wenger, E., McDermott, R. and Snyder, W. (2002) *Cultivating Communities of Practice*. Boston: Harvard Business School Press.

Whitty, G. (2000) 'Teacher professionalism in new times'. *Journal of In-service Education*, 26 (2), 281–95.

-- (2002) *Making Sense of Education Policy*. London: SAGE.

Williams, R. (1983) 'Drama in a dramatized society'. In R. Williams, *Writing in Society*. London: Verso.

Winch, C. (2004) 'What do teachers need to know about teaching? A critical examination of the occupational knowledge of teachers'. *British Journal of Educational Studies*, 52 (2), 180–96.

-- (2006) *Education, Autonomy and Critical Thinking*. Abingdon: Routledge.

Wittgenstein, L. (1967; 2nd edition) *Philosophical Investigations*. Translated by G.E.M. Anscombe. Oxford: Blackwell.

-- (1972) *On Certainty*. Edited by G.E.M. Anscombe and G.H. von Wright. New York: Harper and Row.

Wray, D. (2006) 'Teacher education and primary English: 23 years of progress?' *Journal of Education for Teaching*, 32(2), 133–46.

Wright, L. (1992) 'An analysis of role play and research examined within a historical account of the primary classroom'. Unpublished Master's dissertation, Institute of Education, University of London.

-- (2005) 'An exploration of the learning of primary student teachers: Emerging issues for university and school based teachers'. Unpublished paper.

Yandell, J. and Turvey, A. (2007) 'Standards or communities of practice? Competing models of workplace learning and development'. *British Educational Research Journal*, 33 (4), 533–50.

Yates, S.M. (2007) 'Teachers' perceptions of their professional learning activities'. *International Education Journal*, 8, 213–21.

Zancanella, D. (1998) 'Inside the Literature curriculum'. In A. Goodwyn (ed.), *Literary and Media Texts in Secondary English: New approaches*. London; New York: Cassell.

academic culture and the
   academic community 41–2
academic writing 4–7, 59, 65–8;
   see also literature, academic
action research 12–13, 121, 132–3
Advanced Skills Teacher status 19
agency 43, 52, 59, 61
aims of education 29
Alexander, B.K. 140–1
Alexander, R. 50–1, 54
Anderson, G.L. 140–1
Apple, Michael 19
apprentices 10
'apprenticeship' to teaching 16, 25–6
Aristotle 7, 12
Armour, K. 51–2
Ash, A. 34
assessment of student teachers
   64–5, 70, 128–35
Attard, Karl 51–2
Atxaga, Bernado 107
Austin, J.L. 139
autiobiographical narratives
   by teachers 65–6
Ayers, W. 54

Bakhtin, M.M. 61
Ball, S. 140–1
Barnett, R. 33
Benjamin, Walter 106
Boud, D. 128
Bourdieu, Pierre 95
Britzman, D.P. 34, 61–2
Broadbent, J.E. 90
Burke, J. 44–5
Butt, G. 120

Carnell, E. 44
Carr, D. 36
case studies 19, 67–8. 132–3
classroom management 4, 156
co-constructionist view of learning 75, 87
communities of learners 100
communities of practice 12,
   26–7, 37, 58–9, 74
confidence, professional 88, 165
conservatoire training 125–6, 128
constitutive knowledge and constitutive
   understandings 10–11
Conteh, J. 136
continuing professional development (CPD) 2
core tasks for student teachers 63–4

Cox, G. 127–8
Craft, Anna 43, 110
Creative Partnerships 110, 133
Crick, R.D. 51
critical rationality 13
critical reflection 29–33, 36–7, 40, 46,
   55, 76–84, 87–8, 103, 121, 129, 152
cultural identity and cultural diversity 92–8
culture, definition and interpretations of
   90–1; see also intercultural understanding

Davis, A. 6
Dewey, J. 5, 31, 37
Dinkelman, T. 78–9
Doecke, B. 25, 27
Dunn, I. 129, 132
Dunne, J. 7

Elkjaer, B. 78
end-of-course evaluations 145–6
Engeström, Y. 112–13
essays 103
ethics 8
ethnography 21
evidence-informed practice 13
Excellent Teacher status 19
expert teachers 32, 117

feedback from tutors to student
   teachers 69–73, 132
Fichtman, D. 136
fieldwork 122–3
Finney, J. 133
first person writing 59
Flinkman, Maija 20
foreign language education 99–101
Freebody, Peter 19
Freire, P. 37
Furlong, J. 18, 78

Gallegos, B.P. 140–1
geography teaching 114–24
Gewirtz, S. 140
Ghaye, A. and K. 78–9, 88
Giddens, A. 31, 37
Goffman, E. 140
Goodson, I. 114, 134
government intervention in
   education 18, 164–5
Gregory, S. 134
Guildhall School of Music and Drama 133
Gundara, J.S. 90, 95

Hagger, H. 57
Hardcastle, John 23–4
Hatton, N. 78
Haynes, B. 5–6
Hextall, I. 141
Hillgate Group 16, 20
Hirst, P. 3, 29
Hoyrup, S. 78
Huddersfield University 133–4

identities
    of teachers 6, 20, 59–61, 64–8, 72–3
    of pupils 92–8
inclusive pedagogy 97–101
Institute of Education (IOE), University of
    London 17, 74, 104, 115, 126, 128–9, 142
intercultural understanding 91–101

Jackson, Tony 103–4, 109
Jones, C. 17
Jorgenson, E.R. 136
journal articles 42–7

Kemmis, S. 12
Kemp, A. 129
knowing-in-action 32
knowing-that and *knowing-how* 9–11
knowledge, *theoretical* and *practical* 10–11
Kress, G. 60

labelling theory 139
Lambert, David 117, 120, 122
language, power of 67; *see also*
    foreign language education
Lave, J. 15, 26
Lawes, Shirley 5, 91, 93
Lawlor, S. 16
learner-centred teacher education 57
lesson planning 93, 118–19, 140–3
'lifelong learners' 136
Lillis, T.M. 44–6
literature, academic, engagement with 82–7
Lum, Gerald 10
Lyotard, J. 140

MA in Geography Education 115–16
McDermott, R. 74
McIntyre, D. 57
McLaughlin, T. 36
McNight, L. 25, 27
Mahony, P. 141
Maîtrise Français Langue Etrangère 155–62

Marsden, W.E. 114–15, 122
Marshall, J.D. 139
Master of Teaching course
    (MTeach) 74–7, 87–8
Master of Teaching and
    Learning initiative 155
Master's level accreditation 9–10, 13–14,
    21–2, 42, 57, 77, 88, 102, 112, 116,
    123, 127–9, 136–56, 160, 164–6
mentoring 34–7
Moon, J. 88
Moore, A. 24, 34, 60, 110
motivation of pupils 36
music colleges 125–6
music departments in schools 127
Music Manifestos 1 and 2 133
music teachers, training of 125–37
musicians as distincrt from music
    teachers 128–9, 136

Nash, Robert 48
national curriculum 29
New Right thinking 15–18
Nias, J. 46
Nicholson, Helen 106, 112
Noddings, N. 6

Office for Standards in Education (Ofsted) 115
O'Hear, A. 15–16, 18, 21, 25

Paynter, J. 136
performance, concept of 139–40
performativity, culture of 138–41, 150–3
personal philosophies of teaching 53–4
'philosophical statements' by
    student teachers 76–80
phronesis concept 7
'physical theatre' 109
portfolios, use of 40–57, 74–80,
    86–8, 131–2, 144
Power, M. 141
practical judgement of teachers 7–12, 37
'principled practitioners' 154–6
Pring, R. 13, 54
professionalism in teaching 17–18, 120, 161
progression in education 118–19
propositional knowledge 10, 13
Purcell, Sonia 128, 136

qualified teacher status (QTS) 2, 30, 41;
    see also standards for award of QTS

racism 99–100
reading programmes 66–8
reflection 13, 22–4, 160–4
  contexts for 32–3
  different uses of term 31
  well-grounded 33–8, 164
  writing as a tool for 48–51
  see also critical reflection
reflective practice and reflective practitioners
  30–1, 37, 59–60, 126, 130, 136, 161–4
research literacy 12–13, 120–1
Ritter, J.K. 42
Roth, R. 30
Ryle, G. 9

Sachs, Judyth 120
Schechner, R. 140
schemes of work 143, 153
Schön, D. 30–2, 37
school-based teacher training
  16–18, 30, 154–7, 160, 165
Scott, D. 33
self-esteem of teachers 88
Sikes, P. 134
situated learning 26
Smith, D. 78
Smith, R. 8
Snyder, W. 74
socio-political context of learning 85–7
standards for award of QTS 2–6,
  18–19, 29–30, 70–2, 98–9, 136,
  139–41, 155–6, 160–4
Standish, Alex 115
statements of teachers' professional
  attributes, knowledge and skills 17–18
storytelling 105–7, 112
subject knowledge of teachers 15–16, 95
Swanwick, K. 136
'synoptic capacity' of expert teachers 117, 119

'tactful teaching' (Van Manen) 8, 36
'teacher education', use of term 5
Teachers TV 19
teaching practice 16, 21–2
theatre in education (TIE) projects 102–13
  definition of 103–4
  framing and initiation of 103–6
  as a means of teaching and learning 107–9
  role in teacher development 109–13
theatre for young people (TYP) 108, 111

theory
  distrust of 16
  role of 11
Training and Development Agency for
  Schools (TDA) 2, 4–5, 17–19, 155, 165
Turvey, A. 20
tutors for PGCE, role of 158–64

values 36, 86–7
Van Manen, M. 8

Watkins, C. 49, 55–7
Wenger, E. 15, 26, 74
Williams, Raymond 90, 113
Wilson, K. 51
Winch, C. 13
writing by teachers 48–51, 59–73;
  see also academic writing

Yenol-Hoppey, D. 136

Zancanella, Don 23–4